The European Union and Democratization

Over the last decade, the European Union (EU), through its example of political and economic success and through its external activities, has attempted to promote democracy in neighboring states. In some cases, there has been apparent success; in others, the road has been much rougher.

This volume looks at EU efforts to promote democracy in seven cases, in order to further our understanding of how external actors, and specifically the EU, can best encourage political change in targeted states. The book includes case studies on Latvia, Slovakia, Romania, Turkey, Croatia, Ukraine, and Morocco, each of which is engaged in significant ways with the EU but has been or is a "reluctant democratizer." Major issues that are covered are each state's democratic shortcomings, EU diplomatic initiatives, aid programs, links between the EU and non-governmental organizations, and how the offer of membership in the EU affects calculations of domestic political elites.

By examining these cases, this innovative volume adds to our understanding of processes that are as yet undertheorized and unexplored systematically in either the international relations or democratization literatures.

Paul J. Kubicek is Associate Professor of Political Science at Oakland University, USA. He is the author of numerous works on post-communist and Turkish politics, and is the author of *From Solidarity to Infirmity: Organized Labor in Post-Communist States*.

Europe and the Nation State
Edited by Michael Burgess and Lee Miles
Centre for European Union Studies, University of Hull

This series explores the complex relationship between nation states and European integration and the political, social, economic, and policy implications of this interaction. The series examines issues such as:

- the impact of the EU on the politics and policy-making of the nation state and vice versa
- the effects of expansion of the EU on individual nation states in Europe
- the relationship between the EU and non-European nation states.

1 **Poland and the European Union**
    Edited by Karl Cordell

2 **Greece in the European Union**
    Edited by Dionyssis G. Dimitrakopoulos and Argyris G. Passas

3 **The European Union and Democratization**
    Edited by Paul J. Kubicek

4 **Iceland**
    The reluctant member of Europe
    Baldur Thorhallsson

5 **Norway and an Integrating Europe**
    Clive Archer

The European Union and Democratization

Edited by Paul J. Kubicek

Routledge
Taylor & Francis Group

LONDON AND NEW YORK

First published 2003
by Routledge
11 New Fetter Lane, London EC4P 4EE

Simultaneously published in the USA and Canada
by Routledge
29 West 35th Street, New York, NY 10001

Routledge is an imprint of the Taylor & Francis Group

Typeset in Times by Exe Valley Dataset Ltd, Exeter
Printed and bound in Great Britain by Antony Rowe Ltd,
Chippenham, Wiltshire

British Library Cataloguing in Publication Data
A catalogue record for this book is available
from the British Library

Library of Congress Cataloging in Publication Data
The European Union and democratization / Paul J. Kubicek, editor.
    p. cm.
  Incudes bibliographical references and index.
  1. Democratization–European Union countries.   2. Human
rights–European Union countries.   3. European Union countries–Ethnic
relations.   4. Post-communism–Europe, Eastern.   5. European Union
countries–Foreign relations–Europe, Eastern.   6. Europe,Eastern–Foreign
relations–European Union countries.   I. Kubicek, Paul.
D1060.E8683 2003
940′.009′049–dc21   2003003641

ISBN 0–415–31136–5

Contents

List of figures and tables   vii
Notes on contributors   ix
Preface   xi

1   **International norms, the European Union, and democratization:
    tentative theory and evidence**   1
    PAUL J. KUBICEK

2   **The European Union, democratization, and minorities in Latvia**   30
    NILS MUIZNIEKS AND ILZE BRANDS KEHRIS

3   **The ambivalent influence of the European Union on
    democratization in Slovakia**   56
    KEVIN DEEGAN KRAUSE

4   **The European Union and Romania: the politics of constrained
    transition**   87
    WILLIAM CROWTHER

5   **The politics of conditionality: the European Union and human
    rights reform in Turkey**   111
    THOMAS W. SMITH

6   **The European Union and Croatia: negotiating "Europeanization"
    amid national, regional, and international interests**   132
    STEPHEN M. TULL

7   **The European Union and Ukraine: real partners or relationship
    of convenience?**   150
    PAUL J. KUBICEK

8 The European Union and democratization in Morocco   **174**
BRADFORD DILLMAN

9 Conclusion: the European Union and democracy promotion   **197**
PAUL J. KUBICEK

Index   216

Figures and tables

Figures

3.1 Freedom House civil liberties scores for selected Central and
    Eastern European countries, 1990–2000   58

3.2 Distrust toward the European Union by party preference in
    Slovakia, 1992–1999   78

Tables

1.1 Summary of hypotheses on democracy promotion   20

9.1 Summary of hypotheses on the European Union and
    democratization   199–200

9.2 Evaluation of hypotheses in seven countries   202

Contributors

William Crowther is an Associate Professor of Political Science at the University of North Carolina-Greensboro and Co-Director of the Parliament Documents Center for Central Europe. He received his PhD from UCLA in 1986. He is the author of a number of works on various aspects of politics in Moldova and Romania and is currently engaged in a comparative study of the role of legislative institutions in the post-communist transitions.

Bradford Dillman is an Assistant Professor in the School of International Service and the School of Public Affairs at American University. He is the author of *State and Private Sector in Algeria: The Politics of Rent-Seeking and Failed Development* (Westview, 2000). He holds a PhD in Political Science from Columbia University.

Ilze Brands Kehris is a researcher at the Latvian Centre for Human Rights and Ethnic Studies in Riga. She holds an MA and MPhil in Political Science from Columbia University, where she specialized in international relations and Soviet studies.

Kevin Deegan Krause teaches comparative politics at Wayne State University. He received a PhD in Government and International Studies from the University of Notre Dame. His current research focuses on political and social cleavages in political party systems and the relationship among nationalism, authoritarianism, and economic reform in Central and Eastern Europe.

Paul J. Kubicek is an Associate Professor of Political Science at Oakland University. He holds a PhD from the University of Michigan, and has published widely on post-communist and Turkish politics. His most recent book is *From Solidarity to Infirmity: Organized Labor in Post-Communist States* (forthcoming).

Nils Muiznieks has been director of the Latvian Centre for Human Rights and Ethnic Studies since 1994. He received a BA in Politics from Princeton University in 1986 and an MA (1988) and PhD (1993) in Political Science from the University of California at Berkeley.

Thomas W. Smith is an Assistant Professor in the Department of Government and International Affairs at the University of South Florida. From 1997 to 2000 he taught at Koç University in Istanbul, and is the author of numerous journal articles and *History and International Relations* (Routledge, 1999).

Stephen M. Tull has studied and worked throughout the former Yugoslavia over the course of twenty years. He holds a PhD in Political Science from the University of Michigan, where his work focused on ethnopolitics, self-determination, and sovereignty. He has worked for the United Nations since 1996, in Peacekeeping, Human Rights, and Humanitarian Affairs with assignments in Geneva, Croatia, the Federal Republic of Yugoslavia, Rwanda, and Afghanistan.

Preface

In the course of living and doing research in a number of countries waiting in line for membership in the European Union, I was struck by the difference between the heady rhetoric of democracy and reform from the EU and the cynicism and suspicion of people on the ground in these countries, many of whom were not particularly impressed by EU efforts to promote reforms. Indeed, public opinion in a number of prospective EU members – not to mention in some EU countries as well – reflects great ambivalence, if not hostility, to the EU. This gap between the rhetoric and hopes of the EU and the views of those the EU is ostensibly trying to help provided the initial impetus for this volume.

Our specific set of questions revolves around EU efforts to promote democracy in cases we label "reluctant democratizers," those countries where democratization faced or still faces some formidable hurdles. Our goal is to use these cases – cases of success and failure – to illuminate how external promotion of democracy can work and how it may be limited. Surprisingly, this is an area that lacks extensive treatment in the literature, falling as it does between the gap of comparative politics and international relations. Moreover, when one looks at the issue of EU democratization efforts, one finds little rigorous research, with most works limited to the successful cases of democratic transition in Southern and Central Europe. By looking at some less well-studied cases, we hope to broaden both our empirical and theoretical understanding of the nexus between international and domestic politics on questions of democratization.

Initial versions of Chapters 1, 3, 5, and 6 were originally presented at the Annual Conference of the International Studies Association in New Orleans in March 2002. Afterwards, we found additional collaborators for this project to extend our coverage of the issue. While this volume was initially grounded with some skepticism of EU efforts, we recognize that in many cases the EU has played a positive role in promoting democracy, and we remain hopeful that it can do better in those countries that remain "reluctant democratizers." We hope that this volume can make a contribution in that direction.

PJK

1 International norms, the European Union, and democratization

Tentative theory and evidence

Paul J. Kubicek

Numerous states, international organizations, and international non-governmental organizations take an active interest in promoting democracy and human rights across the globe. Alliances, trade pacts, and economic assistance are offered as means to encourage political liberalization or foster democratic consolidation. Whereas in the initial literature on democratization international factors and agents were assigned an "indirect, usually marginal role,"[1] in the post-Cold War environment these variables have arguably become "more decisive" and exerted a "more profound" influence.[2] This has been most obvious in the countries of Eastern Europe, where one can speak of the international influences of Gorbachev's reforms, the role of transnational communications, the "contagion effect" that led communist regimes to fall like dominoes across the region, and the moral example of Western democracies as factors that spurred political change. More generally, one can argue that the changes of 1989–1991 have created a new international environment more conducive for democratization, and indeed in the past decade one has witnessed numerous efforts to establish democratic systems throughout parts of Africa, Asia, and Latin America. The notion that democracies do not fight each other gives an added justification for democratic states to encourage the formation of democracies elsewhere.

Among international actors interested in democratization, a leading role should be assigned to the European Union (EU). The EU itself, of course, is composed of fifteen democratic states, and in recent years it has made several efforts to transform itself from primarily a trading bloc into an important international actor in the political arena. Among changes in the EU's foreign relations have been an emphasis on democratization, human rights, genuine pluralism, and the rule of law. These concerns have been enshrined in European Council declarations dating from 1991, Association and Partnership and Cooperation Agreements with former Communist states, the Maastricht Treaty, the most recent Lomé Convention, and in the 1993 Copenhagen Criteria establishing democratic requirements for EU membership.[3] Development aid has been made increasingly conditional on the recipients' respect for human rights. Programs, such as PHARE (Poland and Hungary Assistance for the Restructuring of the Economy), have been created to give the EU an "extensive portfolio of support mechanisms for the new democracies to the East,"[4] and obviously EU membership is dangled as a carrot to encourage political liberalization. Even in cases where membership is not being proffered, as in Ukraine or in North Africa, the EU hopes that it can provide some incentives to further political reform.

Have EU efforts paid off? This is a tough question to answer, as it can be difficult to untangle the various domestic and international factors that work for and against democratization. In Eastern Europe, one can point to a host of factors – the legacy of communism, corruption, economic difficulties, weakness of civil society, heterogeneous populations – that will affect democratic consolidation. In Turkey and North Africa, one might add cultural factors and problems of religious and ethnic conflict. However, at least when looking at the spread of democracy to this point in Europe, most observers have been inclined to the give the EU credit for fostering or promoting democratization. Many point to the role of the EU (then the European Community [EC]) in encouraging regime change in Southern Europe, by providing moral, political, and economic support to democratizers in Greece, Portugal, and Spain. The line of reasoning is usually rather straightforward: the prospect of EC membership was attractive enough to help democratizers win any argument against would-be opponents. In Whitehead's words, the EC acted as a "powerful catalyst" for change in Southern Europe, by providing "an elaborate structure of economic and social incentives," so that strategies and calculations of political elites have been "strongly shaped by the pressure of externally designed rules and structures."[5] However, some would contend that the EC's role was not necessary or decisive (democracy was "over-determined" by a number of variables) and a few have even pointed to problems engendered by EC interference in these transitions.[6] One proponent of EU activity concedes that the EU's role has been "more assumed than proven."[7]

When one turns to more recent transitions in Eastern Europe, again one sees the EU playing a prominent role, and certainly there are signs of success. Poland, the Czech Republic, Hungary, and Slovenia appear to have met the democratic criteria for membership (and, together with several other states, seem poised to join the EU in 2004), and the discourse of "returning to Europe" has played a prominent role in numerous countries, where prospective EU membership has arguably re-enforced domestic political and economic reform efforts. However, as two observers note, the effect of EU enlargement on democratization is "a topic that remains mostly unexplored, due principally to the crypto-political nature of most discussions of the matter among policymakers."[8] Even Whitehead, perhaps backing away from his previous claim, noted that the role of the EU in democracy promotion was "undertheorized" and that its work in post-communist states was far more "risky," as it carried potentially high costs with no guarantees of success.[9] In other words, one should not operate with simple assumptions and lines of causality, pointing exclusively to the EU's wherewithal and incentives to push forward democratization efforts. Such arguments are in need of more rigorous examination.[10]

More to the point of this volume, however, is the simple fact that not all states have rushed to accede to EU demands. These are what we have labeled "reluctant democratizers," countries that for any number of reasons have been reticent to push forward important aspects of political liberalization despite the presence of external encouragement in the form of the EU. Examples would include Slovakia under Vladimir Mečiar, Croatia under Franjo Tudjman, and Ukraine during its first decade of independence. These cases – together with four others – make up the bulk of this work, although one could consider others in this mold as well (e.g. Tunisia, Albania, Russia). Today, one can note that some of these countries, such as Slovakia, are moving ahead with democracy and the EU's agenda, and one could even argue that the EU was instrumental in encouraging the 1998 change of government in Bratislava that removed Mečiar from office. Other states, however, such as Turkey, Ukraine, and Morocco, remain more obdurate toward change in the face of EU encouragement and pressure.

Many who would praise the EU overlook these failures or shortcomings. This is unfortunate, however, because they base their conclusions on the basis of incomplete evidence, unconsciously perhaps selecting cases on the dependent variable. In other words, if one focuses only on the EU role in Poland, Hungary, Spain, or Portugal, where a consolidated democracy emerged without any serious trouble, one could easily contend the EU plays an important role in democratization. Not all cases, however, are so simple, and by looking at more problematic cases, and implicitly comparing them with the "success stories," one can get a better grasp of how and under what conditions EU encouragement of democracy can be effective. Better understanding of the external dimension of democratization, however, is important not only when thinking of the EU, but has relevance to a host of other actors that champion democracy. Thus, by analyzing EU interaction with reluctant democratizers, we aim to make a contribution to an important policy question: what are the potential and limits of external agents and international norms in contributing to democratization efforts?

The remainder of this chapter is composed of four parts. The first defines various means by which international factors and actors, and in particular the EU, can influence domestic politics on the question of democratization. The second part briefly looks at the record of the EC/EU in Southern Europe and the more successful cases of East Central Europe, as these experiences form the bulk of the conventional wisdom on the EU's role. The third part, drawing on both that experience and international relations theory on the spread of international norms, will delineate some hypotheses and variables that should inform our examinations of interaction between the EU and more reluctant democratizers. Finally, a few words will be devoted to the issue of democratic consolidation and why the cases selected fit into the category of "reluctant democratizers."

Conceptualizing the international dimension

A substantial literature has developed around the international dimensions of democratization. Much of this has been devoted to labeling and defining mechanisms through which international factors are relevant to democratization within states. A partial list of these would include notions such as diffusion, contagion, demonstration effect, incorporation, consent, adaptation, complex interdependence, *zeitgeist*, convergence, emulation, socialization, learning, and conditionality.[11] Some of these notions are more actor-oriented or policy-driven. Some are better conceived as impersonal forces or simply background variables. Some concepts overlap with others, so it is often hard to employ them in analysis in a discrete fashion. Moreover, it is debatable to what extent one can treat any of these factors as truly catalysts or "independent" variables, as in many circumstances they may depend upon a domestic opening or crisis in order to come into play.[12] And, of course, international factors may only play a supportive role in democratization efforts, as the more crucial factors would be the will of political elites, political cleavages in a given state, and public support for democratic norms and institutions. Singling out the precise role of international factors is therefore difficult. They cannot be treated in isolation from home grown phenomena. Thus, our discussion of the EU's role will inevitably be interspersed with a discussion of domestic politics, a sphere that is often made complex by a host of country-specific variables.

Bearing these issues in mind, however, it is still useful to conceptualize how international actors may shape processes of democratization. One can generally point to four, broad, alliterative categories: control, contagion, convergence, and conditionality.

Control

One method by which international actors can facilitate democratization (or inhibit it, as in the case of postwar Soviet policy in Eastern Europe) is by directly taking control of a state's political institutions. Historical examples would be the role of Allied occupation in West Germany and Japan, states whose institutions were molded by outside actors and initial years of democratic transition were guaranteed by a foreign military presence. More recently, one can point to the incorporation of the German Democratic Republic into a united, democratic Germany.

While the EU does not aspire to take over any given country directly (although some critics may suggest this is the case), one could contend that incorporation into the EU – which would imply a certain degree of EU control over state policy – would be an important guarantor of democracy. While that may be true, the point is that by the Copenhagen Criteria any new member would already have to have effective democratic institutions. EU membership, once bestowed, may thus help "underwrite" democracy,[13] but there is no direct control mechanism by which the EU can impose democracy on any state while it is still struggling to consolidate a new political regime. For the states in this volume then, the notion of control lies at best in the future, when they have already gained EU membership. Thus, we had better turn our attention to mechanisms and processes that are more relevant to the initial periods of democratic transition and consolidation.

Contagion

One notion that is widespread in much of the literature on democratization is democratic contagion, sometimes called diffusion, a demonstration effect, or even the global *zeitgeist*. The notion here is that events or systems in one country or group of countries, to the extent that they are seen to be attractive or achievable, can spread across borders.[14] The language of a democratic "wave" captures this, as does the logic of globalization. Much of Latin America, for example, began the transition to democracy at roughly the same time, and much can be made of the demonstration effects in Eastern Europe, when democratic winds moved quickly from Warsaw and Budapest to Berlin and Prague, and (eventually, and with less certainty) to Bucharest and Sofia.

While contagion can be based on events (i.e. transition in one country inspires actors in another), one can also speak of a demonstration effect of outside actors as well. For example, many have pointed to the Western democracies, and the countries of the EU in particular, as a source of inspiration, given their wealth, security, and stability. These attributes, of course, might be quite attractive to states looking ahead to an unpredictable post-communist period. Institutions may be copied wholesale, as they have a proven, successful track record in the West. Often, but not necessarily, contagion works with a certain geographic logic as well, as the likelihood of "infection" is greater for states that border on democratic states.[15]

While there may be something behind the notion of contagion, it is at best an incomplete theory. While it can address certain correlations, the casual mechanisms are unspecified. It is a "supply-side theory"[16] and overlooks the demands/preferences of human agency, aside perhaps from a simple psychological drive to copy a successful neighbor. It ignores the role of historical memory or how local conditions may filter foreign influences.[17] By itself it cannot explain the presence of democratic "outliers" in a certain region. It neglects the agency and intent of international actors. A pure contagion theory, for example, assumes that the international actor – in our case the EU – is primarily passive, going on with its business, without any overt policy to influence actors beyond its borders. We obviously know this to be false, and we are also well aware that the EU has put more political and economic effort into some countries than others. Thus, it would be a mistake to assume that international factors act uniformly through some sort of contagion effect. Pridham concedes that contagion may play some role in the initial transition phase, but that in general reliance on sweeping global or regional conditions overlook national diversities and a host of other factors that account for different outcomes.[18] For example, contagion arguments – short of a very strict geographical determinism – have a hard time accounting for the problems of consolidating democracy in Slovakia, Croatia, and Romania. Thus, we need to look closer at the actors – both external and internal – and how their preferences and policies, as well as structural factors within the state, impinged upon democratization efforts.

Convergence

The idea of convergence can be viewed as a refinement on the more simple notions of contagion. Whitehead defines this as the "enlargement of a pre-existing democratic community of sovereign states."[19] Pridham offers that it is "gradual movement in system conformity based upon established democracies with power to attract and assist regimes in transition," and that the EU may be the "most ambitious example" of convergence.[20] Incorporation could be a manifestation of convergence, but democratic principles can also "converge" due to socialization through the growth of transnational networks, involvement of EU agencies in political, legal, and economic reform efforts, the internalization of democratic norms, as well as more impersonal changes fostered by globalization. The key difference between contagion and convergence lies in the fact that the latter aspires more explicitly to account for the motivation of the change in "targeted" states. Convergence explanations, unlike those for contagion, thus identify causal mechanisms.

The variety of means by which convergence can occur may lead to some confusion, but for our purposes we can distinguish two primary tracts.[21] The first of these is convergence through a rational, instrumental calculation of domestic elites, responding to either "objective" political or economic pressures ("adaptation" to lower transaction costs)[22] or those purposefully applied by external actors (conditionality, discussed below). The other is more "ideational," constructivist, based upon learning, consciousness-raising, socialization, and the internalization of democratic norms. The difference is thus in the motivation to change. Instrumental convergence can be understood as "Do X to get Y," whereas convergence through socialization would occur when actors accept that "Good people do X."[23] The specific motivation of an actor, of course, may be mixed and often may be difficult for an analyst to uncover, although Checkel has shown through detailed process-tracing how one can distinguish between change through instrumental calculations and change through argumentative persuasion.[24] This latter process can be perhaps best understood as the spread of international norms, a topic around which there is a burgeoning literature in international relations theory. Democracy, if not a global norm, certainly has become one espoused by the EU (the EU's own "democratic deficit" need not concern us here), and the EU hopes and expects that its engagement with other states, irrespective of explicit efforts of conditionality, will foster the spread of democratic values. The notion of convergence is thus one that we should bear in mind, and later in the chapter some hypotheses based on the general literature of international norms will be proffered as ways of thinking about under what conditions convergence would be more likely.

Conditionality

This is perhaps the most developed of all approaches relating to international aspects of democratization and can also be considered the most visible and proactive of policies explicitly designed to promote democratic convergence. By conditionality, one refers to the linking of perceived benefits (e.g. political support, economic aid, membership in an organization) to the fulfillment of a certain program, in this case the advancement of democratic principles and institutions in a "target" state. Conditionality is most clearly enshrined in the Copenhagen Criteria for membership,[25] but one can point to a number of EU foreign policies built around the notion of democratic conditionality, particularly observance of human rights.[26] Conditionality is used to exert direct leverage on others, and "carrots" and "sticks" are employed to persuade, induce, and at times coerce states into adopting the desired policy. Conditionality thus works on a cost/benefit analysis, and democracy results from a rational calculation; it is apt to produce, at least initially, instrumental adaptation of policy and not an internalization of norms.[27] To the extent that EU membership, good ties with Europe, or economic assistance are valued by elites and publics in target states, one could imagine that the EU could utilize a variety of blandishments and sanctions to influence political developments in other states.

One can point to some examples where conditionality may have been a motivating factor for political change. Rupnik suggests Slovakia as the clearest case of this, and Kevin Deegan Krause in Chapter 3 will critically assess this conclusion.[28] However, states do not always roll over when confronted with conditionality requirements, as seen perhaps most clearly in the Turkish case, analyzed in Chapter 5 by Thomas W. Smith. Thus, while the logic of conditionality seems straightforward, many variables must be in place in order for it to work effectively, and the EU's record in this regard is, as we shall see, mixed. One can posit a number of inductively and deductively derived hypotheses on the probable effectiveness of conditionality. These will be developed in a subsequent section of this chapter.

Before jumping to these hypotheses, let us turn briefly to an examination of previous efforts to promote democracy, most of which have been judged "success stories." This effort will allow us to produce some empirical backing for many of the hypotheses on the EU and democratization, as well as serve as a basis for comparison with EU engagement with the more "reluctant democratizers."

The EU and democratization: the historical record

The EC/EU has always been an organization for democratic states. This was first made explicit in 1962 in its Birkelbach Report, in which it rejected a membership bid from Spain and noted that only states which guarantee truly democratic practices and respect for fundamental rights and freedoms can become members of the Community. This was re-affirmed in its 1964 Association Agreement with Turkey. However, as Smith notes, the EC did not make political conditionality a cornerstone of its relations with non-member states.[29]

That policy has obviously changed, and now conditionality is upheld, at least rhetorically, both for would-be members and for states ineligible for membership. The first real example of EC/EU activity in the sphere of democracy promotion was in Southern Europe in the mid-1970s, when Portugal, Spain, and Greece threw off the shackles of dictatorship and quickly consolidated democratic regimes. The causes of these changes were many – ranging from international crises (Portugal in Africa and Greece in Cyprus), economic problems, death of longstanding leaders, socio-economic modernization, and public discontent with authoritarian government. Certainly, however, many have noted the role played by individual member governments and the EC as a whole in this process – by providing support to democratic politicians such as Soares in Portugal, Juan Carlos in Spain, and Karamanlis in Greece, by forging links with political parties, by advancing important economic and political incentives, and by granting external guarantees to business and propertied classes who might have been worried about the consequences of democratization. Membership was held open to these democratizing states, but was conditional upon democratic consolidation. Greece joined the EC in 1981; the others followed in 1986. Whitehead notes the important role of the EC in this process, suggesting that the EC provided the "most powerful, immutable, and long-run incentives for democratic transition and consolidation in southern Europe."[30]

However, one might ask how necessary external agents were to this process. Linz and Stepan note that the Southern European states enjoyed favorable initial starting conditions, making their transitions to democracy far less problematic than the ones we will be examining. While they echo Whitehead in that the EC provided rewards and incentives, they note that international influence was "not crucial" in Spain and that the domestic weaknesses of the junta in Greece best explain the causes of democratization there, not EC pressure.[31] The "pacted transition" of Spain encouraged domestic actors to keep external backers at a distance, and in Greece the interjection of foreign policy questions and debates over the EC became divisive and eventually complicated democratic consolidation. Tsingos argues, "if the EC and its members states were actively promoting democracy in Greece, they were doing so in a most curious fashion."[32] Aside from the EC, one can point to other elements that facilitated democratization, including social support for democracy (as far as can be determined), and the lack of a powerful ideological challenger to democracy.

Ultimately, although there is some overlap of domestic and international factors, one must note that the primary causes of democratization in these cases were domestic. Even Whitehead concedes that these cases "confirm that the unfolding of what appear as primarily domestic political processes largely accounts for the establishment of new democratic regimes, and also for their consolidation."[33] Thus, while these cases may allow one to identify mechanisms through which international actors may play a role, it does little to advance hypotheses about how important or decisive a role it was or can be. To invoke a metaphor, the EC served as a guardrail for states that were already intent upon traveling the road of democratization. Had the road been bumpier, the guardrail may have been crucial to keeping these states on their path, and we would have been able to tell if it was strong enough for this task. However, the EC never faced the tests that it has faced more recently with the "reluctant democratizers."

Mention could be made here of the Turkish case in the 1980s. The military, which launched a coup in 1980, handed power back to the civilians in 1983, and in 1987 Turkey submitted a membership bid to the EC. This bid was rejected in 1989, and the EC cited Turkey's economic and political shortcomings, although the criticism on the political side was rather muted.[34] Turkish leaders, however, did not rush out to overhaul their political system, even though such efforts would have been looked upon favorably by the EC. Why not? Several answers could be suggested, and Thomas W. Smith will discuss the Turkish case at length in Chapter 5, but for now one should note that the prospect of membership was not on the table, EU criticism was viewed by many Turks as meddlesome and marked by prejudice, and Turkey could rely upon support from the United States.[35] In short, the carrot was insufficient, international–domestic linkages were weak, and Turkey could feel confident it could circumvent any EC sanction.

The collapse of communism in Eastern Europe would provide a rich opportunity for the EC (EU after 1993) to promote democratization. Member states formed the EBRD (European Bank for Reconstruction and Development) in 1989, PHARE was established in December of the same year for Poland and Hungary, Trade and Cooperation Agreements were put into place, and in 1991 the first Association Agreements were signed with post-communist states. PHARE would quickly expand its activities beyond its initial two countries, and a TACIS (Technical Assistance for the CIS) program extended EU efforts into the former USSR. By 1996, eleven Association Agreements had been signed with Central and East European States, Cooperation Agreements had been established with countries such as Russia and Ukraine, and the EU found itself to be the largest supplier of aid to the region.[36] Moreover, pressures to grant membership in the EU itself to these states was mounting, and eventually the norms of integration prevailed over the self-interest of some EU states that did not want to move beyond the Association Agreements, which only noted that EU membership was the final objective of these states.[37] By December 1997, the EU had proffered its *avis* on the numerous applications, putting Estonia, the Czech Republic, Poland, Hungary, and Slovenia in the front of the queue for membership, while rejecting another Turkish bid and singling out Slovakia for its political shortcomings.

What lessons can be drawn from this? Superficially, one might note EU success. The EU engaged in dialogue and institution-building with former communist states, and the Association Agreements spelled out terms of political conditionality, noting that they were dependent upon respect for democratic procedures, the rule of law, and human rights. In turn, some Central and East European states can boast of successful democratic consolidation. Surely, one could note, the EU played some important role in this, as witnessed by the fact that geographic proximity to the EU is perhaps the best explanation of post-communist success.[38]

As tempting as it may be, there are several problems with reaching this conclusion. As with Southern Europe, correlation does not prove causality, and on closer inspection some of the supposed causal links break down. One would have thought EU aid would be important in fostering democracy, but it is notable that from 1990–1996 PHARE aid for civil society and democratization for the seven non-Yugoslav countries of Eastern Europe totaled a paltry ECU8.2 million, compared with 1.12 billion for infrastructure, 925 million for the finance sector, and 4.14 billion in the whole program.[39] True, all the economic and technical assistance may have helped create a more hospitable environment for democratization (although Janine Wedel's work is a strong indictment against aid programs), but one is tempted to agree with John Pinder, who noted "too little thought has been given to the question of how the West can contribute to this [democratization]," and that the rhetoric of support for democracy has not been matched with real substance.[40] Mayhew also notes that PHARE aid was not based on any conditionality, although others would dispute this.[41] This, arguably, has changed as discussions moved from aid to membership, but it is interesting to note how reticent the EU was initially to employ sticks.[42] Moreover, the causal logic misses a key point: all the "success stories" were well on their way to being successful by 1991, when the Association Agreements were first signed and membership was not on the table. Again, the EU served as a guardrail, "underwriting democracy" in states where democratic progress, for a variety of reasons, had already been substantial. Indeed, if one had to guess which post-communist countries in 1989 would turn out to be most successful (due to factors such as historical heritage, economic development, elites, political culture), one would likely name those that today enjoy consolidated democracies.

Again, there are some analytical problems. One cannot wholly dismiss the notion that the model of the EU and its various norms has been an important inspiration for democratizing elites. There may thus be a demonstration or contagion effect. Moreover, history and culture, to the extent they are causal elements in the story of democratization, may be shaped by Europe or the notion of a "return to Europe." Overall, one can note that democracy seems to be over-determined in a number of states,[43] with EU support one element in a very complex equation where many factors bode well for democracy. Determining how crucial EU support actually has been and disentangling it from other factors (e.g. is economic success affected by EU support, and in turn does that contribute to democracy?) are nearly intractable tasks.

However, one can note a few items that may be useful for our purposes. One is that the EU has no doubt benefited in the successful countries from a ready acceptance of EU norms. There was no cultural disconnect or rival program (e.g. parochial nationalism) that would challenge the principles upheld by the EU. EU norms were congruent with the agenda of most elites. Obviously, had there been an alternative discourse to that of the EU, matters would have been more complicated. Most accepted the legitimacy of EU conditionality, although of course they would dispute whether they had met EU criteria. The publics also backed the EU, although most observers note that people generally knew very little of the EU and that support for the EU has begun to decline in states such as Poland where the prospect of membership is no longer a dream but seems likely to happen soon.[44] However, one might not want to give that much weight to public opinion, given the fact that from 1991 to 1996 Romania scored the highest of Central and Eastern states in terms of public support for the EU, and a problematic state such as Slovakia scored better than Hungary or Estonia.[45] One element that stands out in most of the successful democratic consolidations is leadership turnover in the initial elections, with the post-communist elites less beholden to the norms and structures of the past.[46] Arguably, as I will posit below, new states or new leaders are more likely to accept externally promoted norms. This factor, however, while potentially relevant to Ukraine and Romania, holds up less well for Slovakia and Croatia. One might mention the stronger performance of established states versus "new" ones such as Ukraine, Slovakia, and Croatia, and there is some evidence to suggest that at least the EU is less popular in "new" states.[47] However, the Baltic states have largely done well, as have Slovenia and the Czech Republic.

Of course, not all post-communist states have proven to be success stories. Some have experienced a bumpier road toward democratization, at times falling off the path. In these instances, the guardrail failed, although in some cases (e.g. Slovakia, Romania) they have returned to a more democratic path. Other states (e.g. Croatia, Turkey, Morocco) have been democratic holdouts for an extended period (Croatia has made good progress of late), and the question here is how the EU might be able to influence domestic politics so that targeted states begin to undertake fundamental reforms. One needs to account for these cases in order to have a complete picture of EU efforts to promote democracy in neighboring states as well as, in academic parlance, variation on the dependent variable (democracy). Our cases are thus those of "reluctant democratizers." Some can now be seen (tentatively perhaps) as successes. Others are failures, or, more kindly, works-in-progress. For the most part, the factors affecting democratization do not line up in one direction in these states, and thus one can see how EU efforts interact with other variables. The next section attempts to highlight these variables and formulate hypotheses relevant to the case studies in this volume.

The EU and democratization: hypotheses

The historical record of the EU in promoting democracy provides one source of ideas for hypotheses about how the EU can foster political change outside its borders. Of course, this project – the spread of democracy – is not unique to the EU, and one can put such efforts into a wider context in order to develop additional hypotheses. What follows is an effort to put together some hypotheses that will help guide our exploration of EU relations with "reluctant democratizers." We shall focus on processes of convergence and policies that promote conditionality, as these two concepts are the ones most useful for our work and also those that lend themselves best to the formation of testable hypotheses.

Convergence

As discussed above, convergence can be understood as system conformity produced by the spread and acceptance of democratic norms. It can be distinguished from conditionality in that convergence results less from a cost/benefit assessment and more from a genuine internalization of norms, the result of persuasion, dialogue, and socialization, or exposure to new ideas. Of course, the adoption of any norm may have a material or instrumental motivation, particularly if elements of conditionality are in play at the same time. However, those who subscribe to constructivist or ideational theories, who maintain that interests are not fixed or given but are the product of complex social forces, would argue that norms can play an important, independent role. As Risse and Sikkink note, "material factors and conditions matter through cognitive and communicative processes, the 'battleground of ideas,' by which actors try to determine their identities and interests and to develop collective understandings of the situation in which they act and of the moral values and norms guiding their action."[48]

How then might these norms work? Specifically, how might the norm of democracy, espoused by the EU, take hold in "reluctant democratizers"? Note that in our cases we are talking about cases in which there has been real resistance by important political actors to democratic principles; there was not, as in Spain, Poland, or the Czech Republic, a virtually automatic acceptance of all the trappings of democracy and thus no need to engage in moral persuasion or norm promotion since the norms were already in place. Thus, the issue is how norms can overcome obstacles and become accepted by elites and masses in a given state.

In order to answer these questions, we can draw upon the burgeoning literature on international norms. Of course, much of this literature concerns the spread and effect of norms on international behavior (e.g. conflict management, economic cooperation, reducing international transaction costs) and suffers from problems of establishing causal links, but there are studies that focus on spread of norms in the domestic arena such as inclusive citizenship and human rights.[49] What do these studies suggest? In general terms, the main points are that the effectiveness of international norms will be conditioned by the saliency of the norm as well as structural context of the domestic policy debate. Salience means that a given norm will have a "durable set of attitudes toward the norm's legitimacy" so that the norm is widely "accepted as a guide to conduct."[50] The importance of salience, however, may be both obvious and too vague, and thus one needs to understand how norms become salient and how they are filtered through domestic politics.

With liberal borrowing from some of this literature, one can posit a number of testable hypotheses, both inductively and deductively derived, that are relevant to our concerns. These include the content of the norm, the structure of domestic politics and transnational coalitions, and the methods of norm promotion. Strands of thought floating around in several works can be lumped together into the following hypotheses.[51]

Cultural match

By this, one means that the international norm must resonate or be proximate with pre-existing domestic norms and must have some degree of domestic "authorship."[52] Another way of putting this is that the norm must be uncontested, and be able to travel easily from the temporal and cultural context in which the norm was constructed. Of course, to the extent that democracy is less an international than a *domestic* norm (as it governs domestic political behavior), one can run into problems of tautology – democratic norms do not take root because the state is not democratic. One can avoid this, however, and preserve some notion of cultural match or norm contestation by referring to the extent to which some aspects of democratic norms (i.e. competition, tolerance, individual rights) are given space within a given domestic discourse. If these norms receive at least lip-service, there is more chance that they can acquire genuine salience than if there is no pre-existing space for them or they have previously been rejected as incompatible with a given state's culture or perceived interests. One set of authors, reviewing efforts to promote democracy from the outside, notes the diffusion of norms and democratic practice decisively depends upon their interaction with local norms and practices.[53] In our context, one way of assessing cultural match is to examine how Europe is "constructed" by local actors, and whether the given country fits into this construction (e.g. the "return to Europe" mantra) or whether Europe is portrayed exclusively as a foreign institution, one that has little in common with the given country.

Novelty of the environment

This notion includes two arguments, both of which may be viewed as a corollary of the cultural match hypothesis.[54] The first is that norm-based persuasion from outside agents is more likely to be effective in new, uncertain environments, when state leaders will be more open to new ideas. The second is that if state leaders themselves are new and therefore may lack firm, ingrained beliefs (what Checkel calls "novice agents") the more likely they will be open to international persuasion. Hypotheses of this type have obvious relevance for the new, post-communist states, which are confronted with a new situation on several levels (e.g. demands of reforms, novelty of statehood) and are led by political "novices," as well as Morocco under its new king, Mohammed VI. They also could be applied to post-Franco Spain and post-Salazar Portugal, in the sense that old norms were being discarded and political authorities were forced to seek new means of legitimation. They may, however, have less relevance for Turkey, a state with more enshrined political traditions. Yet, while we may be able to see the logic at work in this hypothesis, one should note a counter-hypothesis on this score. This would be:

Nationalism of new states

New states (e.g. Slovakia, Ukraine, Croatia) need to develop a basis for their own legitimacy. This will often mean fostering nationalism, perhaps stressing the state's uniqueness and/or desire to remain apart from integrative structures, such as the EU. In the three states named above that will be described in this volume, one perhaps might add that their recent experience in a federation as junior partners would make them hesitant to surrender sovereignty to the EU. Thus, one confronts the possibility of a counter-norm, another discourse, one that may lessen the attractiveness of both the EU as an organization and the norms it espouses. Indeed, studies of other newly independent states testify to the fact that re-integrative schemes may be putting the cart before the horse, and that new states will be more concerned with pursuing a nationalist project.[55] Thus, according to the logic of both hypotheses presented here, one needs to look at how external norms are filtered through preexisting ideas.

Status of the persuader

This hypothesis is rather straightforward. If the persuader, in our case the EU, is seen as authoritative and/or successful, its norms will carry more credibility and therefore, *ceteris paribus*, be more influential. Thus, one needs to consider the prism – ideological, political, cultural – through which the EU is viewed in order to assess how likely it is that it will be able to influence a state's domestic politics. This assessment of the EU – ranging from heroic savior to well-meaning meddler to agent of neo-colonialism – will vary from state to state and (importantly) among actors within a state. Moreover, one might note that some of the EU's own domestic problems, notably its "democratic deficit," might undermine the EU's credibility as an agent of democratization, especially as prospective members gain a better under-standing of how the EU operates in practice.

Spillover from rhetoric to real change

Repeated invocation of a given norm by political elites or social actors will increase the norm's salience. The invocation initially may be cynical or self-serving, but the very fact that the norms are given voice will affect their resonance and lead to greater chances for internalization. Risse and Sikkink suggest that the more state elites "talk the talk," the more "they entangle themselves in a moral discourse which they cannot escape in the long run."[56] as the rhetoric legitimizes the norm and provides a ready-made discourse for regime opponents who seek liberalization and/or democratization. This hypothesis may seem obvious and overlaps a bit with the idea of cultural match, but it is worth noting because one can measure the extent to which external norms are incorporated into the discourse of domestic actors.

Transnational networks

While rhetoric from both the international actor and domestic actors is important, the adoption of a given norm is more likely if there is some sort of activity or support mechanisms behind that norm. This is especially true when current domestic authorities are not truly committed to implementing the given norm. Thus, one needs to discuss efforts to empower other actors to promote the norm. On this score one assesses ties between the inter-national actor and domestic ones, including state elites, political parties, and non-governmental organizations (NGOs) in civil society. These transnational networks transmit the norm, socialize domestic actors, and become an important agent of change. These points are developed best by Risse and Sikkink in a "spiral model" with a "boomerang effect," in which they suggest that political change comes about from both outside encouragement and pressure from below within a society or target state, generated by opponents to the status quo who become empowered by both use of a international norm (gaining moral legitimacy) and access to external actors (who provide logistical and political support and greater leverage to domestic actors).[57] "Reluctant democratizers" – or, in Risse and Sikkink's case, human rights violators – are thus caught in a pincer between external and internal actors, who by working together strengthen the norm and can force concessions from state elites. Of course, the effectiveness of these transnational coalitions – present to varying degrees in all our case studies – will be conditioned on some of the factors enumerated above (e.g. general views of the EU, alternative norms and discourses, rhetorical use or disdain of EU norms by current elites). Again, the point may be obvious, but what we want to look for is both what the EU says and what the EU actually does in order to engage actors in the target state and thereby advance its democratic agenda. Critics of democracy promotion assistance have noted that money from abroad often results in "troughs" at which local elites feed or "ghettoized" communities of NGOs that serve more the foreign donor than any domestic constituency.[58] Programs such as PHARE, TACIS, or the Euro-Mediterranean Partnership thus need careful examination to see how successfully the EU has been able to empower local agents for democratization "from below."

Soft tactics

This hypothesis is more concerned with the method of norm promotion, rather than the norm's substance. Here again I combine two of Checkel's hypotheses.[59] Checkel maintains that norm promotion will be more successful if the external actor refrains from lectures and demands, and instead engages in sustained, principled argumentation. Persuasion is to be preferred to coercion, in part because coercion may enforce some sort of compliance but not genuine internalization of the norm. Checkel also suggests that the less politicized the environment and the more insulated interactions are from intense scrutiny, the more receptive the state will be to the norm. Here one is concerned with the often delicate matter of diplomacy, and that the target states have some means to save face and not appear to be caving in to outside actors.

The logic of this hypothesis, however, is at odds with most conceptions of conditionality, in which an outside actor imposes certain standards or demands on a target state, and compliance, rather than negotiation over the norm's substance, is expected. Thus one can posit an additional hypothesis:

Open and tough tactics

Norm promotion should not be shrouded in diplomatic niceties, standards should be clear, and tough talk (and sometimes action) can be used effectively as a complement or even as an alternative to softer efforts of persuasion. While many of the concerns of the norm's substance and building transnational ties are relevant for conditionality, conditionality is best distinguished from convergence – as I have defined the term – by its methods. This provides a segue into a discussion of how conditionality might work.

Conditionality

Conditionality works along instrumental lines, and thereby falls more into a "rational actor" model of politics than a constructivist one. The goal is less moral persuasion than offering carrots and sticks to compel a state to adopt a given policy, and thus is often easier to identify in practice than methods associated with convergence. Obviously, the EU has employed conditionality, most clearly in the case of Copenhagen Criteria for membership, but also in relations with states such as Ukraine and Morocco where membership in the EU is not on the table (although Ukraine, unlike Morocco, can dream of eventual membership). Conditionality, of course, has been used by many other actors as well, as states are offered incentives or threatened with sanctions if they do not adopt policies ranging from respect of human rights to economic austerity. The questions, however, are whether and under what conditions can conditionality actually work? As we did with the idea of convergence and the acceptance of norms, one can posit several hypotheses.

Carrots must constitute a sizeable benefit

This is a rather simple idea. If external actors are going to offer incentives for policy change, the blandishments must be compelling. In our case, the reward must be substantial enough for elites to be willing to risk, in Dahl's terms, the "costs of toleration," since democratization opens up the possibility that current elites may lose power.[60] Moreover, borrowing from Przeworski, who argues that actors must see at least a possibility of winning if they are to play the democratic game, one might hypothesize that elites who are relatively certain that they would lose under genuine democratic contestation will be less likely to push ahead with democratization, even in the face of external pressure.[61] This idea, of course, opens up the tricky question of whether the EU would have been able or would be able to offer sufficient incentives to leaders such as Kuchma in Ukraine, Tudjman in Croatia, or Mečiar in Slovakia, a point that we shall return to in the conclusion. Finally, one should note that the prospect of receiving the reward must be real; that is, there must be certainty that political change will be rewarded. In the 1970s, Spain, Greece, and Portugal had such hopes; Turkey did not, and thus, arguably Turkish democracy remained less consolidated. However, in East Central Europe, substantial movement toward democracy was made even before Association Agreements were signed with the EU. Today, among our "reluctant democratizers," one sees different carrots on offer – ranging from almost certain membership in the EU (although the absence of a firm date for new members to accede is beginning to create tension in some states' relations with the EU) to unspecified economic reward. These may be important factors in determining how successful policies based upon conditionality will be.

Sticks must be real

If the carrots must be real, so must the sticks. In other words, state leaders need to know that rewards will be withheld or punishments will be meted out if the desired policy change is not adopted. This may seem perfectly obvious, because if states have no fear of sanction, then they will be less willing to bend to EU pressure. However, despite EU rhetoric on such issues as human rights, the record shows that the EU has been reluctant to employ sanctions against violators.[62] In Eastern Europe, the EU has shown some backbone in singling out states for criticism (e.g. delays in concluding Association Agreements with Romania and Bulgaria, Slovakia's lack of fulfillment of Copenhagen's political criteria in 1997), but this has not been universally true (e.g. acceptance of Turkey's candidature despite short-comings on the Copenhagen Criteria, lack of sanction in wake of Ukraine's recent problems). What might be especially important to note here is that the EU may be reluctant to play hardball with a state because other concerns (e.g. security) may trump democratization. Certainly, this has been the case for North Atlantic Treaty Organization (NATO), whose commitment to a democratic membership wavered during the Cold War in order to keep Portugal, Greece, and Turkey as members.[63] Similarly, one might imagine that if there are concerns about security or geopolitical alignments (e.g. will EU pressure push Ukraine into Russia's arms?) or simple fears that pressure may be counterproductive (e.g. might EU interference strengthen Romania's nationalists?), then the power of the sticks and conditionality will be severely circumscribed.[64]

Lack of alternatives for target states

This hypothesis can be seen as a corollary of the previous one. If states have other alternatives for economic or political support, they may be able to withstand pressure from a single international actor. Self-reliant states may also be less susceptible to outside pressure. To put the matter more concretely, EU influence may be weakened if a state can find support from other states that do not apply standards of conditionality. This may be true for Turkey (US), Ukraine (Russia), and Morocco (the Arab world). This problem – that sanctions can be circumvented – has led some to argue that economic sanctions are an ineffective tool of international politics.[65] If the EU, on the other hand, is viewed as vital to the state's economic and political standing and the influence of other actors is limited, then EU demands may carry more weight.

Transnational networks II

Conditionality is more likely to work when external actors can find domestic allies, who in turn can apply pressure to the existing authorities and whose actions can defuse potential claims that the outside demands somehow do not correspond with the state's identity or interests. This idea, of course, is similar to the aforementioned "boomerang effect," although in this case the stress would be less on norms and moral persuasion than playing upon interests of domestic actors. Granted, the line between norms and persuasion and interests may be a fine one, but even those operating from a norm-based perspective refer to the importance of fulfilling some sort of domestic interests.[66] This proposition is also given wide-ranging empirical support, especially from those who study "two-level" games and the necessity of finding a common "win-set" (common interests) between actors in the international and domestic arenas.[67] In our cases, one could anticipate a number of political and economic actors interested in meeting EU demands; the question then becomes whether their voices will be heard or if they can become sufficiently empowered.

Problems of "gray zone" democracies

A special problem potentially relevant to many of our cases occurs when a state meets some minimum standard of democracy (e.g. it has elections and a largely democratic constitution) but in practice there may be some significant democratic shortcomings (e.g. restrictions on competition, barriers that prevent emergence of genuine pluralism). These "democratic" systems can be qualified by many adjectives – illiberal, electoral, delegative, limited, constrained, directed – but the point is that they fall in a gray zone in between consolidated democracy and open authoritarianism. Pridham calls these states "hybrid regimes," and notes that they pose real problems for external actors interested in advancing a broader or more complete notion of democracy.[68] These states may be able to avoid sanctions because external actors might not want to make matters worse and risk the limited democratic gains or wholly alienate the regime. This would be especially true in cases where the regime can plausibly claim some degree of democratic progress from a wholly authoritarian regime. Moreover, because these states may enjoy a wide measure of domestic support or legitimacy, they may be better able to withstand any push to "deepen" democracy or force through a complete democratic breakthrough. To the extent that the EU is interested in a wider notion of substantive democracy (development of parties, the media, civil society, respect for minorities, etc.), the EU may find it more difficult to deal with these quasi-democratic states, whose leaders may formally embrace democratic norms but argue that special circumstances limit the applicability of some democratic principles (especially minority rights) to their country (e.g. this has been the case in Turkey in its battles with Kurds and Islamists and arguably true in Croatia as well during the wars in the Balkans). The issue then is how far can the full demands of conditionality be pushed against states that are partially democratic and claim (in rhetoric at least) to be generally supportive of democratic ideas.

A final word before closing this section. Reality may not always correspond to neatly drawn typologies or hypotheses that attempt to treat phenomena or processes as discrete categories. Simple dichotomies such as "interests versus norms" will fail to capture the interplay between the two. Norms are likely to appeal to interests, and democratization may be promoted, both because it is the "right thing to do" and because it will bring tangible benefits. Norm-based approaches such as "shaming" may produce pressure similar to that of conditionality or actually lead to some sort of material sanction. At times, norms that initially were adopted under pressure for only instrumental reasons will become over time internalized by actors and incorporated into the dominant discourse of the state. Thus, echoing Risse and Sikkink, we will likely encounter "a mixture of instrumental and argumentative rationalities,"[69] in terms of both EU policy to target states and the states' own responses to the EU. For the reader's convenience, a summary of these hypotheses is presented in Table 1.1

Table 1.1 Summary of hypotheses on democracy promotion

Convergence	*Spread of norms*
Cultural match	External norms have some resonance with preexisting ones
Novelty of environment vs. Nationalism	New elites/states more open to new norms or does nationalism in new states work against outside influence?
Status of persuader	External promoter should be held in high regard
Spillover	Rhetoric of support for norm will build momentum for policy shift
Transnational networks	External promoters need allies (governmental or non-governmental) in the target country
Soft tactics preferred	Softer tactics will be more effective than overt pressure
Conditionality	*Instrumental calculation leads to policy shift*
Sizable carrots	External promoter must offer strong incentives
Real sticks	External promoter must be able and willing to sanction
Lack of alternatives	Targeted states cannot turn to others for help and support
Transnational networks	External promoters need allies (governmental or non-governmental) in the target country
Gray zone democracies	Pseudo-democracies can confuse policy by pointing to "progress" and thus escape sanction and win benefits

Democratic consolidation and reluctant democratizers

Up to this point, we have focused mainly on the processes and policies by which the EU may be able to shape political outcomes in other states. In other words, we have put forward hypotheses about independent, causal variables, and have not engaged in an extended discussion of the dependent variable, consolidated democracy. Before closing this chapter and examining the case studies, we should devote some space to defining this concept and noting how our cases of "reluctant democratizers" represent states where democratic consolidation has been quite problematic.

Democratic consolidation can be best understood as the final stage of the process of democratization. As an ideal type, one can break democratization into three stages. Liberalization is the initial period when political restrictions are relaxed and alternative voices and groups are given freedoms to express themselves and organize. Transition can be understood as the process of regime change itself, when the authoritarian system gives way to new democratic institutions and procedures. Consolidation refers to the process, often a lengthy one and in a certain sense always ongoing, of stabilizing and institutionalizing democratic institutions and practices, as well as the internalization of democratic norms by elites and masses. In Linz and Stepan's words, democracy becomes "the only game in town," meaning that non-democratic alternatives are impossible to contemplate, endorsed by no significant political actors.[70] Of course, this game is not only played during elections. Its rules must be observed each day, meaning that democratic norms and behavior (rule of law, respect for opposition and pluralism, etc.) must be observed at all times. However, for Linz and Stepan, democratic consolidation is not only about political behavior; it depends upon support mechanisms such as civil society, political society (well-established political parties), economic society (market institutions along with effective government regulations), and a democratic political culture. Kaldor and Vejvoda go even further, distinguishing between procedural and substantive democracy: procedural democracy is more concerned with rules and institutions; and substantive democracy focuses on civil society, free media, social pluralism, observance of human rights, and effective administration.[71] In their view, movement toward substantive democracy is essential to underwrite the promises of procedural democracy. Labels aside, the important point here is that democratic consolidation means a genuine deepening of democracy, a move beyond promulgation of new rules and toward sustained, meaningful democratic practice. Notably, in both its programs and in its Copenhagen Criteria, the EU has put emphasis on aspects of substantive democracy, such as civil society, development of political parties, and protection of minorities.[72] In our cases, we largely adopt this focus on democratic practice and supporting elements, although in some cases (Morocco, Ukraine) there have been serious shortcomings in procedural democracy as well.

Recognizing that no democracy will be perfect on these more substantive dimensions, one can nonetheless distinguish between more and less consolidated democracies. In Eastern Europe, Poland, the Czech Republic, Estonia, and Hungary rank as democratic "leaders," states where democratic consolidation is well under way and where no significant threat to democracy has emerged since the end of the previous communist regime. Opposition is free to organize, there have been multiple transfers of power from party to party, civil society is *relatively* strong (compared to most of our cases), minority rights have been largely respected, independent media are well established, and constitutional stability has been maintained. Of course, one can point to some problems (e.g. Czech treatment of Roma minorities, Wałęsa's authoritarian blustering in Poland), but these pale next to the democratic shortcomings in the states we will be considering. With good reason, we can call these states "reluctant democratizers," cases where democratic consolidation has been seriously delayed and/or never really gotten off the ground. The difference between the two groups of states are made clear in the rankings of Freedom House, which has characterized the states of our study "Partly Free" or "Not Free" for significant time periods. By the time of this writing, some of these states, notably Latvia, Slovakia, and Romania, have made progress, now ranked "Free" by Freedom House, as their neighbors in Central Europe have been ranked since communism's collapse.[73] In others, however, such as Ukraine, one might argue the transition period of democratization is not even fully completed, and in Morocco the results of ostensible liberalization have been equivocal and one has yet to see any significant movement to democracy. Let us now consider our cases in more detail.

The first country we will examine is Latvia. In many respects, Latvia constitutes a democratic success story – especially compared to most other former Soviet states – and thus may seem out of place in this study. Elections are held, there is genuine political pluralism, civil rights are respected, there has been no political violence, and economic reforms have progressed to the point where Latvia has joined NATO and is on the threshold of EU membership. However, Latvia has had one major blemish on its record which makes it an "issue-specific" reluctant democratizer: state policy that denied citizenship to ethnic Slavs and others who had emigrated to Soviet Latvia and did not know Latvian. As originally formulated, these policies could have disenfranchised over a third of the country's population, and they drew criticism both from Moscow and from Brussels. Indeed, European intervention is often credited with being decisive in forcing the Latvian government to soften its position and make concessions to the non-ethnic Latvians. While there are still tensions around this issue, outside observers, including the EU, have given Latvia's democracy passing marks. Chapter 2 by Nils Muiznieks and Ilze Brands Kehris takes up these issues, demonstrating how Latvia is a case of an initially "reluctant democratizer" succumbing (apparently) to outside pressure.

Slovakia is an obvious case to include among "reluctant democratizers." Whereas its Visegrad neighbors of Poland, the Czech Republic, and Hungary moved ahead with their democratization programs and have joined NATO, Slovakia suffered under the rule of Vladimir Mečiar and his Movement for a Democratic Slovakia. The country's democratic shortcomings became especially notable after 1994 parliamentary elections, after which Mečiar spearheaded an effort to concentrate executive power in his hands, economic reform was compromised by clientelistic practices, the independent media and the Hungarian minority found themselves under assault by state policy, and state administration became extremely politicized. In 1997, the country's problems on this front precipitated the EU to single it out as the only post-communist applicant for membership which failed to meet the political criteria of Copenhagen. Arguably, this decision, which promised to exclude Slovakia from EU enlargement, galvanized Mečiar's opponents and led to his defeat in 1998. Since then, Slovakia has made significant democratic progress, and the country is now a member of NATO and will join the EU in 2004. In Chapter 3 Kevin Deegan Krause will analyze what credit, if any, the EU can take in this transformation.

Romania's transition away from communism has been troubled since the end of the Ceaușescu regime. The initial post-Ceaușescu government, led by President Ion Iliescu and the National Salvation Front, was accused of being a haven for former communists and members of the Securitate, and engaged in practices inimical to political opponents and the country's ethnic-Hungarian minority. Romania clearly was a democratic laggard, and under this government was not seriously considered for NATO or EU membership. In 1996, a center-right party came to power, and there was hope that it could transform the political landscape and court European institutions. While the country's image improved, its economy did not, and in 2000 Iliescu and the reformed Communist Party returned to power. More disturbing, perhaps, was the strong showing of the neofascist Greater Romania Party in parliamentary and presidential elections. While the new government acknowledges the need to undertake political reform and Romania is now a NATO member, the domestic political environment is not wholly auspicious. William Crowther will examine in Chapter 4 how the EU is trying to encourage reform in Romania, dealing with a leadership with a shady past and some elements of the opposition with even fewer democratic credentials.

Turkey has had both a problematic relationship with the EU and decades of difficulties in consolidating a democratic government. The military has intervened to "save" democracy four times since 1960, Kurdish and Islamist political parties have been banned, there are a host of restrictions on free speech, and the Kurds are denied what they view as their legitimate cultural rights. Turkey's human rights record has been a subject of EC/EU interest for years, and the impact of European pressure on Turkey is widely debated. The EU, at its 1999 Helsinki Summit, agreed to entertain Turkish candidacy for membership, reversing a rejection of Turkey in 1997. However, the EU noted that of all candidates in 1999, only Turkey failed to meet the political components of the Copenhagen Criteria. The question now is whether

Turkey will accede to key EU demands, particularly ending restrictions on speech and political competition and granting some rights to its Kurdish citizens. These issues are hotly debated, and in Chapter 5 Thomas W. Smith will examine the possibilities and limits of the EU to produce political change in Turkey.

Croatia represents an interesting case. Although part of the motivation for Croatian independence was the desire to escape from Slobodan Milosević's authoritarianism, democracy did not fare very well under the rule of Croat President, Franjo Tudjman (1991–1999). Opposition was circumscribed, power concentrated in the president's hands, and minority rights were not protected. These policies were justified and fed by war inside Croatia and in Bosnia, where Croat armies and militias engaged in massive human rights violations. The end of the war augured well for change, but it took the death of Tudjman to open the door to new leadership committed to transforming Croatia from pariah state to candidate for EU membership. While it is still premature to speak of Croatian EU candidacy and all the problems of the Tudjman era have not been overcome, there is good reason to think that Croatia will soon "return to Europe." In Chapter 6 Stephen M. Tull traces a contested and occasionally nebulous EU policy toward Croatia, and assesses how much the EU can take credit for recent changes there.

Most observers would agree that Ukraine's democratic record has been a disappointment. President Leonid Kuchma, elected in 1994, has promoted himself as a "reformer," yet at the same time has centralized power in the executive branch, looked askance at rampant corruption, engaged in vote-rigging, clamped down on media, and has been implicated in the disappear-ance and murder of an opposition journalist. His opponents in Ukraine accuse him of authoritarianism. However, in the midst of domestic "Belarusification," Kuchma has also trumpeted Ukraine's "European course," and under his presidency in 1999 an EU–Ukraine "Common Strategy" ack-nowledged the country's "European aspirations" and Ukraine became a major recipient of EU and US aid. At present, however, EU membership is not on the table, and given the morass that Ukrainian politics has become since 1999, one might wonder what, if anything, the EU can do to put the democratic transition back on course. In Chapter 7 I will highlight these issues, focusing in particular on the willingness and capacity of the EU to push itself into the struggle for democratization in Ukraine.

Morocco is a bit different from the above cases. It has applied for EU membership, but was rejected because it did not geographically qualify as a European state. Thus, the carrot of membership will not be on the table. However, it is linked to Europe through history and trade, and values good relations with the EU as a source of economic benefits. For its part, the EU has made an effort to reach out to Morocco and its neighbors with a "Mediterranean Partnership." While primarily an economic project, it none-theless has its political components, with the EU hoping at least for some political liberalization in the Arab states to its south. Morocco, however, does not qualify as a democracy, as the king remains supreme and political competition is circumscribed. However, there is a multiplicity of political parties and pluralism in the media and civil society, thus making Morocco a better candidate for democratization than, for example, Algeria. Moreover, Mohammed VI has pledged that he would like to consolidate democracy, although his meaning of the term and that understood by the EU may be quite different. That being said, the questions Bradford Dillman takes up in Chapter 8 are whether Morocco's engagement with the EU has done anything to open up possibilities for political change, whether the political norms of the EU carry any sort of cross-cultural resonance, and how and whether the transfer of power in the country will bode well for a democratic opening.

Each of these chapters will attempt to engage the hypotheses offered in this chapter, as well as pointing to some country-specific factors. Each author will be posting his own conclusion, while the overall goal is to use this volume as a comparative case study to identify the strategies, policies, and conditions that best facilitate EU efforts to encourage democratic reform and to suggest as well the relevance of these findings for other international actors. The concluding chapter will serve to draw together the findings of our case studies and suggest how the EU might rethink some of its efforts directed at those states that continue to be "reluctant democratizers."

Notes

1 P. Schmitter, G. O'Donnell, and L. Whitehead, *Transitions from Authoritarian Rule*, vol. 1, Baltimore: Johns Hopkins University Press, 1986, p. 5.

2 G. Pridham, "The International Dimension of Democratization: Theory, Practice, and Inter-regional Comparisons," in Pridham, G. Sandford, and E. Herring eds, *Building Democracy? The International Dimension of Democratization in Eastern Europe*, London: Leicester University Press, 1994, p. 7.

3 K. Smith, "The Use of Political Conditionality in the EU's Relations with Third Countries: How Effective?" *European Foreign Affairs Review* 3, 1998, 253–274, and K. Arts, "Development Cooperation and Human Rights: Turbulent Times for EU Policy", in M. Lister, ed., *New Perspectives on European Union Development Cooperation*, Boulder, CO: Westview Press, 1999.

4 G. Pridham, *The Dynamics of Democratization*, New York: Continuum, 2000, p. 293.

5 L. Whitehead, "Democracy by Convergence: Southern Europe," in Whitehead, ed., *The International Dimension of Democratization: Europe and the Americas*, Oxford: Oxford University Press, 1996, p. 261.

6 See J. Linz and A. Stepan, *Problems of Democratic Transition and Consolidation*, Baltimore: Johns Hopkins University Press, 1996, pp. 74–75, 139, and B. Tsingos, "Underwriting Democracy: The European Community and Greece," in Whitehead, op. cit.

7 Pridham, "The International Dimension of Democratization," op. cit., p. 7

8 J. Kopstein and D. Reilly, "Geographic Diffusion and the Transformation of the Postcommunist World," *World Politics* 53, October 2000, 25.

9 L. Whitehead, "The Enlargement of the European Union: A 'Risky' Form of

Democracy Promotion," in Whitehead, ed., *The International Dimensions of Democratization*, Expanded Edition, Oxford: Oxford University Press, 2001.

10 There are a number of works focusing on EU expansion efforts to the East, most of which are primarily descriptive in nature. Examples include H. Grabbe and K. Hughes, *Eastward Enlargement of the European Union*, London: Royal Institute for International Affairs, 1997; A. Mayhew, *Recreating Europe: The European Union's Policy towards Central and Eastern Europe*, Cambridge: Cambridge University Press, 1998; K. Henderson, ed., *Back to Europe: Central and Eastern Europe and the European Union*, London: UCL Press, 1999; and J. Rupnik, "Eastern Europe: The International Context," *Journal of Democracy* 11, April 2000, 115–129.

11 Good sources include S. Huntington, *The Third Wave: Democratization in the Late Twentieth Century*, Norman, OK: University of Oklahoma Press, 1991; G. Pridham, ed., *Encouraging Democracy: The International Context of Regime Transition in Southern Europe*, London: Leicester University Press, 1991, and "The International Dimension of Democratizattion," op. cit.; Whitehead, "Enlargement of the EU", op. cit.; Linz and Stepan, op. cit.; J. Grugel, ed., *Democracy without Borders: Transnationalization and Conditionality in New Democracies*, London: Routledge, 1999; M. Ottoway and T. Carothers, eds, *Funding Virtue: Civil Society and Democracy Promotion*, Washington, DC: Carnegie Endowment, 2000.

12 See L. Whitehead, "Three International Dimensions of Democratization," in Whitehead, *The International Dimensions of Democratization,* op. cit., and Pridham, *The Dynamics of Democratization*, op. cit., p. 286.

13 Tsingos, op. cit.

14 One could at least note as well that anti-democratic notions, such as ethnic-based, intolerant nationalism, can also become contagious and sweep across national borders.

15 Kopstein and Reilly, op. cit., for example, maintain that a post-communist state capital's proximity to Berlin is the best explanatory factor of that state's reform progress in the post-communist period.

16 H. P. Schmitz and K. Sell, "International Factors in Processes of Political Democratization," in Grugel, op. cit., p. 35.

17 Whitehead, "Three International Dimensions," op. cit., pp. 5–8.

18 Pridham, *The Dynamics of Democratization*, op. cit., 287, 296.

19 Whitehead, "Democracy by Convergence," op. cit., p. 266.

20 Pridham, *The Dynamics of Democratization*, op. cit., p. 296.

21 This follows J. Checkel, "Why Comply? Social Learning and European Identity Change," *International Organization* 55, Summer 2001, 553–588. See also D. Drezner, "Globalization and Policy Convergence," *International Studies Review* 3, Spring 2001, 53–78.

22 Schmitz and Sell, op. cit., p. 36.

23 J. Fearon, "What is Identity (As We Now Use the Word)," Manuscript, Stanford University, 1997.

24 Checkel, op. cit.

25 The Copenhagen Criteria of 1993 note that the candidate countries must achieve "stability of institutions guaranteeing democracy, the rule of law, human rights, and respect for and protection of minorities." See Commission of the European Communities, *Bulletin of the European Communities* 26, no. 6, 1993, 13.

26 Smith, op. cit.

27 For a rational choice-based theory of democratization, see A. Przeworski, *Democracy and the Market*, Cambridge: Cambridge University Press, 1991.

28 Rupnik, op. cit., p. 126. See also G. Pridham, "Complying with the European Unions' Democratic Conditionality: Transnational Party Linkage and Regime Change in Slovakia, 1993–1998," *Europe-Asia Studies* 51, November 1999, 1,221–1,244, and K. Henderson, "Slovakia and the Democratic Criteria for EU Accession," in Henderson, ed., op. cit.

29 Smith, op. cit., p. 258.

30 Whitehead, "Democracy by Convergence," op. cit., p. 271.

31 Linz and Stepan, op. cit., pp. 139, 113, 135.

32 Tsingos, op. cit., p. 323.

33 Whitehead, "Democracy by Convergence," op. cit., p. 272.

34 Ibid., p. 269.

35 A. Karaosmanoğlu, "The International Context of Democratic Transition in Turkey," in *Encouraging Democracy*, op. cit.

36 For data, see Mayhew, op. cit., pp. 132–160, and J. Wedel, *Collision and Collusion*, New York: St. Martin's, 1998, pp. 199–204.

37 For an interesting piece on how norms can prevail over instrumental, cost-benefit policies, see F. Schimmelfennig, "The Community Trap: Liberal Norms, Rhetorical Action, and the Eastern Enlargement of the European Union," *International Organization* 55, Winter 2001, 47–80.

38 Kopstein and Reilly, op. cit.

39 Wedel, op. cit., p. 201.

40 J. Pinder, "The European Community and Democracy in Central and Eastern Europe," in Pridham *et al.*, *Building Democracy?*, op. cit., p. 132.

41 Mayhew, op. cit., p. 144. Pridham disputes this, noting that the EU has "stood out as the one with the most comprehensive approach and effective policy in pursuing democratic conditionality." See *The Dynamics of Democratization*, op. cit., p. 68.

42 True, conclusion of an Association Agreement with Romania and Bulgaria was delayed to 1993 because of political problems in these states, but both received a sizable share of PHARE funds in 1990 once the program was expanded to include them. EU relations with former Yugoslav states (Slovenia excepted) are in a different category.

43 Linz and Stepan, op. cit., p. 75, note that democracy is not "over-determined," even by factors such as a supportive *zeitgeist*.

44 A. Szczerbiak, "Polish Public Opinion: Explaining Declining Support for EU Membership," *Journal of Common Market Studies* 39, March 2001, 105–122.

45 H. Grabbe and K. Hughes, "Central and East European Views on EU Enlargement: Political Debates and Public Opinion," in Henderson, ed., op. cit., pp. 186–187.

46 For the critical role of the founding election, see M. S. Fish, "The Determinants of Economic Reform in the Post-Communist World," *East European Politics and Societies* 12, Winter 1998, 31–78.

47 Grabbe and Hughes, op. cit., p. 188.

48 T. Risse and K. Sikkink, "The Socialization of International Human Rights Norms into Domestic Practices: Introduction," in Risse, S. Ropp, and Sikkink, eds, *The Power of Human Rights: International Norms and Domestic Change*, Cambridge: Cambridge University Press, 1999, p. 7.

49 See A. Cortell and J. Davis, "How Do International Institutions Matter? The Domestic Impact of International Rules and Norms," *International Studies Quarterly* 40, December 1996, 451–478; M. Finnemore, *National Interests in International Society,* Ithaca: Cornell University Press, 1996; P. Katzenstein, ed., *The Culture of National Security: Norms and Identity in World Politics*, Ithaca, NY: Cornell University Press, 1996; A. Yee, "The Causal Effects of Ideas on Policies," *International Organization* 50, Winter 1996, 69–108; Finnemore and Sikkink, "International Norms Dynamics and Political Change," *International Organization* 52, Fall 1998, 887–917; J. Checkel, "Norms, Institutions, and National Identity in Contemporary Europe," *International Studies Quarterly* 43, Spring 1999, 83–144; Risse *et al.*, op. cit.; A. Gurowitz, "Mobilizing International Norms: Domestic Actors, Immigrants and the Japanese State," *World Politics* 51, April 1999, 413–445; Cortell and Davis, "Understanding the Domestic Impact of International Norms: A Research Agenda," *International Studies Review* 2, Spring 2000, 65–87; Checkel, op. cit.

50 Cortell and Davis, "Understanding," op. cit., pp. 66, 69.

51 This is not inclusive of all works or hypotheses, of course, and some may overlap with each other. The goal is to enumerate several prominent hypotheses and those that will likely be most useful for considering how EU norms of democracy might work.

52 See Checkel, "Norms," op. cit., and Cortell and Davis, "Understanding," op. cit.

53 S. Mendelson and J. Glenn, eds, *The Power and Limits of NGOS*, New York: Columbia University Press, 2002, p. 8.

54 This is an amalgam of the first two hypotheses suggested by Checkel, "Why Comply?" op. cit., pp. 562–563.

55 P. Kubicek, "Regionalism, Nationalism, and *Realpolitik* in Central Asia," *Europe-Asia Studies* 49, June 1997, 637–655.

56 Risse and Sikkink, op. cit., p. 16.

57 Ibid.

58 P. Stubbs, "NGOs and the Myth of Civil Society," cited in Mendelson and Glenn, op. cit., p. 6.

59 Checkel, "Why Comply?" op. cit., p. 563.

60 R. Dahl, *Polyarchy*, New Haven: Yale University Press, 1971.

61 Przeworski, op. cit., Chapter 1.

62 Smith, op. cit.

63 D. Reiter, "Why NATO Enlargement Does Not Spread Democracy," *International Security* 25, Spring 2001, 41–67.

64 G. Crawford, "Foreign Aid and Political Conditionality: Issues of Effectiveness and Consistency," *Democratization* 4, Autumn 1997, 69–108.

65 R. Pape, "Why Economic Sanctions Do Not Work," *International Security* 22, Fall 1997, 90–136.

66 Cortell and Davis, "Understanding," op. cit.

67 The classic source is R. Putnam, "Diplomacy and Domestic Politics: The Logic of Two-Level Games," *International Organization* 42, Summer 1988, 427–460. See also P. Evans, Putnam, and H. Jacobson, eds, *Double-Edged Diplomacy*, Berkeley, CA: University of California Press, 1993.

68 Pridham, *The Dynamics of Democratization*, op. cit., p. 298. See also his "Uneasy Democratization: Pariah Regimes, Political Conditionality, and Reborn Transitions in Central and Eastern Europe," *Democratization* 8, Winter 2001, 65–94, and F.

Zakaria, "The Rise of Illiberal Democracy," *Foreign Affairs* 76, November–December 1997, 22–43.

69 Risse and Sikkink, op. cit., p. 14.

70 Linz and Stepan, op. cit., p. 5. A similar conceptualization can be found in R. Gunther *et al.*, *The Politics of Democratic Consolidation: Southern Europe in Comparative Perspective*, Baltimore: Johns Hopkins University Press, 1995.

71 M. Kaldor and I. Vejvoda, "Democratization in Central and East European Countries: An Overview," in Kaldor and Vejvoda, eds, *Democratization in Central and Eastern Europe*, London: Pinter, 1999.

72 Pridham, *The Dynamics of Democratization*, op. cit., p. 300.

73 Rankings are available at http://www.freedomhouse.org. Latvia was ranked "Partly Free" from 1992–1994, during its citizenship controversy, but since that time has been ranked "Free." Slovakia was ranked "Partly Free" in 1993–1994 and 1996–1998, as was Romania from 1990–1996, Turkey since 1980, Ukraine and Croatia since 1991, and Morocco since 1972 (when the rankings first began). These scores are reported through 2000 and are regularly updated.

2 The European Union, democratization, and minorities in Latvia

Nils Muiznieks and Ilze Brands Kehris

Latvia has made undeniable progress in consolidating democracy since the restoration of independence in 1991, moving successfully toward integration into both the European Union (EU) and North Atlantic Treaty Organization (NATO) at an unexpectedly fast pace. Since 1997 the EU has repeatedly noted that Latvia has fulfilled the political criteria for membership. A fundamental reason for successful democratization has been the high domestic motivation to conform to democratic standards and the wish to regain what is seen as Latvia's rightful place among the Western democracies. In general, this process has been characterized more by eagerness to make a rapid transition to a stable liberal democracy, rather than by any reluctance to democratize. However, Latvian politicians have encountered the most difficulty in amending laws and practice in the realm of minority policy, and it is with this perspective that Latvia could be termed an issue-specific reluctant democratizer.

More than fifty years of Soviet occupation, policies of linguistic Russification, and a precarious demographic situation (in 1989 ethnic Latvians represented only 52 percent of the population and were a minority in seven of the eight largest cities) generated a broad consensus on the necessity of reasserting national identity. The rights and perceptions of Russians and other minorities were not high on the agenda and liberalization of minority policy, particularly in the realms of citizenship and language policy, took place slowly. It is in the area of minority policy that the direct influence of the EU and other international organizations has been particularly evident.

The role of the EU in promoting the gradual adoption of legislation and policy consistent with European values and norms cannot be seen in isolation from that of other international organizations, namely the Conference on Security and Cooperation in Europe/Organization for Security and Cooperation in Europe (CSCE/OSCE) and the Council of Europe (CE). Other organizations, such as the United Nations, the Council of the Baltic Sea States, and NATO, have undoubtedly played a significant role as well. However, the focus here will be the influence of the European Union and its primary partners, the OSCE and the Council of Europe, on Latvian minority policy. Undoubtedly, coordination between these three organizations led to a significantly greater policy impact than when action was taken separately. This will become clear through the documentation of coordinated official statements (and visits) in the substantive sections below. Close cooperation between these organizations is also confirmed by other observers and participants, as is the primacy of the role of the OSCE, at least in the early years of democratic development.

The OSCE and, in particular, its High Commissioner on National Minorities (HCMN) has been described as the "gatekeeper" for the European Union.[1] A close observer has explicitly fixed the High Commissioner's direct link to the EU:

> . . . the High Commissioner could also usually count on the support of, and exert pressure through, or with, the European Union and/or the Council of Europe. As the protection of persons belonging to national minorities is a consideration for EU accession, the High Commissioner was able to use his links with the European Commission and EU Presidency to great effect.[2]

The High Commissioner's cooperation with the Council of Europe and the European Commission was conducted through frequent high-level meetings. In the case of the Council of Europe, it was explicitly to coordinate their action: "[The High Commissioner] also had frequent contacts with the Council of Europe's Director of Political Affairs, which allowed the two to co-ordinate strategy and tactics and to ensure that they were sending the same signal."[3] With the European Commission cooperation was beneficial both to supply the Commission with expertise on human rights and minority issues, while gaining direct backup from the Commission for the High Commissioner's recommendations. This cooperation was especially intense when the EC was preparing opinions on the state of possible future members.[4]

Another analyst stresses the link of the High Commissioner, Max van der Stoel, to the EU, through direct use of his contacts with EU officials.

> Most significantly, however [the High Commissioner] contacted officials of the European Union (EU) and ensured that they would link Latvia's admission to the EU, a primary goal of that state's foreign and economic policy, to implementation of his recommendations on citizenship and language.[5]

The cooperation was close to the point of occasional joint working groups, which were also used to bring home the point of coordinated action to the country visited.[6] Apart from inter-organizational coordination, there was also the crucial backing of key OSCE states, both unilaterally and multilaterally, which gave the High Commissioner greater leverage with Latvian state representatives. The explicit coordination included occasional High Commissioner requests for backing statements by states or organizations:

If the High Commissioner felt that his recommendations were not being sufficiently implemented, he would follow-up (either with a further letter or visit) and/or lobby sympathetic OSCE States or partner organizations [which the author subsequently identifies with the Council of Europe and European Commission], to approach the Government with the same message.[7]

In the two main sections below, we discuss the influence of the European Union, largely through its cooperation partners the OSCE and the Council of Europe, on the two main minority rights legislative and policy areas of the 1990s: citizenship and language. The narrative suggests that both conditionality and convergence were at work.

Citizenship

Events through 1991

In the dramatic events in 1989 and 1990, the Latvian Popular Front won a majority of seats in elections to the Supreme Soviet of the Latvian Soviet Socialist Republic, elected by all residents. On May 4, 1990 this majority adopted a resolution declaring the restoration of Latvia's independence with a transition period to de facto independence. In an inclusive referendum on March 3, 1991, 73.8 percent of the entire population voted in favor of Latvian independence, which became legally established (and promptly internationally recognized) on August 21, 1991 after the failed coup in Moscow. On October 15, 1991 a Supreme Council resolution determined that exclusively those who held citizenship of the Republic of Latvia in 1940 and their descendents would constitute the polity, while other permanent residents would have to naturalize (without determining the procedures or exact requirements for naturalization). This resolution was based on the premise of legal continuity – Latvia was not a newly established state, but a restored state whose occupation by the Soviet regime was never recognized by most Western democracies.

A vivacious debate then erupted between those who argued for an inclusive approach of granting citizenship to all residents (the "zero-option") and radical nationalists opposed to any extension of citizenship to postwar settlers and their descendants. Based on the logic of legal continuity and the restoration of the prewar republic and its citizenry, a consensus emerged that the Supreme Council lacked the legitimate authority to further extend citizenship to former Soviet citizens who were not entitled to Latvian citizenship through restitution. The consensus was that this could only be done by a new parliament to be elected in June 1993 by "restored" citizens alone. As a result, for the first three years of independence, Latvia did not have a citizenship law and approximately 700,000 residents who had arrived after 1940 could not naturalize. The Soviet Union, the country of their previous citizenship, no longer existed, but Latvian citizenship was not yet accessible. The uncertain political status of these "non-citizens" evoked considerable international concern.

Although Latvia became part of the CSCE in 1991, in this early phase it is safe to say that decisions regarding citizenship were almost exclusively determined by domestic variables and political sparring, in which the more liberal, inclusion-oriented political forces lost out. However, in 1992 Latvia was not accepted into the Council of Europe explicitly because of the lack of a well-defined citizenship law. Henceforth, the international factor became more visible and politicians learned their first lesson regarding the consequences of not conforming to the standards and norms of the institutions to which they aspired.[8]

1994 legislation

The first post-independence debate on the citizenship law took place within the context of critical but precarious negotiations on withdrawal of Soviet/Russian troops from Latvia and decommissioning the Skrunda early warning radar station. In 1992, the CSCE Helsinki Summit Declaration called for the conclusion of an agreement with a specific timetable on the withdrawal of troops from Latvia. Subsequent Russian–Latvian negotiations took place with the explicit assistance of the CSCE (after 1995, the OSCE) and especially the Swedish government, which coincidentally held the Chairmanship-in-Office position in 1993 and had a strong interest in regional security.

The attitude of Latvian politicians towards the CSCE was basically positive in 1993, but tensions with Russia were running high. The first High Commissioner on National Minorities, Max van der Stoel, took office in January 1993, and CSCE long-term Missions were established first in Estonia, and in the fall of 1993 also in Latvia. The Missions would allow close on-site monitoring, with a mandate to address citizenship issues, while providing a reliable source of information to Western countries. Both the High Commissioner and the Mission were seen primarily as conflict prevention instruments, not as guardians of international democratic standards per se. At this stage consolidating independence was as much on the agenda as consolidating democracy.[9]

The precarious demographic situation and recent experience of alien rule fostered strong nationalistic sentiments and fueled disbelief in the loyalty of a large part of the non-Latvian population. The assistance of the CSCE and major CSCE countries in achieving the troop withdrawal underscored the correctness of the belief that the only guarantee to independence would be close cooperation with Western states and speedy integration into Western structures and organizations. In the events preceding the final adoption of the Citizenship Law in 1994, these two motivating forces can clearly be seen competing. A significant part of the Latvian political elite, animated by exclusionary nationalism, accepted international standards only very grudgingly and saw their adoption more as the heavy price that had to be paid in order to guarantee the acceptance and cooperation of key Western nations.

Max van der Stoel visited Riga between January 15 and 20, 1993, and then again on April 1 and 2, consulting with high-level governmental and parliamentary representatives. Out of these visits came his first written recommendations, in the form of a list attached to a letter dated April 6, 1993, addressed to Latvian Foreign Minister Georgs Andrejevs. The recommendations clearly focus on the citizenship issue, urging speedy adoption of a new citizenship law, with clear provisions for naturalization and lenient language and residency requirements in line with European standards. The recommendations also highlight the need to grant children born in Latvia citizenship without naturalization and to exempt persons over the age of 60 from language exams.[10]

The Foreign Minister replied that "Most of your conclusions appear to be reasonably grounded, especially those concerning the lack of a new citizenship law in Latvia." But the clear reluctance to heed the recommendations is evident, as the letter then goes on to point out that the Supreme Council as a "transitional parliament" has no mandate to expand the citizenry, indicating that this could be considered only after the June 1993 Saeima elections.[11] Apart from the direct contacts by the High Commissioner and trusted interested observers, this correspondence was also made available to all CSCE participating states by the CSCE Chairman-in-Office ahead of a meeting of the Committee of Senior Officials at the end of April that year, where the situation was to be discussed. International multilateral coordination evolved rapidly.

Meanwhile, in Latvia, heated discussions led to the submission of five widely different citizenship law drafts by parliamentary factions to the Saeima committees for review on September 23, 1993.[12] The new law was adopted in the first reading (there are usually three readings of laws) on November 25, although 23 (out of 100) members of parliament unsuccessfully attempted to block consideration of the draft law, opposing any law that would extend citizenship. Some more moderate representatives of the ruling coalition[13] indicated clearly in the debates that the law adopted in the first reading would be submitted for comments to "international institutions," but most who participated in the debates sounded the nationalist alarm bell. Illustrative of the prevailing atmosphere, even proposals from the moderate opposition Harmony party did not suggest the automatic granting of citizenship, but included naturalization requirements, such as a ten-year census, knowledge of language and the Constitution. Some MPs occasionally referred to international standards, but the extensive debate focused almost exclusively on domestic demographic issues.

After the draft law was adopted in the first reading, the High Commissioner again got involved. In a letter to the Foreign Minister dated December 10, 1993, the High Commissioner warned the government not to adopt too restrictive a policy on naturalization, connecting the citizenship issue directly to democracy. If the right to become a citizen would be denied to the majority of non-Latvians, he states, "the character of the democratic system in Latvia might even be put into question." The High Commissioner suggested that a reasonable approach would be to require moderate Latvian language skills, basic knowledge of the Constitution, and an oath of loyalty to the Republic of Latvia. He also expressed his reservations about the unspecified annual quotas to be set by the government which would lead to uncertainty. He proposed instead a set timetable for various groups of residents depending on their length of residence in the country, thus still ensuring gradual naturalization. He again stressed the importance of granting citizenship to children born in independent Latvia.[14]

In his response, Foreign Minister Andrejevs assured the High Commissioner that his recommendations would be taken into account and distributed to all eight Saeima factions, but then stated that an expert opinion from the Council of Europe was still expected. He continued "I request your understanding in our reserved approach in expressing our views to your submitted recommendations."[15] This illustrates the priority given to the Council of Europe and membership therein at this time, but also an underestimation on the part of Latvian officials of the degree of cooperation and coordination among international organizations.

During the first half of 1994, the press reported on additional intense Latvian contacts with the CSCE and the Council of Europe. Gradually, the idea that there was a direct connection between the citizenship law and the potential for membership in the Council of Europe began to circulate more frequently, as the High Commissioner and Council of Europe representatives, as well as bilateral CSCE states sent signals with increasing clarity. Thus, on February 26 Latvian National Independence Movement (LNNK) MP Alexander Kirsteins discussed in the media whether Latvia should agree to CSCE recommendations regarding citizenship in order to ensure membership in the European Union.[16] On March 9, Latvia's Ambassador to the United States Ojars Kalnins related that a note he had received from US Secretary of State Warren Christopher expressed concern over the rights of Russian-speaking residents who could not vote.[17]

On June 7, 1994, a delegation of Latvian MPs returning from a visit to the Council of Europe provided information to the media and parliament that there were serious Council of Europe reservations regarding the naturalization provisions of the draft law. Governing coalition member Janis Tupesis expressed directly the conditionality put on amending the law:

> first, everyone wants Latvia in the Council of Europe; second, if Latvia will be accepted, then Council of Europe stances have to be adhered to; third, the present Latvian draft law on citizenship is not acceptable to the Council of Europe, fourth, if the draft law will not be amended accordingly, Latvia will not be accepted into the Council of Europe.[18]

In a clear case of direct influence, the decision was taken to postpone review of the draft law, while the nationalist opposition Fatherland and Freedom party complained about crude pressure and interference in Latvian internal affairs.

In the second reading of the law, explicit reference was made to the recommendations of the High Commissioner and the Council of Europe. However, many MPs of the nationalist opposition and some governing coalition representatives dismissed the recommendations as based on an insufficient understanding of Latvia's specific situation, and some expressed disparaging remarks regarding Max van der Stoel as too concerned with the interests of Russians.[19] Debate still focused on domestic issues, and actors showed little understanding of the connection between the recommendations and membership in the international normative community and organizations, with the exception of a couple of individuals from the ruling coalition and the moderate opposition. The ruling parties were divided in their expressed views, sometimes even lacking intra-party consensus. But the existence of some liberalizers in positions of power was key to successful continued international influence and the possibility to establish an effective transnational coalition.

In the end, the law adopted in the third and final reading on June 21, 1994 included a yearly quota of 0.1 percent increase in the citizenry and stringent naturalization requirements. Although this draft ignored the High Commissioner's concerns, nationalists attacked it as too liberal. Under intense international pressure, Latvia's President Guntis Ulmanis then employed his constitutional prerogative to return the legislation to parliament. On July 1, a Latvian parliamentary delegation visited Strasbourg and consulted once more with the Council of Europe's Parliamentary Assembly and experts.

A reworked version of the law was then adopted at an extraordinary session of the parliament on July 22, 1994. This time, much of the discussion focused on Europe and included explicit references to Council of Europe and OSCE recommendations, but the results were mixed. The law included a timetable for naturalization based on length of residence called the "window system," but no fixed maximum number of persons who could naturalize as in the previous draft. However, instead of the High Commissioner's compromise recommendation of spreading naturalization over three years, the final version extended the timetable to seven years from 1996 through 2003.[20]

This first phase of citizenship legislation in Latvia represents a mixed case of influence. On the one hand, the urgent need for specific legislation was taken into account and severe restrictions on possible naturalization applications were abolished. On the other hand, the latter change took place only after a first law was already adopted that contradicted clear recommendations by Max van der Stoel. The repeated recommendation to grant citizenship to children born in Latvia was not heeded, and naturalization requirements were also significantly more stringent than recommended. Moreover, the final result came only after intense consultations and explicit linkage of adoption of an acceptable law to the coveted membership in the Council of Europe.

Parliamentary discourse was dominated by domestic demographic concerns and the perceived threat of disloyalty, while the tendency to opt for a restrictive law was almost unanimous. The goal of joining the European community of nations was almost universally accepted by the political elite, but at this point usually not directly connected to the issue at hand. The second round concentrated on the international dimension, but the focus was almost exclusively on arguments of conditionality – there were very few attempts to discuss specific norms, shared values, or democratic prerequisites within the context of citizenship. Despite a lack of detailed understanding of liberal democratic norms, the consensus on democracy as the only possible option for Latvia remained unchallenged. This is an important point in order to understand the high level of motivation to cooperate with Western institutions, while also explaining the tendency by most politicians at the time to focus on the tactical and instrumental dimensions of norm adaptation.

1998 legislation

Latvia's membership in the Council of Europe in February 1995 and Romano Prodi's statement to President Ulmanis at the OSCE summit in Lisbon in December 1996 expressing support for Latvia's membership in both the European Union and NATO shifted the Latvian focus from the Council of Europe to the European Union. The OSCE retained a conspicuous role both through the continued active involvement of the High Commissioner on National Minorities and the OSCE Mission to Latvia. Moreover, when the European Commission delegation office in Riga was opened in April 1997, it provided for closer direct involvement by the European Commission in developments in Latvia.

Because of the unexpectedly slow pace of naturalization, in 1996 the High Commissioner came forth with recommendations to ease the language and history exam requirements for naturalization and to lower naturalization fees.[21] In his answer, Foreign Minister Valdis Birkavs expressed good will in principle, but pointed to the undesirability of amending the citizenship law at the present time. But already that fall, in a letter dated 28 October 1996, the High Commissioner, while expressing understanding of the political difficulties with amending the Law on Citizenship, also suggested abolishing the window system.[22] Again, the Foreign Minister's reply in December suggested that political considerations made this unfeasible for the time being.[23]

After his visit to Riga in April 1997, the High Commissioner, as usual, followed up with written letters and recommendations. In May, the High Commissioner's letter includes the repeated recommendation to grant citizenship to children born in Latvia, while also reiterating the view that the naturalization exams should be simplified.[24] In September, the Foreign Minister reported back that the fees had been reduced for select groups of naturalization applicants. During his visit to Riga at the beginning of April and at later times, the EU Commissioner for External Relations Hans van den Broek also called attention to the citizenship issue as a major issue for the EU and made the link between the OSCE High Commissioner's recommendations and the Council of Europe and the European Commission explicit.[25]

The coordinated effort by various institutions and OSCE participating states in sending a unified message to Latvian leaders was in evidence once more, when President Ulmanis returned from Helsinki in April 1997 and spoke to the press of the necessity to abolish the window system, which had increasingly been stressed by OSCE and EU officials. At the same time, several ruling coalition politicians resisted the message. Alexander Kirsteins, member of LNNK, who held the post of special task minister on European Union affairs, claimed that the pressure from such high-level Western officials on Latvia regarding the non-citizens issue was a sign that Russia had pressured the USA in top-level meetings in Helsinki. He also proceeded to reject the idea that the non-citizen issue could become an obstacle for Latvia's EU accession and suggested that the EU should not interfere in Latvia's domestic affairs. A foreign affairs advisor to Latvian Prime Minister Skele also said that although the large non-citizen population could present a problem when approaching the EU, it would not pose any real obstacle for membership. Only a couple of representatives from the moderate ruling party, Latvia's Way, called for evaluating why naturalization was proceeding so slowly, admitting that this would be a major problem on the way to the European Union.[26]

The discourse still focused on resistance to liberalization and international pressure and arguments of conditionality, which tended to be dismissed by nationalists, who had gained a greater say in Prime Minister Skele's government than previously. On the other hand, the international agents who attempted to transmit the message to take the issue seriously were more clearly heard by pro-liberalization domestic agents, the President and some politicians from the ruling coalition parties. These were not only perceiving the linkage of the citizenship issue and membership in the EU, but were also more open to persuasion and normative arguments due to their self-perception as liberal democratic politicians. Thus, there were shared norms between some domestic and international agents, but many more remained reluctant democrats when it came to "minority-related" issues.

Pressure to amend the citizenship law mounted throughout 1997, and the response by Latvian politicians was sometimes contradictory. OSCE Mission head Charles Magee in an interview stated that the Latvian President as well as the Foreign Minister and other officials had expressed their support for the abolition of the window system.[27] In May, however, President Ulmanis announced that amendment of the citizenship law would not be feasible, since it would require the agreement of all ruling coalition partners (including the nationalist Fatherland and Freedom and LNNK). The domestic discussion intertwined with credible international signals. In June the Director of the European Commission on Multilateral Issues Anhel Vinhas visited Riga and clearly expressed conditionality, stressing that although citizenship issues are domestic concerns, entering the EU would entail both economic and political costs, and would not be possible with such a large number of non-citizens.[28]

On July 15, 1997, the Commission Opinion on Latvia was published, signaling that the European Commission would be paying attention to the naturalization of non-citizens, since the 1994 Law on Citizenship was evidently inadequate in addressing the problem. Although no specific demand to amend the law was included, a number of recommendations aimed at the facilitation of naturalization were, and the general evaluation states that the citizenship issue burdens Latvia's claim to democracy: "With the reservation that steps need to be taken to enable the Russian-speaking minority to become better integrated into society, Latvia demonstrates the characteristics of a democracy."[29]

On August 7, 1997, the merged nationalist party Fatherland and Freedom/ Latvian National Independence Movement (TB/LNNK) formed a coalition government under Prime Minister Guntars Krasts, while coordinated OSCE and EU pressure continued concerning the citizenship law. In October, a majority of deputies rejected a draft law complying with international recommendations that called for the abolition of the window system and the granting of citizenship to children born in Latvia.[30] Shortly thereafter, Chairman of the Saeima Committee on Science, Culture and Education Dzintars Abikis indicated that citizenship law amendments should be considered, indicating that the pressure and message of conditionality was starting to convince a few more domestic actors.[31]

Parallel to this, there was also mounting domestic opposition to the pressure, with negative comments on the OSCE at the end of the visit in October by the High Commissioner by both President Ulmanis and the Foreign Ministry, the domestic "allies" of the international actors.[32] However, the President continued to support the abolition of the window system.[33] Prime Minister Krasts, caught between the international pressure and his allegiance to his party's nationalistic stance, tried to maneuver between resistance to citizenship law amendments and the need to appear eager to cooperate fully with the EU and other institutions. He tended stubbornly to make statements to the media that the non-citizens issue would pose no obstacle to the accession to the EU and that it was not a requirement by the European Commission.[34] At the same time, party purists criticized him for being too weak in defending the nationalist position and for alleged cooperation in the citizenship issue with the President.[35] The Prime Minister's nationalist party had frequently gone on record saying that no amendments to the citizenship law would be made while it was in power.[36] The pressure by Russia in the spring of 1998 was not helpful, either, and the argument that European views were influenced by Russia was a long-lived one in some quarters. The opinions among the different ruling parties were so contradictory that there was speculation about the imminent fall of the government.[37]

At the same time, awareness was spreading among moderate politicians that "European recommendations" should be taken into account. The perception of all the recommendations as "European" indicated the success of coordination between the High Commissioner, the Council of Europe and the European Commission.[38] As conditionality became more difficult to ignore, some "skeptical liberalizers" (or "tactical liberalizers") were joining ranks with the initial, more normative ones.

OSCE and European Commission recommendations on required law amendments had been reiterated numerous times in public and in private. But this time, the influence brought to bear on the government to ensure that the amendments were submitted to parliament included unprecedented, coordinated action. Bilateral statements were made by the ambassadors to Latvia of the USA, Sweden and United Kingdom (which was the EU presiding country at the time), while the British and Swedish prime ministers also weighed in.[39] Finally, the government accepted the draft amendments providing for the abolition of the window system. A week later, after further consultations with the High Commissioner, the government also acquiesced to the granting of citizenship to children born in Latvia after August 21, 1991.

Parallel to the international pressure on the government, another government crisis came with a call for a vote of no confidence in Prime Minister Krasts' cabinet in order to pressure him to accept the amendments in the name of the government. The deputy head of the TB/LNNK party Juris Dobelis even accused the coalition partner Latvia's Way of putting pressure on the Prime Minister's party to accept the OSCE recommendations because it wanted to flex its muscles and appear as the only European-oriented party in Latvia.[40] Thus, only parts of the political establishment were firmly on the side of liberalization, the ruling coalition was internally divided over the issue, and pushing the amendments through involved both external and internal pressure on recalcitrant nationalists. To this extent, the liberalization of the legislation was dependent on the precarious domestic balance of power, which succeeded in keeping nationalist impulses in check. The domestic liberalizers had gained the upper hand in the first round.

After the proposed amendments were submitted to parliament, international pressure was maintained over the course of legislative deliberations. In the beginning of June, European Commission representative Catherine Day declared that the European Union would be satisfied if Citizenship Law amendments in compliance with international standards would be adopted, and would not put forth any further political demands.[41] Bilateral attention also continued throughout the process, and after the adoption of the amendments in the second reading, the media reported that Finnish President Ahtisari and German Chancellor Helmut Kohl had phoned President Ulmanis expressing satisfaction at the progress and reminding him that international observers expected the final reading promptly.[42] The European Union president also made official statements, commending the adoption of the amendments in the second reading, but expressing concern that the third reading would not be considered as an urgent matter.[43] A small scandal was caused by the leaking of a letter to Prime Minister Krasts from British Prime Minister Tony Blair, in which he urged the Latvian Prime Minister to ensure the passing of the amendments in parliament.[44]

Although Latvian political discourse focused on international recommendations, international pressure or domestic demographic fears, there were a few voices among the normative liberalizers who also stressed domestic stability and democracy, like Foreign Minister Birkavs and several other MPs.[45] Their internalized democratic values and the convergence of their views with those of the international agents was a necessary prerequisite for the successful domestic acceptance of international recommendations.

Despite loud contestation and attempts at filibustering by nationalists and the Prime Minister's own party, the amendments were adopted in a final reading on June 22, 1998.[46] The adoption of the amendments was hailed as a positive development by the European Union, the OSCE and the United States. The nationalists and their allies were not so easily defeated, however, and immediately collected enough signatures (by thirty-eight parliamentary deputies) to force the President to halt the proclamation of the amendments for two months and issued a call for a referendum.

While preparing for the referendum the intense international pressure was repeated, both through the organizations – the OSCE, the EU – and bilaterally, in an unprecedented case of coordinated international involvement. European leaders and their ambassadors to Latvia issued statements and comments, waiving the stick of non-membership in "their" organizations. Latvian delegates returning from visits to European institutions also regularly repeated the reassurance that no additional requirements regarding citizenship would follow. After Prime Minister Krasts and President Ulmanis also expressed worry about the possibility of further recommendations, High Commissioner Max van der Stoel issued an unusual official statement that no others would follow on the citizenship issue.[47] Meanwhile, in an apparent attempt at showing his nationalist credentials before the referendum, Prime Minister Krasts allegedly accused the High Commissioner of instigating questionable actions against Latvia and of lying.[48]

But conspicuous international support for the High Commissioner's recommendations continued. European Union Commissioner Hans van den Broek during a visit to Riga in July said that a "no" outcome to the referendum on the citizenship law amendments would be very negatively viewed by the European Union, and he explicitly tied the EU view to the recommendations by the OSCE High Commissioner.[49] A letter to the

Foreign Minister by Max van der Stoel and statements on television by US Secretary of State Madeline Albright in support of the citizenship amendments illustrated the broad transatlantic pro-amendment lobby.[50] On September 4, President Ulmanis received a letter from US President Clinton expressing clear support for the citizenship amendments and reiterating that the USA would not support any changes in the law that would not correspond to OSCE requirements.[51] On the eve of the referendum, a veritable barrage of statements in favor of the amendments were also issued by European Parliament representatives, the European Commission – which, in addition, directly threatened that a negative outcome could adversely influence the report on Latvia under way in the Commission – and by Italian Prime Minister Romano Prodi.[52] Despite this onslaught of statements on conditionality, Prime Minister Krasts and the nationalists continued voicing their conviction that failure to adopt the citizenship law amendments would not mean exclusion from the European Union.[53]

On October 3, 1998 the referendum was conducted, parallel to parliamentary elections, and the amendments to the law were left in place. However, despite massive international pressure and internal struggles between liberal and nationalist forces, the vote was only slightly in favor of retaining the amendments (53 percent in favor, 45 percent against). Nevertheless, a relieved outpouring of congratulations followed from all previously involved international actors and the foreign ministries of European countries. In the beginning of November, head of the work group on EU enlargement Mr Van den Pass signaled that Latvia had a good chance of being included among the first group of candidates for EU accession talks.[54]

Noting that the requirement to facilitate naturalization was included in both the 1997 Opinion on Latvia and the Accession Partnership, the European Commission regular progress report on Latvia in the fall of 1998 expressed satisfaction at the adopted amendments to the citizenship law. However, the need to simplify naturalization procedures and to provide information on naturalization to non-citizens was also noted.[55] Although it devotes a section to naturalization and the still large number of non-citizens, the 1999 progress report nevertheless states that "Latvia now fulfils all recommendations expressed by the OSCE in the area of citizenship and naturalization," making it clear that Latvia fulfilled the Copenhagen political criteria for membership.[56] Finally, at the EU Council Helsinki Summit in December 1999, Latvia was invited to start accession negotiations, which began in February 2000.

The 2000 and 2001 European Commission reports reiterated the fulfillment of the political criteria, but indicated that further actions to increase the rate of naturalization would be desirable. The large number of non-citizens, who by 2002 still constituted 22 percent of the population, continued to present a problem. The European Commission subsequently ceased its involvement in the issue, leaving it to the OSCE High Commissioner and the OSCE Mission to Latvia. Until its closure at the end of its mandate in

December 2001, the Mission continued to work with the Latvian government on the policy and implementation aspects of naturalization. Measures adopted through its direct involvement included the 2001 reduction of naturalization fees and recognition of the secondary school centralized Latvian language exam as the naturalization language exam. The first large-scale attempt to reach out publicly with an information campaign on naturalization was also initiated by the Mission before its closure.

While EU attention to the citizenship issue waned after the October 1998 referendum, the EU and its partner organizations became increasingly involved in seeking to influence Latvian language policy. In part, this shift derived from Latvian legislative initiatives in 1999 and 2000. However, the shift in international attention also reflected an emerging international consensus that the most difficult aspects of the citizenship controversy had been dealt with and other, more neglected minority policy areas could be tended to.

Language

Language issues in European Union–Latvian relations

In the latter half of the 1990s Western efforts focused not only on preventing language policy from impinging on minority rights, the right to private life and freedom of expression, but also on ensuring that measures to defend the Latvian language did not inhibit the free flow of goods, services, and people between Latvia and its (future) partners in the EU. As with the citizenship issue, the European Union and its member states relied heavily on the OSCE to engage Latvia, which it did not only through sustained, principled argumentation, but also through forcefully wielding the club of political conditionality.

In order to understand the sensitivity of language as a political issue in Latvia, it is necessary to mention the legacy of Soviet language policy. The mass influx of Russophone settlers during the Soviet era, the declining share of ethnic Latvians, and Soviet policies of Russification transformed Latvia's linguistic environment. Soviet policy not only drastically reduced the role of Latvian in the public domain, it also resulted in asymmetric bilingualism: by 1989 almost all Latvians were bilingual speakers of Latvian and Russian, while most non-Latvians were monolingual speakers of Russian.[57] Since independence in 1991 Latvian language planners have pointed to the weakened status of the Latvian language, the entrenched position of Russian, and the looming presence of Russia to justify an active state regulatory role in promoting the Latvian language.[58]

Soon after independence, in March 1992 the Latvian parliament adopted far-reaching amendments to the 1989 Law on Languages making knowledge of Latvian a prerequisite for many posts in both the public and private sectors. The law created a government body called the State Language Center and granted it the authority to conduct inspections and levy fines, thereby institutionalizing considerable state intrusion into society to regulate language use.[59] International and regional organizations, including the EU, gave scant attention to the human rights concerns raised by language policy until the late 1990s, opting to focus instead on issues related to citizenship.

A United Nations fact-finding mission to Latvia concluded in November 1992 that "the language law itself is not incompatible with international law nor with generally accepted human rights standards."[60] In his early correspondence with the Latvian authorities from 1993 through 1996, OSCE HCNM Max van der Stoel focused almost solely on citizenship issues, making only passing reference to problematic aspects of language legislation.[61] In its 1997 *avis* on Latvia's readiness to join the EU, the European Commission concluded that Latvia met the political criteria and that Latvia's primary political task was promoting naturalization of non-citizens. Again, language policy was mentioned only in passing.[62]

Language law controversy, 1997–2000

International "benign neglect" of language issues ceased in October 1997, when Latvian authorities passed in the first reading a new draft language law that envisaged expanded government regulation of language use in the private sector. Representatives of international organizations and Latvian legislators were quick to draw the link between the new law and EU accession. Council of the Baltic Sea States Commissioner for Human Rights Ole Espersen announced that the language law, if adopted in its current form, would be a serious obstacle to EU membership.[63] First Deputy Speaker of the parliament Andris Ameriks concurred, saying that he was "ashamed of the law."[64] Dzintars Abikis, the chairman of the parliamentary commission responsible for the law, vowed to vet the law with the Council of Europe and the OSCE Mission to Latvia before conducting a second reading.[65]

On March 24 and 25, 1998 representatives of the European Commission worked side by side with colleagues from the office of the OSCE HCNM and the Council of Europe in an expert group that visited Latvia and drafted a highly critical report on the draft state language law.[66] The report noted that many provisions "take insufficient account of the distinction between the public and private spheres" and risk "contravening international legal standards of human rights, most notably freedom of expression." The experts recommended either "limiting the scope of the draft Law on the State Language exclusively and clearly to the public sphere" or "identifying [. . .] all situations where a legitimate public interest can be demonstrated for measures requiring the (additional) use of the State language." As will be seen below, eventually, the Latvian authorities chose the latter option.

In response to the report, never made public, Abikis complained that the European experts did not take into consideration Latvia's fifty-year occupation and argued that the Oslo Recommendations regarding the Linguistic Rights of National Minorities, prepared under the auspices of the OSCE High Commissioner, sanction government regulation of language use to protect consumer rights.[67] This was not only a plea for special circumstances, but also an attempt to challenge gray areas in the argumentation of the OSCE High Commissioner – to challenge him on his own terms. Max van der Stoel, in turn, warned that ignoring the recommendations of European organizations concerning language and citizenship might lead to Latvia's international isolation.[68]

In mid-1998, as disagreement between Latvian officials and European experts on draft language legislation grew more acrimonious, controversy over proposed amendments to the citizenship law exploded and further debate on the language law was postponed until after the elections and citizenship referendum in October 1998. In February 1999, not long after taking office, the new parliament conducted a second reading of the problematic draft language law, thereby evoking the engagement of international and regional organizations once again. While the OSCE Mission to Latvia and the OSCE HCNM took an active consultative role, so did the European Commission's legal service.

According to a former advisor to the OSCE HCNM, on April 12, 1999 Latvian Foreign Minister Valdis Birkavs met with the HCNM in The Hague and "Birkavs requested Van der Stoel to provide the Latvian Ministry of Foreign Affairs with further written arguments about the incompatibility of the draft law with international standards." Van der Stoel obliged and in his letter, dated April 13, 1999, he reiterated his previous legal arguments and pointed to potential problems "in terms of accession to the European Union which has specific requirements relating to the effective functioning of the single market."[69]

During a visit of Latvian Prime Minister Vilis Kristopans to European Commission President Jacques Santer on April 22, 1999, Kristopans requested a legal analysis of the draft language law. Soon thereafter, the EC legal service drafted and forwarded to the Latvian authorities "an informal copy" of an analysis of the compatibility of the draft language law with the Europe Agreement (EA). The ten-page analysis, never made public, concluded that certain provisions were "disproportionate" and "may result in a significant limitation of certain rights and freedoms guaranteed by Titles III, IV and V of the EA."[70] Both the Prime Minister's request of the EU and that of the Foreign Minister with regard to the OSCE High Commissioner suggest the emergence of a transnational network in which European-oriented Latvian officials worked hand in hand with Western organizations, which provided ammunition to the former to face down domestic critics and opponents.

To reinforce the importance attached by the EU of amending the draft law, Joschka Fischer, foreign minister of Germany, pointed out to visiting Latvian officials in early May the necessity of harmonizing the draft state language law with the demands of the EU.[71] The European Commission's confidential analysis was then discussed in a closed session of the parliament's European Affairs Commission, after which commission head Edvins Inkens told the press that the draft law contained many vague provisions, that "non-political" proposals would be discussed, but that there was no special need to rush the draft law.[72]

However, in early June 1999, the parliamentary Commission on Education, Culture and Science pushed forward discussion of the law, rejecting some OSCE recommendations and accepting others. On the eve of the third and final reading of the law, scheduled for July 8, 1999, Vaira Vike-Freiberga was elected Latvian president. She would play a critical role, as she had the authority to veto any law and send it back for reconsideration by the parliament. She stated clearly that the two main criteria she would employ in evaluating the law were: (1) whether it defended the Latvian language; and (2) whether it threatened Latvia's chances to receive an invitation to begin accession negotiations with the European Union in Helsinki at the year's end.[73] At the end of June and early July 1999, the European Union forcefully brandished the stick of political conditionality in a coordinated attempt to influence the shape of the language law.

At the end of June, Foreign Minister Birkavs announced that he had received calls from OSCE High Commissioner Max van der Stoel and EU foreign affairs commissioner Hans van den Broek, both of whom had expressed concern about the draft language law.[74] On July 2 the Danish Foreign Minister announced that the "only obstacle" to Latvia being invited to negotiate EU membership could be the new state language law. That same day, the Finnish Ambassador to Latvia, who then represented the EU's rotating presidency, organized a confidential meeting of EU member state ambassadors in Latvia with representatives from all parties in parliament to discuss the draft law. While most parties commented on the Finnish initiative in neutral or positive terms, the nationalist TB/LNNK party termed it "unacceptable."[75]

Several days later, the diplomatic onslaught continued – the EU presidency requested the Latvian parliament to postpone review of the draft language law until the fall. President Vike-Freiberga then portrayed Latvia's options in stark terms: either Latvia follows the recommendations of the OSCE or it risks not being accepted into the EU.[76] Despite the clear request from the EU and abundant warnings from the international community, parliament resisted: on July 8, 1999, 73 deputies voted for the problematic law, 16 were against and 8 abstained.[77] As in the controversy over citizenship several years earlier, it was left to the President to make a critical decision on an unpopular issue.

After the vote, the international lobbying intensified – both the OSCE High Commissioner and the chairman of the Parliamentary Assembly of the Council of Europe Lord Russell Johnston urged the President to veto the law, while the head of the European Commission's delegation to Latvia noted that the EU's position on the language law basically coincided with that of the OSCE.[78] The next day Tarje Halonen, the Finnish Foreign Minister representing the EU presidency, announced that the language law as passed by parliament "is not favorable" for Latvia's invitation to join EU accession negotiations.[79] The same day, Latvian President Vaira Vike-Freiberga vetoed the law and sent it back to parliament for reconsideration, arguing that a number of provisions were vague and contradicted freedom of expression and the right to private life, which were guaranteed in Latvia's Constitution and the European Convention on Human Rights.[80]

In subsequent months, the EU and OSCE continued to engage the Latvian authorities on the draft language law. In a confidential five-page note to the Latvian authorities dated October 5, 1999, the OSCE High Commissioner once again elaborated on the application of freedom of expression and right to privacy guarantees with regard to language policy and invoked the jurisprudence of the United Nations Human Rights Committee and the European Court of Human Rights, as well as the requirements of the Europe Agreement.[81] The European Union, for its part, commented in depth on the language controversy in its 1999 Regular Progress Report, reiterating and elaborating OSCE HCNM arguments with regard to compatibility with the Europe Agreement. In its "General Evaluation," the EU concluded that although "Latvia fulfils the Copenhagen political criteria [. . .] it will be necessary to ensure that the final text of the Language law is compatible with international standards and the Europe Agreement."[82]

As the date for the anticipated invitation to join EU accession negotiations approached at the end of the 1999, pressure built to adopt a final version of the language law that would be acceptable to the EU and other European organizations. However, in mid-November 1999, Dzintars Abikis announced that deputies had not reached agreement with OSCE experts on issues pertaining to state regulation of language use in visual information.[83] As the final reading of the reworked law approached, nationalist deputies from TB/LNNK and the People's Party urged resistance to international pressure. One deputy claimed that "our country has no international legal obligations that would not permit the adoption of a strict State language law,"[84] while another even argued that "not a single paragraph of the Europe Agreement speaks about language problems and the Rome Treaty foresees even stronger action than that pursued by Latvian legislation."[85]

On December 9, 1999, a bare majority of fifty-two deputies passed a final version of a new State Language Law that sanctioned government regulation of language use in the private sphere if there was a "legitimate public interest" and left a number of the most important provisions to be determined by the executive in secondary legislation.[86] The compromise law was applauded by the European Commission and deemed by the OSCE High Commissioner as being "essentially in conformity with Latvia's international obligations and commitments."[87] While this compromise permitted the EU to extend an invitation to Latvia to begin accession negotiations, it merely postponed the issue once again and shifted the focus from the parliament to the government, which would have to adopt implementing regulations acceptable to European institutions by September 2000, when the law was to take effect. Here, Checkel's insight regarding soft tactics is relevant – negotiations with the government would be more insulated and less politicized than with the parliament. Still, the persuasion would not be easy.

The debate over secondary language legislation, 2000–2002

After a March 2000 meeting with EC Enlargement Commissioner Gunter Verheugen, Latvian Foreign Minister Indulis Berzins noted that Latvia must address three priorities to receive a positive EU progress report for the year: adopt implementing regulations to the State Language Law, make progress in social integration, and improve the work of the state administration.[88] While the EU took an active interest in the regulations, there is no evidence that it delegated its experts to consult/cajole the Latvian authorities, relying instead on the services of the OSCE.

Throughout the first half of 2000, a Latvian government working group engaged in intense consultations with OSCE experts and the OSCE High Commissioner sent detailed evaluations of the draft regulations during the summer.[89] The debate revolved around the notion of "legitimate public interests" – whereas the OSCE argued forcefully for a narrow interpretation and very limited state intrusion in the private sector to regulate language use, Latvian officials initially adopted a far broader interpretation.

As the September deadline approached, the Latvian authorities once again decided on a familiar course of action: adopt a decision on those issues in which an agreement with European experts had been reached, while postponing a decision on the most controversial issue. The most controversial issue in this case was drafting a list of professions in the private sector subject to language requirements. On August 22 the government adopted a packet of nine regulations with two annexes covering issues such as the circumstances when translation into Latvian must be provided at conferences and demonstrations, when private organizations are required to provide information in Latvian alongside other languages on publicly displayed signs, and language requirements for various posts in the public sector.[90] The government vowed to adopt a list of private sector professions to be regulated by November, which also happened to be the date of the next EU progress report.

Regardless of the gap in the regulations, international organizations greeted them with relief. In a press statement issued on August 31, Max van der Stoel stated that the regulations were "essentially in conformity with both the Law and Latvia's international obligations" and that "virtually all of my recommendations were accepted by the government."[91] On September 6 the French Embassy in Latvia representing the EU presidency issued a statement that "The European Union fully supports the declaration of the OSCE High Commissioner on National Minorities Max van der Stoel on the State Language Law implementing regulations."[92]

However, the Latvian authorities could not quickly agree on the list of professions in the private sector subject to language regulation by the publication of the next EU progress report on November 10, 2000. The progress report remarked that:

> At the time of adoption of the implementing regulations, the Latvian government also committed itself to introducing further amendments to the regulations before November 2000, and specifically amendments concerning the language requirements for the performance of professional duties in order to further delimit their scope.[93]

On November 21, 2000, the government adopted the list of professions. It was brief and contained thirty-four categories, almost all of which could be termed proportionate and falling within a legitimate public interest.[94] The list included various health care professionals, public safety and security-related professions, as well as notaries and sworn advocates. This step brought to a close one important chapter in the acrimonious debate over drafting basic language legislation with a clearly delimited state regulatory role. In its 2001 progress report, the European Union continued to draw attention to the importance of applying the law and regulations fairly and admonished that "a liberal attitude will also be particularly important with a view to Latvia's accession to the European Union." The report continued by reminding Latvia that "the Court of Justice of the European Community has taken a clear position in relevant cases related to language requirements."[95]

One and a half years after the apparent end of the controversy surrounding Latvian language legislation, a new episode unfolded. In mid-April 2002, the State Language Center sought to reopen the debate by proposing a significant expansion of the list of professions in the private sector subject to language regulation. The proposed list included nineteen new professions, including various municipal level posts, accountants, sales personnel, athletic coaches, and hairdressers. First to sound the alarm bell was a human rights NGO, which termed the proposed amendments a violation of private life pursuing no legitimate public interest. Initially, Justice Ministry officials and politicians saw no problem with the proposals and Dzintars Abikis publicly supported the amendments, even claiming that "The boundary of legitimate public interests is very relative, therefore one should rest on the protection of consumer rights."[96]

Several days later, the press reported that the office of the OSCE High Commissioner had expressed an interest in the proposals. At the same time, Latvian Foreign Ministry officials stated that the amendments would create a negative international reaction and would violate the international legal norms binding on Latvia, while the Justice Ministry stated the amendments would not be adopted, but that it would consult with the OSCE on the legitimacy of regulating the language knowledge of municipal workers.[97] The end of this rearguard attempt to revisit the issue came at the end of April, when core proponent of the amendments and long-time director of the State Language Center Dzintra Hirsa submitted her resignation.

This incident suggests the existence of a network consisting of international human rights organizations, NGOs, and sympathetic officials, primarily in the Foreign Ministry. However, Abikis's reaction also suggests that all the persuading had little impact – only a cold calculation of potential lost international prestige, not the internalization of Western norms stayed the hand of those wanting to regulate language use in a manner inappropriate for a democracy in the EU. Still, this cold calculation could be made without the direct intervention of the OSCE High Commissioner or the EU urging the Latvian authorities to heed their own commitments.

Conclusion

Latvia's evolution from democratization to a consolidated democracy proceeded swiftly, but encountered some obstacles in minority rights-related issue areas. The adaptation of citizenship and language legislation to European standards took place as a result of a process whereby international pressure from European institutions and countries intertwined with domestic political struggles. Conditionality related to EU membership was clearly essential in convincing Latvian politicians that concessions had to be made. It should be pointed out, however, that part of the reason conditionality worked is that even the most nationalistic opponents of concessions never questioned the priority of joining the European Union and adherence to democratic values. The nationalists may appear radical in their occasional stubbornness in denying linkage and conditionality against all indications to the contrary, but they did not espouse an isolationist, particularistic route like right-wing populists elsewhere in Europe. The assumption that there is no viable alternative to democracy and the European Union underlay all debates.

The contagion-type hypotheses should not be dismissed, however. Although some of them, like spillover, do indeed seem to be contradicted by the detailed evidence presented in this chapter, too little time elapsed between the rhetorical change of position to be able to expect that an internalized, normative change would have followed. Indeed, the evolution of stances towards Latvian citizenship and language legislation in the 1990s, although largely tactical for many politicians, may at a later date prove to have been a harbinger of a reworking of values. The cultural match hypothesis, however, is fundamental in understanding the adaptation to the requested legislative amendments. Without the underlying, strong belief in democratic values, the priority of the goal of EU accession and the lack of alternatives would not have remained unquestioned. This is not to say that the public debates did not display a lack of understanding of some specific liberal democratic values. But the subjective need to identify oneself with a pro-Western, democratic orientation appeared across the political spectrum, and the reason these factors are not more readily apparent in the debates is precisely because they represent unquestioned consensual assumptions.

Likewise, the status of the persuader cannot be said to be disconfirmed simply because it is not explicit. The top priority given to joining the EU would not be possible without a parallel high esteem for the active international persuaders, nor would their advice be heeded. One could arguably distinguish here a change over time, in which the OSCE, and especially the High Commissioner, were initially not entirely appreciated or even respected, but later, when the linkage to other European institutions (and especially the EU) became increasingly clear, realization that recommendations could not be ignored led to increased respect. The European Commission and key OSCE countries were effective precisely because of the respect afforded them.

Nationalism, of course, permeates debates about citizenship and language policy. On the other hand, the novelty of the elites with a sharp learning curve is also in evidence – at least for the part of the political elite that were liberalizers by conviction. Indeed, it is the unofficial alliance of these with the international agents that together won over the tactical liberalizers and made the change possible. By overemphasizing Latvian nationalism, one tends to overlook the fundamental fact that sensitive legislation was liberalized in conformity with European standards, liberalizers winning out over the nationalists. This could not have happened without the inclination and ability to learn and adapt to European liberal norms by a small, but powerful part of the domestic political elite. Hence, the existence of an internationally oriented domestic political grouping seems in this case to be a necessary condition for the adoption of European Union standards, while the corollary is that the effectiveness of this transnational coalition is dependent on the domestic distribution of power.

Notes

1 W. A. Kemp, ed., *Quiet Diplomacy in Action: The OSCE High Commissioner on National Minorities*, The Hague: Kluwer Law International, 2001, p. 27.
2 Ibid., p. 73.
3 Ibid., p. 98.
4 Ibid., p. 99.
5 S. R. Ratner, "Does International Law Matter in Preventing Ethnic Conflict?" *New York University Journal of International Law and Politics*, 32:3, Spring 2000, p. 639.
6 Kemp, op. cit., p. 79.
7 Ibid., pp. 59, 79. The same point is made by Ratner, op. cit., p. 638.
8 L. Barrington, "The Making of Citizenship Policy in the Baltic States," *Georgetown Immigration Law Journal*, 13:2, 1999, p. 172.

9 R. Zaagman, *Conflict Prevention in the Baltic States: The OSCE High Commissioner on National Minorities in Estonia, Latvia and Lithuania*, Flensburg: European Centre for Minority Issues, 1999, pp. 21–24; speech by former Swedish Prime Minister Carl Bildt at the conference "OSCE and Latvia: Past, Present and Future," in Riga, March 20, 2002.

10 Letter of CSCE High Commissioner on National Minorities to HE Georgs Andrejevs, Minister for Foreign Affairs of the Republic of Latvia, April 6, 1993, found at http://www.osce.org/hcnm/documents/recommendations

11 Letter by Georgs Andrejevs, Minister of Foreign Affairs to The Hon. Max van der Stoel, ibid.

12 Saeima Plenary Session transcript September 23, 1993, available at http://www.saeima.lv/Latvian/steno/st_2309.html

13 The government at the time was formed by two parties: Latvia's Way and the Farmers' Party, leaving the nationalist Latvian National Independence Movement (LNNK) and the extreme Fatherland and Freedom (TB) in the opposition, together with the moderate and more radical anti-nationalist parties.

14 Letter by the CSCE High Commissioner on National Minorities to HE Georgs Andrejevs, Minister of Foreign Affairs of Republic of Latvia, December 10, 1993 at http://www.osce.org/hcnm/documents/recommendations/latvia/1994/10c084.html

15 Letter January 25, 1994, ibid.

16 *Integration Monitor*, February 26, 1994, http://www.policy.lv

17 Ibid., March 9, 1994.

18 "Pilsonibas licloci" ("The twists and turns of citizenship"), *Rigas balss*, June 7, 1994.

19 Saeima Plenary Session transcript from June 9, 1994, at http://www.saeima.lv/latvian/steno/st_94/st0906.html

20 Saeima Extraordinary Session transcript, July 22, 1994, http://www.saeima.lv/latvian/steno/st_94/st2207.html

21 Letter by OSCE High Commissioner on National Minorities to HE Valdis Birkavs, Minister for Foreign Affairs of the Republic of Latvia, March 14, 1996 at http://www.osce.org/hcnm/documents/recommendations/latvia/1996/33hc56.html

22 Letter from the High Commissioner on National Minorities to Minister for Foreign Affairs Valdis Birkavs, October 28, 1996 at http://www.osce.org/hcnm/recommendations/latvia/1997/42hc27.html

23 Foreign Minister Valdis Birkavs letter to the High Commissioner on National Minorities, December 24, 1996 at http://www.osce.org/hcnm/recommendations/latvia/1997/42hc27.html

24 Letter from the High Commissioner on National Minorities to HE Valdis Birkavs, Minister for Foreign Affairs of the Republic of Latvia, May 23, 1997, http://www.osce.org/hcnm/documents/recommendations/latvia/1997/48hg17.html

25 Ratner, op. cit., p. 639.

26 "Saasina delikato jautajumu par nepilsoniem" ("The delicate question of non-citizens is sharpened") *Diena*, April 12, 1997.

27 "Naturalizacijas parsteidzosa nepopularitate" ("The Surprising unpopularity of naturalization") *Diena*, April 18, 1997.

28 "ES uztrauc nepilsonu skaits Latvija" ("The EU is concerned about the number of non-citizens in Latvia"), *Diena*, June 21, 1997.

29 "Agenda 2000 – Commission Opinion on Latvia's Application for Membership of the European Union," at http://www.europa.eu.int/comm/enlargement/dwn/opinions/latvia/la-op-en.pdf

30 Saeima Plenary Session transcript October 16, 1997 at http://www.saeima.lv

31 *Integration Monitor*, October 27, 1997, http://www.policy.lv

32 *Integration Monitor*, November 3, 1997, http://www.policy.lv

33 "Iestasanos ES noteiks katras valsts konkretais darbs" ("Accession to the EU will be determined by each country's concrete work") *Diena*, November 17, 1997.

34 *Diena*, December 1, 1997.

35 E.g. "Valdiba sava riciba ir parak pieticiga" ("The government is too modest in its actions"), *Lauku_Avize*, January 20, 1998; "Stridi pilsonibas jautajuma," ("Struggles in the citizenship question"), *Neatkariga Rita Avize*, February 12, 1998.

36 "Nepieciesams sakt diskusiju par grozijumiem Pilsonibas likuma" ("It is necessary to start discussions on amendments to the Citizenship Law"), *Vakara zinas*, February 14, 1998.

37 "Krasta dienas ir skaititas?!" ("The days of Krasts are numbered?!"), *Diena*, March 30, 1998.

38 "Cik daudz Latvijai japiekapjas Eiropas Savienibas rekomendacijam un Krievijas prasibam pilsonibas jautajuma" ("How much should Latvia give way to European Union recommendations and Russian demands in the question of citizenship"), *Vakara zinas*, April 14, 1998.

39 "Vienojas par Pilsonibas likuma grozijumiem" ("Agreement on amendments to the Citizenship Law"), *Diena*, April 15, 1998.

40 "Tevzemiesi neatbalstis automatisku pilsonibas pieskirsanu" ("Fatherlandists will not support the automatic granting of citizenship"), *Nacionala Neatkariba*, May 27, 1998.

41 "EK: Pilsonibas likumu pec ES standartiem" ("The EC: The citizenship law according to European Standards"), *Neatkariga rita avize*, June 3, 1998.

42 "Pilsonibas likuma grozijumi – kas talak?" ("Amendments to the Citizenship Law – What next?"), *Neatkariga rita avize*, June 1998.

43 "Eiropas savieniba apsveic Pilsonibas likuma grozijumu atbalstu Saeima" ("The European Union congratulates the support of the parliament to amending the citizenship law"), *Vakara zinas*, June 10, 1998.

44 *Diena*, 4 June 1998 and "Letter from British PM leaks to press," *The Baltic Times*, June 18, 1998.

45 "Apdraudeti grozijumi Pilsonibas likuma" ("Amendments to the citizenship law threatened"), *Diena*, June 3, 1998.

46 Saeima Plenary Session transcript from June 22, 1998, http://www.saeima.lv

47 OSCE High Commissioner of National Minorities Press Statement, July 16, 1998, http://www.osce.org./news/generate.pf.php3?news_id=1357

48 "Krasts stratosfera" ("Krasts in the Stratosphere"), *Diena*, July 20, 1998; "Premjeram nenaktu par sliktu apmeklet diplomatijas kursus" ("It wouldn"t be bad for the Prime Minister to take courses in diplomacy"), *Diena*, July 25, 1998.

49 "ES kritize Krievijas spiedienu" ("The EU criticized Russian pressure"), *Diena*, 21 July 1998; "Prasa EDSO rekomendaciju izpildi" ("Requesting the fulfillment of OSCE recommendations"), *BNS*, July 21, 1998.

50 "Musu atbalstitaji sobrid saka 'bet'" ("Our supporters presently say 'but'"), *Lauku Avize*, July 28, 1998.

51 "Klinton nosutijis atbalsta vestuli Ulmanim" ("Clinton sends a letter of support to Ulmanis"), *Neatkariga Rita Avize*, September 5, 1998.

52 *Diena*, October 1 and 2, 1998.

53 "ES runa, Krasts nedzird" ("EU speaks, Krasts doesn't hear"), *Diena*, September 4, 1998.

54 *Diena*, November 2, 1998.

55 Regular Report from the Commission on Latvia's Progress Towards Accession, http://www.europa.eu.int/comm./enlargement/report_11_98/pdf/en/Latvia_en.pdf

56 1999 Regular Report from the Commission on Latvia's Progress Towards Accession, p. 17, available at http://www.europa.eu.int/comm/enlargement/report_10_99/pdf/en/lavia_en.pdf

57   According to 1989 Soviet census data, 68.7 percent of all Latvians claimed a command of Russian, while only 22.3 percent of all Russians claimed a knowledge of Latvian. Latvian proficiency among Ukrainians and Belarussians is even less common. See, *1989. gada tautas skaitisanas rezultati Latvija, Statistisks biletens, 2. dala*, Riga: Latvijas Valsts Statistikas Komiteja, 1991, pp. 41–42.

58 See, e.g., Ina Druviete, *Latvijas valodas politika Eiropas savienibas konteksta*, Riga: LU Latviesu valodas instituts, LZA Ekonomikas instituts, 1998, p. 147.

59 For an in-depth analysis of language legislation and its implementation, see Angelita Kamenska, *The State Language in Latvia: Achievements, Problems and Prospects*, Riga: Latvian Centre for Human Rights and Ethnic Studies, 1995.

60 For a "Summary of the Report on a Fact-Finding Mission to Latvia" by Ibrahima Fall, see Hanne Margret Birckenbach, *Preventive Diplomacy through Fact-Finding: How International Organisations Review the Conflict over Citizenship in Latvia and Estonia*, Hamburg: LIT, 1997, p. 302.

61 In the first letter to the Latvian Foreign Minister, dated April 6, 1993, only 2 of 18 paragraphs are devoted to language policy with the emphasis being on the need to clarify imprecise wording and admonishing that it was not "the intention of the legislator" to require the use of the Latvian language "in the internal affairs of all private enterprises and organizations," ibid., p. 367. For the texts of this, another communication in 1993 and one in 1996, see ibid., pp. 361–381.

62 In the section on minorities, the *avis* does note that "some obstacles exist for those who have no command of Latvian: need to know Latvian to receive unemployment benefit, obligation to pass a high-level language test to be able to stand for elections," but does not provide any evaluation of these measures or mention them as problematic in the "General Evaluation." See *Agenda 2000 – Commission Opinion on Latvia's Application for Membership of the European Union* DOC/97/14, Brussels, July 15, 1997, p. 20.

63 *Diena*, October 23, 1997.

64 *Chas*, November 10, 1997.

65 *Chas*, October 23, 1997.

66 See Kemp, op. cit., pp. 63–64. The unpublished twenty-page report, "Report prepared by the team of experts visiting Latvia on 24–25 March 1998 on the Draft Law on the State Language and proposed amendments to the Labour Code," Strasbourg, March 30, 1998, is on file with the authors.

67 *Rita Zinas, Jauna Avize*, March 31, 1998.

68 *Diena, Biznes & Baltiia*, April 1, 1998.

69 Kemp, op. cit., pp. 162–163.

70 Unpublished report and cover letter from Catherine Day of the European Commission's DG1A, dated April 27, 1999, to Andris Piebalgs, Ambassador of Latvia to the EU, on file with the authors.

71 *Diena*, May 8, 1999.

72 *Diena*, May 18, 1999.
73 *Diena*, June 19, 1999.
74 *Diena*, June 30, 1999.
75 *Diena*, July 3, 1999.
76 *Diena*, July 6, 1999.
77 *Diena*, July 9, 1999.
78 *Diena*, July 14, 1999.
79 See "Halonen Advises Latvia Against Strict Language Law," *Deutsche Presse-Agentur*, July 14, 1999.
80 For the official text of the President's veto, see *Diena*, July 16, 1999.
81 The two-part "Note on Selected Issues Concerning the Draft Latvian Law on Language" and "Note on the Compliance with International Standards of the Existing Latvian Law on Language" has the heading "Office of the OSCE HCNM" and is on file with the authors.
82 See "1999 Regular Report from the Commission on Latvia's Progress Towards Accession," October 13, 1999, p. 18.
83 *Diena*, November 19, 1999.
84 See Aigars Kimenis, "Nenodosim savu valodu un tautu" ("Let us not betray our language and people"), *Diena*, December 6, 1999.
85 See Alexandra Kirsteins, "Latviesu valoda tiesam neizmirst?" ("Is the Latvian language really not dying?"), *Diena*, November 25, 1999.
86 For this and other criticisms, see Latvian Centre for Human Rights and Ethnic Studies, *Human Rights in Latvia in 1999*, Riga, 2000, p. 38. For the text of the law, see *Latvijas vestnesis*, December 21, 1999.
87 For the EU view, see *Diena*, December 10, 1999. For the OSCE view, see Press Statement, "High Commissioner welcomes State Language Law in Latvia," The Hague, December 9, 1999, available at www.osce.org
88 *Diena*, March 28, 2000.
89 This was a rare case in which the full text of one of the OSCE HCNM letters was published in Latvian in a timely fashion. See "EDSO augsta komisara nacionalo minoritasu jautajumos Maksa van der Stula vestule," *Lauku avize*, August 10, 2000.
90 *Latvijas vestnesis*, No. 302, 29 August 2000. The full texts of the regulations in English can be found at www.riga.lv/minelres/National legislation/Latvia/latvia.htm
91 Press Statement, "Statement regarding the adoption of regulation implementing the Latvian State Language Law," The Hague, August 31, 2000, available at www.osce.org
92 *Neatkariga Rita Avize*, September 6, 2000.
93 "2000 Regular Report from the Commission on Latvia's Progress Towards Accession," Brussels, November 8, 2000, p. 23.
94 See *Latvijas vestnesis*, No. 435/437, December 1, 2000.
95 Commission of the European Communities, "2001 Regular Report on Latvia's Progress Towards Accession," Brussels, November 13, 2001, p. 26.
96 *Diena*, April 13, 2002.
97 *Diena*, April 18, 2002.

3   The ambivalent influence of the European Union on democratization in Slovakia

Kevin Deegan Krause

During the 1998 parliamentary election campaign in Slovakia, an animated television commercial used by the leader of the country's governing coalition featured a scene of gold stars on a deep blue background closely resembling the flag of the European Union. The image was not a positive one, however. In the animation, lines quickly appear between the stars, revealing the constellation of Leo the lion, which lashes out at passing Slovak children but fails to anticipate their clever evasion. Although the attitudes of Slovakia's population did not differ dramatically from those of neighboring democratic success stories such as Poland, the Czech Republic, and Hungary, the behavior of Slovakia's institutions and political parties did differ sharply. The differences involved not only Slovakia's apparent turn away from democracy during the mid-1990s but also the tense relationship between the government and the EU. Thus, the EU's role in Slovakia's reluctant democratization deserves particularly close attention, as it offers insight into what the EU (and other international actors) can and cannot accomplish in their democratization efforts, and particularly into the unintended consequences of international factors on domestic political life.

This chapter looks briefly at the course of Slovakia's democratization and then at the public efforts made by the European Union during the same period. It then traces the connection between its efforts at the elite and mass levels and the response by the Slovak government. The analysis demonstrates that the EU faced significant barriers in its attempt to encourage the democratization of the 1994–1998 government of Vladimir Mečiar. Despite its active presence – and claims made for the success of its efforts – the EU did not play an indispensable part in the electoral success of Slovakia's opposition in 1998. Nor, however, did its criticism of Slovakia's democratization prove ultimately counterproductive. There is little evidence to support charges that EU criticism actually helped the Mečiar government gain support from those who were outraged by EU "meddling."

Political developments in Central and Eastern Europe during the era of Gorbachev in the Soviet Union provide ample evidence that democratization may depend heavily on what happens elsewhere. Once external barriers that inhibit democracy have disappeared, however, the question that remains is on the effectiveness of external incentives for democracy that will actively encourage its formation. Without waiting for a rigorously tested answer, Western governments and international institutions made the plausible assumptions that such incentives would work without great difficulties and greeted the incipient democratization in Central and Eastern Europe with an outpouring of advice and, in some cases, money. Ten years later, it is possible to begin a more thorough and sober assessment and to draw certain conclusions.

Chapter 1 offers a framework for analyzing the role of external actors – particularly the European Union – in promoting democratization. Kubicek focuses on two processes: convergence, defined as "the spread of international norms"; and conditionality, defined as "the linking of perceived benefits to the fulfillment of a certain program."[1] The first of these is a largely cultural mechanism and involves a shift in values, while the second is primarily structural and involves weighing of costs and benefits. The remainder of this chapter will analyze Slovakia's democratization in the context of these two processes, looking in particular at the domestic conditions faced by the EU in its attempts to promote democracy and the mixed success of its efforts. Before looking at the efforts of the EU, however, it is necessary to understand exactly how Slovakia's development between 1992 and the present and the extent to which internal factors can explain its unique course of development.

Slovakia's democratic arc

Slovakia is unique among the countries of Central and Eastern Europe in the pattern of its political development. During the period from 1990 through 2002, few countries experienced a decline in political freedom as significant and enduring as Slovakia, and none with that experience then achieved such a rapid restoration. In Figure 3.1, which shows Freedom House scores for most countries in Central and Eastern Europe between 1990 and 2000, Slovakia literally stands out from its neighbors. Slovakia's Freedom House score shows a level of "unfreedom" for 1996 and 1997 greater than that of Romania and Bulgaria and surpassed only by countries such as Russia, Croatia and Yugoslavia. Yet by 1999 Slovakia's score had returned to the same level as the Czech Republic, Poland and Hungary. [2] What accounts for this arc?

The institutional answer

It is not a coincidence that the two periods of increasing threats to democratic freedoms coincide exactly with the 1992–1994 and 1994–1998 governments led by the Movement for a Democratic Slovakia (HZDS) chaired by Vladimír Mečiar. A series of analyses of Mečiar's governments in comparison to those that preceded and followed them indicate that Slovakia's

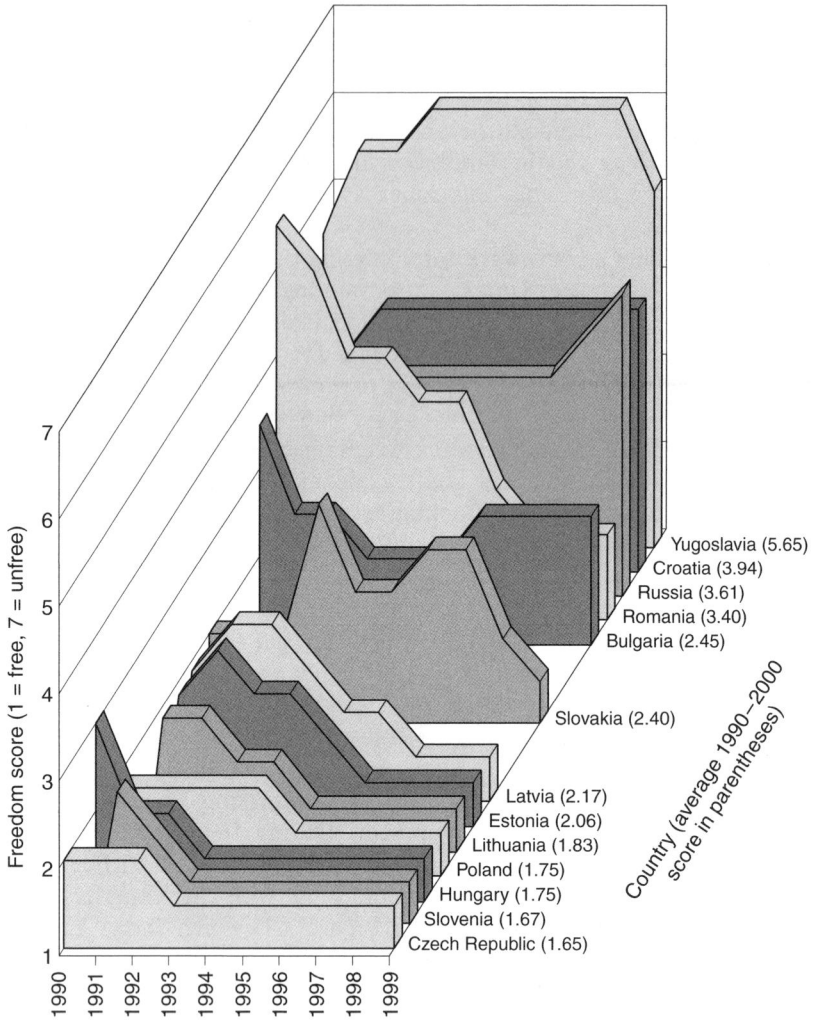

Figure 3.1 Freedom House civil liberties scores for selected Central and
Eastern European countries, 1990–2000.

problems with democracy stem almost entirely from systematic efforts to
dismantle externally imposed restraints on the power of government and
parliament. Furthermore, this destruction of what O'Donnell refers to as
horizontal accountability can be traced almost entirely to the initiative of
Mečiar or one of his immediate subordinates.[3]

The first and second Mečiar governments hinted at the possibility of
institutional encroachment but did not take significant steps in that direction. In 1990 and 1991 Mečiar fought for control within the anti-communist

movement Public Against Violence (VPN), earning a reputation for aggres-siveness[4] and ultimately provoking a split within the movement, but his intra-party struggles did not immediately threaten rival institutions. In his second government, which lasted from June 1992 until April 1994, Mečiar raised concern among observers, but their comments focused on his "authoritarian style" rather than concrete encroachments and focused on *anticipated* rather than actual problems.[5] Actual institutional interference by the Mečiar government remained confined largely to state-owned media, universities, and privatization schemes.[6] Although occurring in sensitive areas, these encroachments remained limited, and Mečiar's government lost as many conflicts as it won. Mečiar's second government did extend its grasp in 1994, particularly in the realm of privatization, but by then the party had already lost its parliamentary majority and faced the strong possibility of a vote of no confidence.

Government encroachments on rival institutions in Slovakia ended almost immediately with the vote of no confidence that ended the second Mečiar government in March 1994. The government that followed, a wide coalition including Christian Democrats, former communists, and former prominent politicians from Mečiar's own party, reversed some of the decisions of its predecessor and did not pursue sustained attacks against its rivals.[7] This government, however, chose immediately to call new elections, and Mečiar's party performed well, returning to parliament in October with a parlia-mentary delegation three times the size of its nearest rival. By November, Mečiar had found two relatively docile coalition partners in the Slovak National Party (SNS) and the Association of Workers of Slovakia (ZRS). It is this government, Mečiar's third, from December 1994 until October 1998, that posed the greatest threat to Slovakia's democracy. Mečiar's "siege" on Slovakia's democracy[8] did not happen all at once, however, and the way the accountability violations progressed through four distinct states offers vital insight into the mechanisms that made Mečiar's encroachments possible and appropriate EU responses difficult.

Stage I: maximum use of legislative and executive prerogative

Politics in Slovakia changed abruptly after the 1994 parliamentary elections. Just over a month after the election, deputies from Mečiar's party (HZDS) joined with deputies from the Slovak National Party (SNS) and the Association of Workers of Slovakia (ZRS) to create an ad hoc majority and used it to solidify the position of those three parties within parliament and other political structures. During twenty-three hours of parliamentary sessions that began on November 3, 1994 and continued until the following morning, parliament took advantage of the full range of its legal powers – including legal loopholes – to place members of the HZDS, SNS and ZRS in the maximum number of legislative, executive, and administrative posi-tions. In the following two years, the third Mečiar government reinforced its gains with the occupation of virtually every position within its immediate purview.

In some respects the third Mečiar government merely followed a pattern that is customary in democracies, placing trusted supporters in key legislative and executive positions. But its efforts went far beyond the still weakly defined precedent of its predecessors in office to deliberately eliminate the potential for independent monitoring and thereby sever ties of horizontal accountability. Although the changes did not in most cases violate Slovakia's still emerging legal structures, they altered the balance of political power within Slovakia's political system, and edged across the line between effective administration and accountability violation. With a stable majority in parliament and without the fear of obstruction from independent monitors, the coalition faced no immediate barriers against the use of executive agencies for its own benefit, particularly in the sensitive areas of privatization, broadcast media, and intelligence. Through its initial efforts in parliament and government, the coalition acquired largely unchallenged access to substantial sums of money, to mass media, and to the more shadowy advantages available through espionage.

Having acquired this access, the coalition did not hesitate to use it. Unencumbered by oversight mechanisms, the majority coalition used the Fund of National Property to take "unambiguous control over the privatization process" and to institute "a system of patronage in which the benefits flow to the politically connected."[9] Likewise, the absence of review allowed Slovakia's public broadcasting to tilt strongly in favor of the coalition[10] and gave free rein to the Slovak Information Service (SIS). In each of these cases and in the other changes detailed above, the elimination of accountability served not only immediate needs – the desire for retribution, rewards for supporters, increased cohesion, and loyalty within the executive – but also established the conditions for further violations of accountability and a further tilting of the institutional balance. Control of privatization provided a source of funds for fending off future election challenges. Control of broadcast media provided a means for limiting criticism and reframing issues in ways that favored the coalition. Control of SIS provided a direct means for close observation of opponents and, when necessary, for intimidation. Through these means and others at hand the coalition moved beyond its nearly complete control over parliament and government institutions to put pressure other institutions that were not formally within its reach.

Stage II: attacks against institutions with accountability potential

Having taken strong control of those institutions closest at hand, the majority coalition in Slovakia sought to maximize its influence over institutions outside its constitutional scope. The coalition devoted the largest share of these efforts toward institutions with the potential for demanding the rudiments of accountability: explanation, justification, and punishment. The targeted institutions included the presidency, the parliamentary opposition, and the constitutional court.

Since a simple parliamentary majority did not suffice to free the majority coalition from the oversight of the president or from other constitutionally imposed limitations, the coalition faced a substantial barrier. Constitutional laws required the support of three-fifths of parliament's deputies (90 out of 150), and the coalition at its most disciplined fell well short. In response the coalition pursued a twin-pronged strategy, simultaneously striving for a constitutional majority by excluding rival parties while also pursuing alternative mechanisms outside the constitutional realm and in some cases outside the ordinary political realm.

The third Mečiar government immediately set to work to remove Michal Kovac from the presidency. When it failed to attract a constitutional majority for Kovac's ouster, it used normal legislative means to limit sharply his powers and prerogatives. Furthermore, evidence strongly suggests that officials in the Mečiar government sought to incapacitate Kovac – or even to force his resignation – by engineering the abduction of his son.[11]

Between early 1995 and the end of the parliamentary term in 1998 the coalition also took a series of steps to discredit and ultimately to expel its opponents in parliament. These efforts began with members of the opposition parties in parliament but expanded to include deputies who threatened to break away from the majority coalition. At the same time that it was fighting to free itself of constitutional limitations, the coalition was also fighting a rearguard action to maintain its majority in parliament. The defections of parliamentary deputies from the ruling coalition produced a strong reaction that led to their exclusion by parliamentary fiat without regard for clear constitutional and legal protections for their positions.

The third Mečiar government refrained from direct action against the Constitutional Court until late in its term. The question whether the defecting deputies should have their positions restored appears to have tipped the balance between the costs of defying the popular Constitutional Court and the cost of preventing deputies from defecting. In order to maintain party discipline and avoid accountability to their own deputies, the coalition parties accepted the risk of open rejection of their accountability to the court.

While all the above institutional encroachments succeeded in releasing the majority coalition from certain important external restraints, they did not achieve the sweeping success that marked the earlier efforts. Despite the limitations and intimidation, Michal Kovac served out his full term as Slovakia's president, and the opposition remained coherent enough to deny the coalition a constitutional majority. Furthermore, the accountability violations began to incur costs of their own. Whereas the coalition's initial efforts within the parliamentary and governmental spheres did not provoke anger beyond the narrow range of staunch opposition supporters, attacks on the president and parliamentary deputies exposed the coalition to negative public scrutiny. The kidnapping and bombings aimed at coalition opponents raised awkward questions that required police investigation. The expulsions of disloyal deputies required increasingly obvious departures from parliamentary procedure and common sense and forced the coalition into serious conflict with the respected Constitutional Court.

Stage III: limiting institutional accountability for the attacks of stage II

In subsequent stages, the attacks on accountability became almost exclusively defensive, as the coalition sought to avoid or undo the consequences of previous encroachments. The dramatic increase in politically related violence in Slovakia in 1995 and 1996 produced a series of investigations by police and prosecutors. The failure of these investigations to produce even a single formal indictment suggests glaring weaknesses in Slovakia's law enforcement, weaknesses that resulted from political interference rather than professional incompetence.

Rather than face responsibility for the kidnapping of the president's son, the coalition became increasingly involved in the previously inviolate sphere of criminal investigation and prosecution. Ministers and prosecutors appointed by the majority coalition removed investigators at the behest of fellow government appointees who were themselves under investigation. The process stopped only when the newly appointed investigators could not or would not perform a detailed investigation. In many cases the coalition did not even conceal the process of seeking out favorable investigators, though at other times it justified the changes on the basis of political bias, opportunism, lack of competence, and other failings.[12] Attempts to block public revelation of details through non-official channels also apparently led to further involvement by Slovakia's intelligence service – including the car-bomb death of a key witness's associate – which in turn led to further politically influenced investigations.

In its fear of future changes in government, the coalition also sought to avoid accountability through the use of blanket grants of amnesty, a power that devolved to the prime minister at the end of Kovac's term in early 1998. All these efforts proved successful to the extent that they prevented the indictment and trial of coalition employees, but they did not add to the coalition's political resources or release it from any restraints that were not of its own making. If anything, the need to avoid prosecution forced the coalition to show its hand and reveal that the absence of accountability mechanisms extended as far as the police and prosecutors.

Stage IV: limiting accountability to voters

For the first two-thirds of its parliamentary term, the HZDS-led majority coalition in Slovakia confined its efforts to undermining horizontal accountability and stayed clear of direct interference with electoral institutions. Earlier efforts against deputies of rival parties and its own defecting members had edged in this direction, but not until 1997 did the coalition look to undermine future elections. In the spring of that year the coalition illegally altered a referendum ballot to avoid losing an important vote. In the summer of the following year the coalition passed a revised electoral law. Although less questionable from a constitutional standpoint than the alteration of the referendum, the electoral law amendment created disproportionately high barriers for the opposition parties.

These coalition actions during its second two years in office demonstrate its increasing awareness that its limit extended beyond mere institutional checks and balances into the electorate. The coalition responded to falling popularity not only by engaging in public appeals but also by changing the rules that transform public opinion into political outcomes. By altering a referendum ballot on the thinnest of pretenses, the coalition admitted its impending defeat. By tailoring an election law to penalize the opposition, the coalition revealed its anxiety that coming elections might bring a change of government (and by granting amnesty in cases that had already been closed, the government further protected itself from such a change). In 1997 and 1998, Slovakia's majority coalition branched out from its encroachments on horizontal accountability to undercut vertical accountability as well.[13]

These violations of vertical accountability required prior violations of horizontal accountability. The referendum alteration depended on prior, unrestricted control of the Interior Ministry and confidence in its ability to avoid any subsequent attempts at prosecution. As with the abductions and other encroachments, the referendum alteration forced the Mečiar government into a repetition of horizontal accountability violations described above, including abrupt shifts in official responsibilities, neglect of Constitutional Court decisions, pressure on prosecutors and judges, and sweeping amnesties. These efforts and the electoral law changes both followed in the coalition's pattern of regarding external accountability as an obstacle to be avoided, whether through legislation or through more complicated use and misuse of other mechanisms under coalition control.

Reversal

Mečiar's efforts to restrict voter choice had only limited effect in the parliamentary election of 1998, and thanks in part to a unified strategy by key opposition parties and a significant voter turnout drive by opposition parties and other organizations, HZDS found itself with only 29 percent of seats in parliament and without a realistic chance of finding coalition partners who would provided the remainder. The new government, led by Mikulas Dzurinda of the Slovak Democratic Coalition took immediate steps to restore most of the institutional barriers that had been eliminated by Mečiar, reverting to proportionality in committee and oversight appointments, creating a directly elected presidency, and otherwise refraining from the sort of attacks on rival institutions that had been common in the previous government. Although certain coalition representatives proved susceptible to embezzlement and other forms of clientelism and corruption, over time the coalition did not renew Mečiar's strategy of institutional encroachment.

The cultural framework

Vladimir Mečiar played a central role in the course of Slovakia's political development, but political parties and their leaders do not appear from nowhere and do not stay in power without public support. Mečiar, for his part, remained Slovakia's most popular politician for the entire decade of the 1990s. Analyses of Slovakia's democratic decline in the mid-1990s frequently see Mečiar not as an explanation but as an "explanandum," the product of a "traditional"[14] and "nationalist-authoritarian" political culture.[15] Such claims broaden the explanation of Slovakia's democratic decline and recovery, linking the contingent decisions of particular leaders to deeper cultural and structural factors.

The role of such factors in creating the framework for political decisions is undeniable, yet the application of most cultural and structural factors to Slovakia has been unsatisfying. It is unlikely that the increasingly wide oscillations in accountability from one government to the next have resulted from corresponding shifts in Slovak values about democracy. Furthermore, even before the most recent shift toward accountable, democratic govern-ment, it had become apparent that overall levels of support for democracy in Slovakia differed little from levels in states such as the Czech Republic, Poland or Hungary that experienced far fewer difficulties with democratic consolidation.[16] To the extent that cultural and structural arguments do help to explain Slovakia's problematic democratization, the mechanisms are indirect and far more complicated.

Surveys of public opinion in Slovakia and the Czech Republic demonstrate the relationship between culture and institutions. These surveys show that while the distribution of opinions of Slovaks and Czechs on questions of democracy remained nearly identical during the 1990s, the relationship between responses on such questions and political party preference increased more dramatically in Slovakia than in the Czech Republic, to the point that Slovakia's political party spectrum could be described almost exclusively in terms of the democratic values of party supporters.[17] Thus the institutional problems discussed above had their roots not in a fundamental difference between the average Slovak and the average Czech – or Hungarians or Poles – but rather in a fundamental difference in the types of values that determined Slovaks' political choices.

Limits of convergence

Of the factors affecting democracy promotion, the only ones that depend most heavily on the underlying values of the democratizing country are the aspects of democratic convergence that Kubicek identifies in Chapter 1 as novelty and proximity (or what he calls "cultural match"). Under the heading of novelty, Kubicek notes that the process of liberalization and democratic transition can produce new circumstances that may either favor or retard adoption of democratic norms from abroad. On the one hand, rapid or far-reaching political change may produce an environment of uncertainty in which both new political elites and mass publics look abroad for new normative systems that make sense of their new circumstances. On the other hand, change that involves creation of altogether new states may lead to a search for national legitimacy that elevates domestic norms (e.g. nationalism) at the expense of those proffered by democracy promoters (e.g. political liberalization). Kubicek also notes the role of proximity, arguing that the more the norms of the democratizing state resemble those of the would-be democracy promoter, the fewer barriers will emerge to acceptance of democratic norms. Within the realm of political norms, this statement seems too obvious even to mention, but the notion extends as well to other realms. Thus significantly different norms in such areas as gender roles, wealth distribution, or national identity may hamper the democratizing country's reception of external norms about democracy as well.

In Slovakia novelty and proximity are closely related and play a significant – if not determining – role in affecting the influence of the European Union. While abrupt change may leave populations and elites in democratizing countries in need of new frameworks for understanding and open to models imported from abroad, abrupt changes that include the creation of a new state may work in the opposite direction by compelling a reliance on home-grown models. Slovakia faced both impulses at the same time. Surveys of masses and elites in both republics of Czechoslovakia show an almost immediate and widespread embrace of Western models of politics and economics.[18] Enthusiasm for such models subsided over time in both republics but only after both populations had internalized to a strong degree the messages they received early on about need for democracy and markets.[19]

Slovaks, however, differed from their Czech counterparts in one important respect: the cultural and political implications of national identity. Although the responses of Slovaks and Czechs on survey questions using generic references to nationalism, national pride, and patriotism show almost identical results, more specific questions about the meaning of those concepts reveals significant differences. Although Czechs endorse nationalism just as strongly as Slovaks, their understanding of the term shows significantly less connection to specific grievances and anxieties[20] and the same pattern appears in analysis of the differences in the rhetoric of public figures in the two countries.[21] The political success in Slovakia of leaders who emphasized the insecurity and injury aspects of nationhood had no significant analog in the Czech Republic. Among a particular segment of Slovakia's political leaders, both before and after independence, the emphasis on Slovak-ness became a dominant theme, first in distinction to Czech or Czechoslovak influences and later in distinction to influences from the West. In this respect the novelty and proximity factors of convergence become identical: while Slovaks overall were no less likely to value democracy than Czechs, Poles, or Hungarians, perceived differences between Slovakia and the EU regarding the value and meaning of national identity may have caused some Slovaks to regard the EU as tainted by anti-national cosmopolitanism and therefore to disregard its other messages as well. It is quite clear from Slovakia's press that certain prominent figures in Slovakia's political elite came by the mid-1990s to regard Western support for specific efforts at democratization as sufficient reason to reject such ideas. Within the population as a whole, these notions have a faint reflection in the slightly stronger belief among Slovaks than Czechs that "We have a good sense of democracy and do not need outside help" and the stronger correlation between this belief and trust in the European Union.[22]

At their strongest, however, questions of proximity and state-building novelty can account for the beliefs of only a small segment of Slovakia's political elite and relatively minor differences in public opinion. Without the other more visible and institutional differences between Slovakia and democratizing countries within the range of EU efforts, such factors would scarcely be noticeable. It is important, therefore, to turn to those questions of convergence and conditionality where the form and content of EU efforts did play a significant role. To do so, however, requires a closer examination of EU democracy promotion in Slovakia during the 1990s.

The diplomatic game

At the outset of the 1990s, the EU's efforts at democracy promotion in Slovakia did not differ meaningfully from its efforts in any other Central European country. Only as the course of Slovak politics changed did the EU policy toward Slovakia diverge from its efforts elsewhere in the region. As Slovakia fell short of EU democracy standards, EU officials became increasingly clear about the possibility of imposing its most severe sanction: exclusion from the Union. Even in the face of these threats, Slovakia's government offered little but reassurance and cosmetic change.

Responding to Mečiar

Between Slovakia's independence and the final months of 1994, EU officials behaved toward Slovakia as they did toward the Czech Republic, Hungary, and Poland, offering encouragement in the creation of a market economy and the consolidation of democracy, and funding various initiatives through programs such as PHARE and TACIS. EU representatives expressed occasional concerns about the activities of the second Mečiar government, but these remained muted. It was not until the first stage of accountability violations described above that EU efforts in Slovakia began to diverge from efforts in neighboring countries, but from November 1994, each new stage of institutional encroachments by the third Mečiar government led to a wave of EU responses. In each new wave – each, coincidentally, beginning in the final months of the year – the rhetoric of EU officials became sharper and the conditional relationship between the call for political reforms and the offer of EU membership became more explicit.

The process of escalation began in November 1994 with an EU expression of concern about Slovakia's political direction in the form of a demarche delivered by the French and German ambassadors. The demarche expressed a series of hopes for the new Slovak government and alluded to concerns about the status of Slovakia's Hungarian minority and "alarm" about "political developments since elections,"[23] which later clarification revealed to mean the coalition's immediate and full use of all legislative prerogatives available to it.[24] The areas of concern defined in the demarche, however, did not prevent the EU from ratifying an Association Agreement with Slovakia and accepting Slovakia as an Associate Member in early 1995. Nor did the EU refuse the application for full membership that Slovakia submitted in June 1995.

Yet by the time Slovakia submitted its application, EU officials had begun to express further concerns regarding the third Mečiar government's use of its prerogatives to limit rival bodies. Tensions rose during summer and fall as such efforts expanded to include outright attacks on rival parliamentary parties and the president and, apparently, the abduction of the president's son. By November 1995, the range of the government's accountability violations were the subject of a resolution by the European Parliament and demarches by both the EU and the United States. In this second round, the demarches presented a more specific set of concerns. Most of these related directly to the government's accountability violations, including: "the possibility that actions could be taken against the president of the Republic that would not be in conformity with the Constitution" and "difficulties encountered by nongovernmental organizations and bodies in the performance of their work."[25] Reflecting the stronger sentiments of the new demarche were a series of strongly worded follow-up comments by EU Commissioner for Foreign Relations Hans van den Broek, German Chancellor Helmut Kohl, EU Commission Chair Jacques Santer, and the Co-Chair of the Joint Parliamentary Committee between the EU Herbert Bosch. These statements included warnings that Slovakia could fall from its position among the prime candidates for integration and called for a series of institutional changes including the scrapping of revisions to Slovakia's criminal code, the enactment of formal guidelines governing minority languages, and the introduction of opposition representatives on a variety of parliamentary committees and oversight bodies.[26]

In December 1996, the European Parliament reacted to the exclusion from Slovakia's parliament of an MP who had resigned from HZDS with rapid passage of a sharply worded resolution. The statement not only called for the reinstatement of the deputy and an investigation of an explosion at his house but also notified the Slovak government "that respecting basic democratic principles, including exercising parliamentary mandates, is a precondition for EU entry and for preserving cooperation with the European Union."[27] Six months later, in 1997, as the EU Commission finalized its report on EU membership applications, EU officials including Bosch and Van den Broek reiterated what appeared to be final warnings[28] about the steps that Slovakia would need to take in order to receive a positive recommendation. Slovakia's government did not pursue any of these suggestions and the EU Commission report issued in August 1997 recommended against Slovakia's admission.

The Commission's recommendations still required the vote of the European Council in its December 1997 Luxembourg Summit, and officials of the EU and its member states spent the last half of the year in repeated efforts to convince the Slovak government that an invitation to membership was still possible and that it required only the reversal of certain (not all) institutional encroachments made during the previous two years. Again, Bosch delivered the familiar set of conditions:

> Key changes which should be made by Slovakia, according to him, are to bolster the stability of the operations of democratic institutions and to allow the opposition to be represented on supervisory bodies and parliamentary committee boards, the resolution of the [expelled deputy] case, and the adoption of the act on the use of ethnic minority languages. Bosch reasserted that the European Parliament would highly value such positive changes and quickly respond. Time for changes is still here.[29]

Again a multitude of high level officials from the EU and its member states repeated the conditions with increasingly visible exasperation. Both the Prime Minister and Foreign Minister of Luxembourg, which at the time held the presidency of the European Council, offered Slovakia the chance of an invitation in exchange for political change. In personal visits EU commissioner Van den Broek, the Danish Foreign Minister, and the Chair of the Swedish Parliament delivered the same message. The Slovak government arranged a brief rapprochement between Prime Minister Mečiar and President Kovac, who wrote a joint letter affirming Slovakia's commitment to integration, but Slovakia's parliament took no action in the specific areas of concern except to make matters worse. In November 1997 the European Parliament called on the European Council to reject Slovakia's membership bid, and in its December meeting the Council announced that formal membership talks would include only Cyprus, the Czech Republic, Estonia, Hungary and Poland.

During the first half of 1998, EU officials repeated the calls for political change but with visibly reduced expectations about their effectiveness, and EU efforts in Slovakia shifted to the electoral arena, a realm discussed below.

The September 1998 parliamentary elections made it impossible for Mečiar to maintain a parliamentary majority and allowed the formation of a new government under the leadership of Mikulas Dzurinda, who began immediately to act upon the EU recommendations. EU officials reacted with cautious optimism. The European Parliament, which had been quick to criticize the Mečiar government, proved equally quick to praise Dzurinda's efforts, and by December of 1998, Joint Parliamentary Committee Co-Chair Bosch announced that "The basic obstacles preventing Slovakia from integrating into the European Union (EU) have been removed."[30] By March 1999 the more cautious EU Commission also had noted "great progress"[31] and in July 1999 the French Ambassador stated that Slovakia had met all political preconditions for accession.[32] In December 1999, little more than a year after the Dzurinda government took office, the European Council in its Helsinki session voted to begin membership talks with Bulgaria, Latvia, Lithuania, Malta, Romania, and Slovakia.

Mečiar's non-response

As the EU became increasingly insistent and specific in its conditions for accepting Slovakia's membership bid, Slovakia's government became increasingly intransigent. The third Mečiar government never demonstrated itself to be particularly responsive to EU concerns, but the level of its responsiveness clearly deteriorated over time. When the first EU demarche arrived in the wake of the first stage of encroachments, Mečiar publicly rejected the notion that it required any political change:

> There is nothing to comment on. The demarche is positive. It recognizes the democratic results of elections in Slovakia, expresses the view that the course on which Slovakia has embarked will continue, and speaks about minority rights. That is all. Basically, all of the negative fuss about the EU's coming to the rescue of those who lost the elections or those who are now infamously leaving the government and begging us to let them go is nonsense. The contents of the demarche are not at all as they have been interpreted by the mass media. Nothing has happened.[33]

Yet within four months, the Mečiar government had conducted a series of intense negotiations with Hungary that led to the signing of a treaty governing Slovakia–Hungary relations and the treatment of minorities that received praise from officials of EU member states.[34] The second round of demarches produced a less conciliatory reaction from Mečiar who sharply criticized the EU for threatening sanctions without seeking out both sides of the issue, before again denying the existence of any problems:

> Naturally, we are interested in the integration into the European structures. We have declared our interest in it, and we are also meeting its

requirements. Nobody, no resolution says that the Slovak Republic fails to fulfill anything or that we are lagging behind in the obligations we have accepted.[35]

The increasingly angry tone of Mečiar's response had its counterpart in the unwillingness of his coalition to make political changes. Some pro-integration Slovak commentators praised the demarches for "positively influencing" Slovakia's parliament by dissuading the coalition from escalating its attacks on the president and the opposition, but even these observers noted that the changes were minor and, probably, temporary.[36] Indeed, subsequent EU critiques proved strikingly ineffective. The increasingly specific lists of desired changes presented by Bosch and Van den Broek evoked a mix of indignation, denials, and promises of change but resulted in no meaningful changes in policy. Nor did the awareness of EU oversight prevent further encroachments. Despite explicit warnings by EU officials that the conduct of the 1997 NATO referendum would influence the 1997 EU Commission report, the Mečiar government nevertheless engaged in electoral manipulation. As EU officials were giving Slovakia final warnings before the 1997 Luxembourg Summit, the government's parliamentary deputies voted in direct contravention of EU specific conditions to ignore the Constitutional Court. Even the government's last-minute promises to make appropriate changes eventually came to nothing, and even in its final days it showed no signs of willingness to accommodate any outside demands.

The limits of conditionality

Explanations of obstinacy on the part of the Mečiar government span a wide range, with some observers allowing for the possibility that the government misinterpreted signals and others suggesting that the government interpreted the signals only too correctly. The debate relates directly to the process of conditionality discussed by Kubicek in Chapter 1. Kubicek argues that unlike convergence, conditionality concerns the provision of tangible incentives for the achievement of particular goals. Since the effectiveness of such conditions depends on clear standards, and since the "internalization of norms" does not lend itself to easy measurement, conditional efforts at democracy promotion most often focus on the creation of specific institutional structures and the achievement of other easily observable milestones. Kubicek notes that the effectiveness of conditionality in democracy promotion depends on three factors:

- *Benefit of the incentive* Efforts that rely on a cost-benefit analysis by the democratizers must use incentives that have genuine value. In practical terms, the benefits (or the avoidance of sanction) must compensate adequately and within a reasonable time for the real costs of democratization faced by political leaders and their supporters. The size of benefit must also take into account the structure of opportunity costs faced by the democratizing country. The existence of alternative sources of international support that do not insist on political change may allow reluctant democratizers to reject the conditions of the democracy promoter at little cost.

- *Certainty of the incentive*   Promoters of democracy must offer reasonable confidence that meeting its conditions will lead directly to the conferral of the promised benefit. Doubt about the ability or willingness of the democracy promoter to follow through on promises will undermine any incentive to meet conditions of democratization.
- *Clarity of the standards*   The conditions set for democratizing countries must be formulated in a manner that allows for a minimum of dispute regarding the success or failure of their efforts. The complexity of issues surrounding democratization makes this goal particularly difficult to achieve, and the question becomes particularly difficult in the case of "gray zone" democracies that exhibit some features of democracy but not others.

Officials in the third Mečiar government argued implicitly that the failure of conditionality in the case of Slovakia can be attributed to a lack of clarity in EU conditions for Slovakia that are alleged to have shifted over time and to have differed from those of other applicant countries.[37] Others suggest a possible lack of clarity regarding the likelihood of sanctions. Samson argues that the leaders of the third Mečiar government believed that Slovakia's geographical position made its inclusion inevitable and saw no credibility in threats that the country's acceptance depended on political reform.[38] As of 1997, this position even received support from Joint Parliamentary Commission Co-Chair Bosch who allowed that "The fact that [changes] have so far not been made may only show that the Slovak Cabinet had slightly underrated the message of the European Union's cautions and warnings on the need to carry them out."[39]

These arguments, however, hold greater explanatory value for the early years of the third Mečiar government than they do for the period that followed. By mid-1997 the message of EU representatives was so specific and resolute that it is difficult to understand any misinterpretation. Not only did members of Slovakia's opposition correctly read the signals as early as 1995 (though the interpretation was also in their best political interest), but so also did at least one of the Mečiar government's own foreign ministers, who explained his resignation as the result of government manipulation of the 1997 NATO referendum that "greatly limited" his ability to prepare Slovakia for EU and NATO accession.[40] To believe in the inevitability of Slovakia's accession even after the explicit 1997 report of the European Commission would have required a superhuman degree of faith (or incomprehension). If the lack of reform simply involved involuntary misunderstanding, then each successive demarche and EU exhortation should have had an ameliorative effect upon the government's behavior rather than the increasing hostility that actually emerged. Furthermore, these observations reflect upon the content of the EU's *public* messages to Slovakia. It is likely that in private discussions Van den Broek and Bosch were more rather than less explicit. Finally, Slovakia's eventual outright rejection by the 1997 Luxembourg council produced not an effort to recover lost ground but rather a series of additional accountability violations.

The clarity explanations thus require at least some additional points. In fact, a closer look at the value of incentives faced by the third Mečiar government offers a sufficient explanation for its increasing hostility in the face of ever stronger and more specific EU conditions. Central to this supposition is the notion that Vladimír Mečiar resolutely pursued the elimination of outside sources of accountability as his primary political goal. In-depth analysis indicates that although Mečiar was capable of making tactical retreats, he never relinquished the goal of direct personal control of Slovakia's politics without restriction and was willing to take major – if not always well-considered – risks toward that end.[41] By the time the EU had become more insistent in its demands, the avoidance of accountability had gone beyond personal preference to political necessity. Mečiar and his allies by then simply had too much to lose from permitting opposition representatives on oversight boards, from allowing party defection to go unpunished, and from the loss of nationalist support that would result from passing a law on minority languages. EU membership still remained a government priority throughout this period, but the government was not willing to pursue it at the cost of the immediate political and economic rewards that resulted from Mečiar's style of rule. As a result, the government first attempted to placate the EU with signs of good faith – such as the Slovak–Hungarian treaty – that did not interfere with the institutional encroachments at the core of its political livelihood. Over time, however, EU understanding of Slovakia's problems improved and its conditions zeroed in on precisely those accountability violations that lay at the heart of Mečiar's political efforts. EU conditions ultimately failed to bring about political reform under the Mečiar government, because its main incentive – membership – depended on the very condition – accountability – that Mečiar sought most to avoid. The EU had nothing to offer Mečiar to compensate for what it demanded from him. This is a key point, and one that the EU has run up against in other circumstances (e.g. Ukraine, Croatia). If the EU's objections go more to policies that can be amended (as in the case of Latvia) and less to personalities (or programs intrinsically associated with a personality), it may have more leverage. However, in the case of Slovakia the EU could offer Mečiar little to push democratization ahead.

The election game

In late 1997 an offhand statement by Arie Oostlander, European Parliament Observer for the European Union Expansion, captured both the frustration of EU officials with Slovakia and the emergence of an alternative strategy. Oostlander told the Slovak Press Agency TASR that the EU resolution recommending against membership negotiations with Slovakia was a signal "that the current Government poses a barrier in the way to Europe," and added in a direct address to Slovakia's citizens, "Please, change either the opinion [that Slovakia seriously wants to join the EU] or change the government."[42] As early as 1995, EU institutions and EU member countries had begun to seek an alternative path to Slovakia's democratization, not by trying to overcome the overwhelming barriers raised by the third Mečiar government, but rather by working with already receptive political forces within the opposition. As Slovakia's elections neared, these efforts became considerably more overt. During 1998, political leaders from EU member countries actively provided expertise and funding to opposition political parties. Official EU institutions, unwilling to completely abandon a position of formal neutrality, pursued the same goals through efforts at voter education, voter turnout, and electoral observation, using these ostensibly non-partisan themes in ways that benefited opposition parties.

Western Europeans and Slovakia's opposition were not the only ones to take EU issues into the electoral arena. The Mečiar government long preceded them there. The two sides, however, faced significantly different challenges in their use of the EU as a political issue. The opposition and its EU supporters needed simply to make the case of that EU membership offered significant benefits and that the opposition had a better chance of leading Slovakia toward that end. In short, they needed only to convince voters of the degree of benefit and the certainty of its conferral according to clear standards. For the Mečiar government in 1998 the task was far more difficult. Having taken the same position during the 1994 election campaign and in its governmental program statement, the government parties faced the prospect of reconciling a pro-EU stance with increasingly vocal criticism from the EU itself. Yet Mečiar appears to have been so confident of his skill in the electoral realm that he would accept the risk of voter unhappiness over the EU rejection of Slovakia rather than introduce accountability into his mode of governing.

Sowing seeds of doubt

The party's strategy became increasingly complex as EU critiques of Slovakia became ever sharper and more detailed. At first the party took the position that there simply was no criticism, and that EU comments had been inadvertently or deliberately misunderstood,[43] but by 1996 such arguments were already difficult to sustain. Where EU criticism could not be dismissed, Mečiar's government officials adopted a variety of strategies to shift the cost-benefit analysis of Slovak voters in such a way as to diminish the impact of the EU's rejection. Over time the mix of these arguments shifted from attacks on the clarity and certainty of conditions to attacks on the benefits of EU membership itself.

Clarity

One of the most frequent HZDS strategies for keeping – even attracting – voters despite EU criticism of Slovakia involved repeated questioning of the basis of EU judgments about Slovakia. These claims took three forms:

- "The EU lacks information." Beginning during the second Mečiar government and intensifying with the demarches of 1994, officials of the coalition parties noted that EU criticisms relied on sources that were "unsubstantiated" or even "not objective."[44] As EU criticisms intensified, this argument relied increasingly on the notion that the failure of the EU to understand Slovakia resulted from deliberate *mis*information provided by Slovakia's opposition.
- "The EU does not understand." Even where EU institutions might receive correct information, Mečiar government officials argued that they did not necessarily possess the cultural context in which to interpret it. In a speech to the Joint EU–Slovakia Parliamentary Commission, the Chairman of Slovakia's Parliament, Ivan Gasparovic asked "Have Western diplomats and observers actually understood the sense of historical developments in Slovakia? Do they understand the essence of these changes? Do they understand Slovak national characteristics? Each nation, each state has some specific features, and these are in general respected."[45]
- "The EU has a double standard." Beginning in 1995, representatives of the Mečiar government increasingly made the argument that regardless of its information or understanding, the EU would not judge Slovakia by the same criteria as everyone else.[46] After the 1997 decision of the Luxembourg council to reject Slovakia, Mečiar attempted to give this argument an even more positive spin by explaining the double standard as the result of his "insistence on equality" in the face of countries that "see themselves as superior."[47]

Each appears designed to lower the cost of failure by making the argument that "If we are excluded, it is not our fault." At their most extreme, these statements go further to make the implicit claim that the fault lies with foreign or domestic actors who seek Slovakia's destruction.

Certainty

A second strategy for defusing EU criticism involved reassurances about the inevitability of Slovakia's accession regardless of any isolated EU statements. As Slovakia's rejection became more likely, however, certain HZDS officials modified these messages by also focusing on the certainty of delays in the process for *all* potential applicants. The claims thus took two forms:

- "The EU will indeed accept Slovakia." These statements began early, even before the third Mečiar government, and continued through and even after Slovakia's rejection from the first group of countries. As Slovakia's accession became increasingly less likely, the claims that Slovakia's accession was merely "a matter of time"[48] became increasingly strained, culminating in Mečiar's statement shortly before the 1998 elections that "In the back rooms they are speaking about a group of countries that could be first. It is an absolutely different group from the one which is now being spoken about publicly. We are first in that group."[49] A frequent element of such arguments was the notion (made by leaders in other countries as well) that "Europe needs Slovakia" because of its "unique geostrategic importance."[50] As late as January 1998, for example, Mečiar noted that logic dictated that the capital of a united Europe could be located in Slovakia.[51]

- "The EU will not accept anybody in the near future." In an apparent effort to reduce concerns over visible setbacks in Slovakia's position relative to other applicants, HZDS officials attempted to reassure voters by noting the ephemeral nature of any delay in the context of a slow accession process. In a 1997 interview, the Chair of Slovakia's Parliament, Ivan Gasparovic, "expressed his doubts that membership will be given to any of the associated countries before 2005."[52] In an elaboration several weeks later, Gasparovic went further to raise doubts about whether expansion would occur at all:

  > If anyone thinks that a state from Central and Eastern Europe will get into the European Union before 2005, then he is naive. At last year's meeting of the European banks, which was attended by representatives from the World Bank, it was even said that you (the states of Central and Eastern Europe) may perhaps enter the EU in 400 years. Some of them even proclaimed that it would be in 700. . . . It goes without saying that this is an exaggeration. The fact, however, is that this is not a question of one year; in my opinion, it is not even a question of 10 years.[53]

  An article by a Mečiar advisor makes an almost identical point: "Today, there is already official talk of the fact that it will be at least in the year 2002 or 2003. There is a Spanish variation which mentions the year 2025."[54]

In contrast to the previous group of claims that absolved blame for failing to meet the EU conditions, these rejected even the possibility of blame by denying that the conditions played any role in determining the outcome.

Benefit

A third HZDS strategy focused on the relative value of EU membership. Some statements pointed out hidden costs connected with integration while others suggested higher opportunity costs by pointing out the potential benefits of alternatives. As EU statements became increasingly sharp and Slovakia's acceptance increasingly unlikely, the mix of comments shifted away from mere caveats toward outright hostility. The claims took three basic forms:

- "Integration will be expensive." As early as 1995, Mečiar began to discuss the costs of joining the EU, though he did not suggest that these outweighed the benefits. Over time, however, party leaders began to discuss a wide range of potential financial disadvantages, with one Mečiar advisor reiterating, "The EU is not a charitable organization."[55] A variant of this argument, heard frequently after mid-1997, contended, "Early integration will be more expensive." In 1997 Ivan Gasparovic stated, "Experienced economists claim that the sooner a country gets into the EU, the more expensive it is for it"[56] and prominent HZDS deputy Augustin Marian Huska noted that delay in Slovakia's accession to the European Union would be beneficial because neither Slovakia nor the EU were prepared to handle the consequences.[57] A representative of one of HZDS's coalition partners, the Slovak National Party, even attempted to turn Slovakia's rejection into a benefit, pointing out in 1998 that it is advantageous to Slovakia that it is not in the first group of countries, since "it will have a chance to monitor the effects on countries in the first group."[58]

- "There are viable alternatives to EU membership." In 1997, Slovak Foreign Minister Zdenka Kramplova reassured Slovaks that rejection by NATO and the EU would not lead to "international isolation."[59] During late 1997 and 1998, Slovak diplomats also began to pursue more intensive bilateral relationships with individual countries[60] and to focus on the possibility of the Central European Free Trade Area (CEFTA) as a possible alternative. Furthermore, although HZDS officials publicly rejected any notion of special ties with Russia, its coalition partners, particularly Jan Luptak of the Association of Workers of Slovakia (ZRS), indicated a willingness to consider security guarantees from Russia over those of Western countries.[61]

- "Integration threatens Slovakia's sovereignty." From the beginning of the third Mečiar government the chairs of both of the minor coalition partners expressed strong reservations about the trade-offs involved in European integration and warned of dangers to Slovakia's sovereignty.[62] HZDS chair Mečiar generally avoided such statements. At times, in moments of apparent anger, he defended Slovakia against foreign interference, noting, "Slovakia is a sovereign country, so no one has the right to give us ultimate orders, not even MPs of the European Parliament who have no power of jurisdiction,"[63] but his statements usually remained ambiguous, often critical of the EU yet in support of Slovakia's membership. The same cannot be said of many who were close to Mečiar. In late

1995, HZDS spokesman Stanislav Haber compared the EU with Nazi Germany in 1938 and the Soviet Union in 1968, both of which sent Czechoslovakia demarches followed by tanks (he resigned after an ambiguous reprimand from the party). Even stronger statements appeared throughout 1997 and 1998 on the pages of the HZDS weekly publication, *Slovensko Do Toho!* According to *Do Toho!* editor Igor Zvach, for example, for Slovakia to accept conditions imposed by the EU, such as a minority language law, "would border on treason."[64]

It is in the company of such statements that otherwise harmless advertising images – such as an aggressive lion emerging from gold stars on a blue field – take on additional and significant meaning. When the EU proved unwilling to confer benefits on HZDS, HZDS cast doubt on the ability of the EU to benefit Slovakia as a whole.

The eight strategies detailed here demonstrate the breadth of HZDS rhetoric during the period. Statements by party leaders and party appointees occupied literally the full spectrum of possible positions toward the EU from the determined and deferential statements of Slovakia's foreign ministers to the fury of HZDS parliamentary deputies on the pages of *Slovensko Do Toho!* Avoiding inconsistencies and even outright contradictions did not appear to play a role in party strategy In fact, the presence of a full range of positions offered wide latitude to party leader Mečiar. He rarely engaged in the debate himself except to express Slovakia's readiness for membership and indignation that the EU might think otherwise. This noncommittal position was possible precisely because he had at his disposal a party with representatives voicing a wide range of positions. Rather than commit himself abroad in a way that could offend some at home (or vice versa), he placed different party officials in front of different audiences (often the one best suited to their messages and methods) and led them as a conductor leads an orchestra.

A mixed harvest

If Mečiar thought that by this means he could shape the attitudes of party supporters in such a way as to minimize the damage of rejection by the EU, he was largely right. If he felt that he could use the same tactics actually to expand the electoral appeal of HZDS, he was wrong.

Few changes on Slovakia's electoral landscape are more striking than the shift in the relationship between party preference and attitudes toward the European Union over the years from 1993 until 1999. Figure 3.2 shows a distinct change over time in the mean assessment of the EU among the supporters of political parties: the support bases of the Christian Democratic Movement (KDH), the Democratic Union (DU), and the Hungarian Coalition parties (MK) shift from moderate trust toward higher levels of trust. The support base of the Party of the Democratic Left (SDL) shifts in the

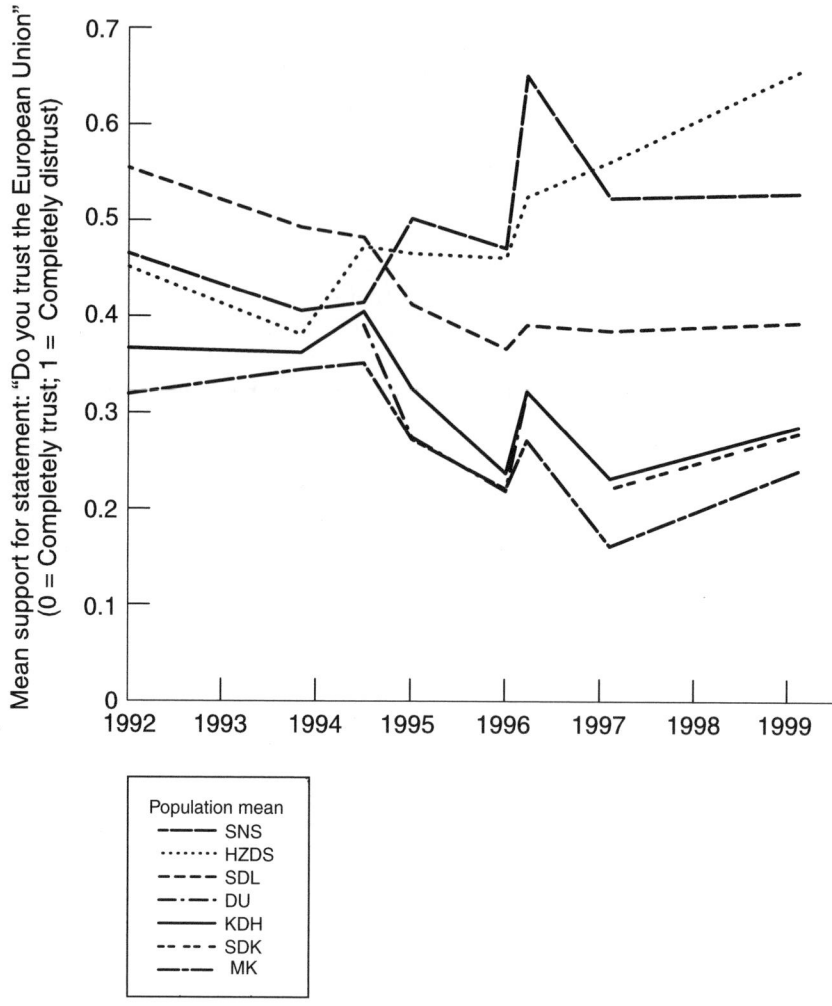

Figure 3.2 Distrust toward the European Union by party preference in Slovakia, 1992–1999.

Source: FOCUS, 'Pubic Opinion Surveys' (Computer file), Bratislava 1992–1999.

same direction and at about the same rate but from an initial position of moderate distrust. The pattern for the Slovak National Party (SNS) and the HZDS is quite different. The support bases of both shift from relative neutrality in 1992 and 1993 to extreme distrust by 1998. For SNS the shift occurred rapidly and then moderated. For HZDS the trend toward ever-higher levels of distrust continued through the most recent available FOCUS survey in 1999.[65] Eastern Eurobarometer surveys conducted during the same period exhibit an almost identical pattern.[66] In four years – the four years coinciding with the third Mečiar government – the HZDS electorate shifted from a position indistinguishable from the population as a whole to become the most vehemently anti-EU electorate of any party in the country. The change thus corresponds precisely with the increasingly sharp EU criticism of the Mečiar government and the increasingly distrustful tone of HZDS comments regarding the EU.[67]

As part of this differentiation process, questions related to the EU became sharply politicized. In fact, they came over time to be the most sharply politicized questions in the country's political life. Of particular note is the relationship between support for the EU and opinions of HZDS and its leader. In a battery of seventeen survey questions on religious, ethnic, economic, and political issues asked in late 1993, responses to questions about EU membership and EU trust ranked ninth and twelfth, respectively, in the strength of their relationship with respondents' trust of Vladimir Mečiar. In 1999 the same two questions ranked first and second. In six regular FOCUS surveys conducted between 1993 and 1999, the level of correlation between Mečiar and trust in the EU rose by regular amounts in every successive survey, increasing from a barely significant correlation of 0.07 in 1993 to an extremely significant correlation of 0.42 in 1999.[68]

Such a politically charged question might be expected to produce a realignment of voters that could explain the shift in Slovakia's electoral balance between Mečiar's 1994 victory and his 1998 defeat. In fact several factors limited the shift of party preference surrounding the EU issue. Shifts in the position of a party's electorate may reflect either changes in the minds of party voters or changes in the composition of the party electorate. Data from FOCUS surveys that include questions of previous voting behavior allows for a rough test of both hypotheses. Restricting the sample only to HZDS loyalists – those who voted for the party in the election preceding the survey and who still support the party – shows an increase in EU distrust over time that closely parallels the change in the party as a whole. Thus (if most survey respondents can be trusted to correctly report their previous vote), much of the attitude change that occurred over time happened *within* the minds of party loyalists. At the same time, the surveys show a parallel change in the composition of the party. Those who stopped supporting the party over time felt less distrust toward the EU than did party loyalists; those who began supporting the party felt more distrust than did the population as a whole. After 1994, however, this movement of persons played an ever-smaller role in comparison to change in the opinion of loyalists. The contours of this shift are important. Only about 15 percent of those who claimed to have supported HZDS in 1994 shifted to other parties, and of those nearly half shifted to other parties within the coalition. Those who shifted to the party amounted to an even smaller share – about 4 percent of HZDS support and nearly half of those shifted from another anti-EU party within the coalition. From these numbers it is possible to make certain broad conclusions:

- The combination of EU criticism and HZDS interpretations of that criticism were enough to change significantly the opinions of party loyalists in the direction of distrust of the EU.
- The party was thereby able to avoid losing significant numbers of voters to parties with more pro-EU positions. (Nearly half the departing voters shifted to an equally anti-EU party within the coalition.)
- The party was not able to use its new position on EU questions to attract voters.

It is possible, too, that the exclusion of Slovakia by the EU and the increasingly hostile response of HZDS drove previously undecided voters into the opposition ranks. Though this is difficult to measure, survey results offer some support. According to a 1999 FOCUS survey, those who did not vote in 1994 but went to the polls in 1998 were considerably more likely than the population as a whole to vote for opposition parties. According to a 1997 survey, non-voters who opted to support opposition parties expressed considerably more trust toward the EU than the population as a whole and almost as much as opposition loyalists. Thus, while Mečiar may have changed the opinions of his base enough to keep its loyalty, he may in the process have mobilized at least some who had previously remained outside the political arena and in the process weakened his own chances for re-election.

The EU in Slovakia's election game

If HZDS was not able to use its public statements to do any more than slow the defection of party loyalists, neither was the EU able to use an outside game to achieve its own goals. Having correctly identified Mečiar as an insurmountable obstacle to Slovakia's democratization and subsequent EU accession, officials from the EU and certain member states sought his replacement by a coalition of parties that expressed active support for the EU and had proven their willingness to accept institutional accountability. Toward that end, the EU and its member states provided well over a million Euros for a variety of direct democracy promotion efforts at mass and elite levels. The effects of most of these efforts at the elite level is difficult to ascertain and even more difficult to quantify. These programs undoubtedly taught policymakers important skills, but Slovakia's political polarization during the 1990s probably diminished the role that such programs actually played in the democratization. Slovakia's democratization occurred through a change from one governing coalition to another very different one, not from change within any particular party or coalition. Those elites who benefited from such programs were already well disposed toward demo-cratization; those who were ill-disposed rarely participated.

At the mass level, democracy promotion programs have claimed Slovakia as a success story.[69] According to these accounts, efforts at increased turnout, particularly among young people, helped lead Slovakia's opposition to the electoral victory that ousted the third Mečiar government. EU programs played a sizable role in such efforts and the EU might thus claim some credit for Slovakia's political change. A closer look at Slovakia's election results, however, suggest that while voter education and increased turnout did clearly help the opposition, they merely built upon a victory that it would have been won in any case. Between the 1994 and 1998 elections, Slovakia's opposition parties gained just over 700,000 votes while its coalition parties lost just over 100,000. Overall turnout over this same period increased by just under 500,000. Even if every one of the new voters preferred the opposition and every one had stayed home on election day, opposition parties would still have gained a clear majority of seats. A more elaborate model based on the retrospective claims of survey respondents in early 1999 indicates that increased turnout contributed only six seats to the opposition's thirty-six-seat margin of victory in 1998.

Ultimately the reason for the opposition victory in 1998 lies less with outside help than with a variety of internal factors including the weariness with incumbents that is shared in all democracies, the emergence of a "middle" party with democratic leanings, and the new-found ability of the opposition to coordinate its efforts. That novelty resulted in no small part from the threat that Mečiar posed to Slovakia's institutional accountability and the continuation of its electoral democracy, the same factor that brought rejection by the EU and EU electoral assistance.

The bigger picture

The account presented here suggests both a surprisingly small role for the EU in Slovakia's democratization process and few alternatives for EU officials. Slovakia's barriers to entry were political rather than cultural, and its political barriers depended on the decisions of a very small circle of political leaders. As EU officials discovered after repeated efforts, there is not much the EU can do to make democracy more attractive to leaders who have decided it is not otherwise in their best interest. They do not have the sort of financial resources to buy off such leaders (and if they did, they would certainly not be permitted by member states to use the funds for that purpose); nor do they have any tangible coercive mechanisms (and could not use them if they did). In essence the only thing the EU can do to such leaders is to threaten them with exclusion, but like Mečiar, leaders such as Tudjman, Kuchma, or Lukhashenka may be immune to such threats before they arrive. "Never," these leaders might note, "join a club that will have you as a member only if you become someone else."

The only short-run options left open, then, are indirect. They involve persuading those who in turn might persuade the reluctant democratizer.

Depending on the circumstances, this can mean coalition partners or financial supporters. In almost all circumstances it means voters. But influencing voters is not an easy task for outsiders in any context and involvement in partisan politics is particularly risky for an organization that claims a degree of political neutrality. In Slovakia, the EU faced coalition partners who were equally resistant to persuasion and found that many of those financing the coalition had their own fears about the consequences of EU integration on their own less-than-transparent business practices.[70] Fortunately for EU efforts, however, Slovakia's opposition rose to the challenge of Mečiar's institutional encroachments and managed to defeat him without requiring significant EU involvement. In other countries, the balance might be reversed and the coalition partners and supporters might provide the best path to political change.

In the long run, the EU's rewards become more powerful and its influence therefore greater. Membership becomes more appealing as it recedes, and the admission of some countries raises the stakes for others who must struggle to avoid the stigma of being left out. Mečiar's mix of party positions, though sometimes uneven in its effects, demonstrates the ability of party leaders to survive the political impact of EU rejection, but only at a price. Such efforts may ultimately be self-defeating to the extent that they preserve the party electoral base by persuading it to accept opinions that become increasingly less palatable to outsiders and thereby limit its electoral potential. In this sense, perhaps, the designers of the HZDS advertisement were correct to see a threat to their party in the stars in the EU flag. Although an aggressive Leo makes for better television, a more appropriate symbol may be found in the constellation of Libra, the balance of which was eventually tipped in favor of the EU and democracy by the actions of *domestic* political leaders.

Notes

1 P. Kubicek, Chapter 1 of this volume, p. 7.
2 Although Freedom House scores raise significant methodological questions, they capture the general course of Slovakia's democratic development. The upward spike recorded for 1993 is almost certainly an overestimate based more on potential than actual developments. Nor do these scores register the period between March and November 1994 during which Slovakia experienced the same extent of political and civil rights as its Visegrad neighbors. The rise between 1994 and 1998, however, does correspond to a significant worsening of conditions under the government of Vladimir Mečiar.
3 G. O'Donnell, "Delegative Democracy?" Kellogg Institute Working Paper, 1992; C. S. Leff, "Dysfunctional Democracy: Institutional Conflict in Post-Communist Slovakia," *Problems of Post-Communism*, September/October 1996; M. S. Fish, "The End of Mečiarism," *East European Constitutional Review* 8(1–2) at http://www.law.nyu.edu/eecr/vol8num1–2/special/endofmec.html, accessed June 20, 1999; K. D. Krause, "Accountability and Political Party Competition in Slovakia and the Czech Republic," Doctoral dissertation, South Bend, IN: University of Notre Dame, 2000.

4 F. Gal, *Z prvej ruky*. Bratislava: Vydavatelstvo Archa, 1991.

5 J. Obrman, "The Czechoslovak Elections," *RFE/RL Research Report,* 1(26), 1992, pp. 12–19; S. Szomolanyi, "Introduction: A Transition to Democracy?" *The Slovak Path of Transition – To Democracy?* in S. Szomolanyi and G. Meseznikov, eds, Bratislava: Slovak Political Science Association and Interlingua, 1994, pp. 5–12; S. Abraham, "Early Elections in Slovakia: A State of Deadlock," *Government and Opposition* 30(1), 1995, pp. 86–100.

6 A. Kalniczky, "Academic Freedom in Slovakia: The Case of Trnava University," *RFE/RL Research Report* 2(11), 1993, pp. 53–65; S. Fisher, "Slovak Television in Disarray," *RFE/RL Daily Reports*, 1994, pp. 29–33.

7 Mečiar partisans immediately assailed the new government as the product of a parliamentary putsch and the forerunner of an authoritarian regime, but these claims do not bear closer examination.

8 N. King, "Mečiar's Power Plays in Slovakia Stir Fears of Democracy's Erosion," *The Wall Street Journal*, Bratislava, January 11, 1996, pp. 1, 8.

9 J. Gould, "Winners, Losers and the Institutional Effects of Privatization in the Czech and Slovak Republics," Working Paper, Robert Schuman Center, European University Institute, 1998.

10 A. Skolkay, "Slovak Government Tightens its Grip on the Airwaves," *Transition,* April 19, 1996, pp. 18–21.

11 Legal controversy about the validity of an amnesty decree issued by Mečiar in 1998 has to date prevented the prosecution of suspects involved in the case, but a variety of witnesses and other circumstantial evidence link the abduction closely to Slovakia's intelligence service, at the time headed by Mečiar appointee Ivan Lexa.

12 *Slovenska Republika*, "Unfounded Objections," Trans. Foreign Broadcast Information Service, Bratislava, December 6, 1995, pp. 1–2; *Slovenska Republika*, "Former Investigators were Supposedly Changing Testimonies," Trans. Foreign Broadcast Information Service, Bratislava, April 16, 1996, pp. 1, 6; *Sme,* "Prime Ministers Promised Universities, Highways, and Theaters to Regional Capitals," Trans. Foreign Broadcast Information Service, Bratislava, September 2, 1996, p. 3.

13 It remains an open question whether HZDS planned to disrupt the 1998 parliamentary elections. In August 1998 the coalition challenged the status of the Slovak Democratic Coalition (SDK), a party created by members of then opposition parties in an effort to circumvent the 1998 electoral law's obstacles to coalition formation. A decision by Slovakia's highest appeals court prevented the exclusion of SDK – at the time the only political formation that could rival HZDS – but it is unclear whether the court faced political pressure in the decision. HZDS also attempted to exclude the presence of election observers before finally accepting them as a condition of its membership in OSCE. Speculation suggests that the coalition did not take any further steps because it remained confident of victory until the final days of the campaign. Furthermore, HZDS may have lacked the personnel willing to engage in deliberate manipulation of a parliamentary election. Unlike the electoral law change or the referendum alteration (and other illegal activities undertaken by the third Mečiar government), deliberate suppression of cast ballots would have required more than just a small core of party loyalists.

14 J. Elster, C. Offe, and U. Preuss, *Institutional Design in Post-Communist Societies*, Cambridge: Cambridge University Press, 1998.

15 M. Carpenter, "Slovakia and the Triumph of Nationalist Populism," *Communist and Post-Communist Studies* 30(2), 1997, pp. 205–220.

16 G. Evans and S. Whitefield, "The Structuring of Political Cleavages in Post-Communist Societies: The Case of the Czech Republic and Slovakia," *Political Studies* 46, 1998, pp. 115–139; K. D. Krause. "From Another Dimension: Public Opinion and Party Competition in Slovakia and the Czech Republic," American Political Science Association, Boston, MA, 1998; D. Smeltz, J. Bell, N. Mendrala, A. Sweeney, and M. Teare, "10 Years After the Fall of the Wall," Washington, DC: Office of Research, United States Department of State, 2000.

17 K. D. Krause, "Public Opinion and Party Choice in Slovakia and the Czech Republic," *Party Politics* 6(1), 2000, pp. 23–46.

18 AISA, "Surveys of Public Opinion" (Computer file), Prague, 1990; Institute of Sociology, Czechoslovak Academy of Sciences "Economic Expectations and Attitudes Survey II" (Computer file), Prague 1990.

19 R. Rose, W. Mishler, and C. Haerpfer, *Democracy and its Alternatives: Understanding Post-Communist Societies*, Cambridge: Polity Press in association with Blackwell Publishers, 1998.

20 ISSP, "National Identity" (Computer file), 1995; K. D. Krause, "Accountability and Political Party Competition in Slovakia and the Czech Republic," op. cit.

21 N. Nedelsky, "The 'Free and Equal Citizen' versus the Sovereign Nation: Political Cultural Roots of Czech and Slovak Definitions of State Sovereignty," American Association for the Advancement of Slavic Studies, Crystal City, VA, November 15, 2001.

22 FOCUS, *Aktualne problemy Slovenska*, Bratislava, FOCUS, 1994.

23 *Sme*, "The Demarche from the European Union that was Handed by the Ambassadors of Germany and France to the Slovak President, the Prime Minister, and the Parliament Chairman in Bratislava on 23 November," Trans. Foreign Broadcast Information Service, November 24, 1994, p. 2.

24 In a moment of unusual candor, the Chair of the Slovak Parliament, Ivan Gasparovic, explained that the German Ambassador had acknowledged "that the Constitution or laws have not been violated" but nevertheless expressed surprise at the dismissals of "the supreme officials of the National Property Fund, the Supreme Control Office, the prosecutor general, and the director of Slovak Radio . . . immediately one after the other," *Rozhlasova Stanica Slovensko*, Trans. Foreign Broadcast Information Service, Bratislava, 2030 GMT, November 24, 2004.

25 *Slovenska Republika*, "What was in the Suitcases with the Diplomatic Correspondence?" Bratislava, November 8, 1995.

26 *TASR*, Trans. Foreign Broadcast Information Service, Bratislava, 1845 GMT, October 15, 1996.

27 *TASR*, Trans. Foreign Broadcast Information Service, Bratislava, 1843 GMT, December 12, 1996.

28 *TASR*, Trans. Foreign Broadcast Information Service, Bratislava, 1404 GMT, May 30, 1997.

29 *TASR*, Trans. Foreign Broadcast Information Service, Bratislava, 0953 GMT, September 10, 1997.

30 *TASR*, Trans. Foreign Broadcast Information Service, Bratislava, 1330 GMT, December 4, 1998.

31 *TASR*, Trans. Foreign Broadcast Information Service, Bratislava, 1637 GMT, March 7, 1999.

32 *TASR*, Trans. Foreign Broadcast Information Service, Bratislava, 1432 GMT, July 20, 1999.

33 E. Zelenayova, "He who has Lost Trust at Home is Looking for Support Abroad," *Slovenska Republika*, Trans. Foreign Broadcast Information Service, Bratislava, November 28, 1994, pp. 1, 2.

34 *STV 1*, Trans. Foreign Broadcast Information Service, Bratislava, 1628 GMT, March 19, 1995.

35 M. Tvarozek, *Rozhlasova Stanica Slovensko*, Trans. Foreign Broadcast Information Service, Bratislava, 1740 GMT, November 17, 1995.

36 J. Hrabko, "The Falling of Slovak Myths," *Sme*, Trans. Foreign Broadcast Information Service, Bratislava, November 13, 1995.

37 *TASR*, Trans. Foreign Broadcast Information Service, Bratislava, 1132 GMT, May 6, 1997.

38 I. Samson, "Slovakia: Misreading the Western Message," *Democratic Consolidation in Eastern Europe: International and Transnational Factors*, in J. Zielonka and A. Pravda, eds, Oxford: Oxford University Press, 2001, pp. 363–382.

39 *TASR*, Trans. Foreign Broadcast Information Service, Bratislava, 0953 GMT, September 10, 1997.

40 *TASR*, Trans. Foreign Broadcast Information Service, Bratislava, 1656 GMT, May 26, 1997.

41 M. S. Fish, "The End of Mečiarism," op. cit.; K. D. Krause, "Accountability and Political Party Competition in Slovakia and the Czech Republic," op. cit.

42 *TASR*, Trans. Foreign Broadcast Information Service, Bratislava, 1809 GMT, December 4, 1997.

43 B. Panik, "Vladimir Mečiar Described as Nonsense the Claim that he is Not Accepted in the West," *Narodna Obroda*, Trans. Foreign Broadcast Information Service, Bratislava, November 3, 1995.

44 *Rozhlasova Stanica Slovensko*, Trans. Foreign Broadcast Information Service, Bratislava, 2030 GMT, November 24, 1994.

45 *STV 1*, Trans. Foreign Broadcast Information Service, Bratislava 2100 GMT, November 22, 1995.

46 *TASR*, Trans. Foreign Broadcast Information Service, Bratislava, 1132 GMT, May 6, 1997.

47 *TASR*, Trans. Foreign Broadcast Information Service, Bratislava, 1653 GMT, December 22, 1997.

48 *TASR*, Trans. Foreign Broadcast Information Service, Bratislava, 1831 GMT, September 11, 1997; M. Ivanickova, "Slovakia's Entry to EU is a Matter of Time – The World Diplomatic Conference to Meet in Slovakia," *Slovenska Republika*, Trans. Foreign Broadcast Information Service, Bratislava, November 25, 1997, p. 3.

49 *TASR*, Trans. Foreign Broadcast Information Service, Bratislava, 1815 GMT, August 28, 1998.

50 I. Samson, "Slovakia: Misreading the Western Message," op. cit.

51 *TASR*, Trans. Foreign Broadcast Information Service, Bratislava, 1427 GMT, January 11, 1998.

52 *TASR*, Trans. Foreign Broadcast Information Service, Bratislava, 1920 GMT, March 5, 1997.

53 I. Gasparovic, "My Comments on the Issues that are being Discussed in Slovakia and in Relation to Slovakia Today," *Slovenska Republika (Slovensko Do Toho!*

Supplement), Trans. Foreign Broadcast Information Service, Bratislava, March 26, 1997.
54 J. Cerna, "Slovakia Wants to be Part of the European Union," *Slovenska Republika*, Trans. Foreign Broadcast Information Service, Bratislava, June 17, 1997.
55 Ibid.
56 *TASR*, Trans. Foreign Broadcast Information Service, Bratislava, 1920 GMT, March 5, 1997.
57 *TASR*, Trans. Foreign Broadcast Information Service, Bratislava, 1316 GMT, November 12, 1998.
58 *TASR*, Trans. Foreign Broadcast Information Service, Bratislava, 1553 GMT, January 11, 1998.
59 *TASR*, Trans. Foreign Broadcast Information Service, Bratislava, 0952 GMT, September 24, 1997.
60 *TASR*, Trans. Foreign Broadcast Information Service, Bratislava, 1528 GMT, October 23, 1997.
61 *Narodna Obroda*, "Jan Luptak does not Rule Out Slovakia's Neutrality," Trans. Foreign Broadcast Information Service, Bratislava, October 12, 1995, p. 6.
62 *Narodna Obroda*, "Juraj Schenk Disassociates Himself from Jan Slota's Statements," Trans. Foreign Broadcast Information Service, Bratislava, October 18, 1995, p. 1.
63 *TASR*, Trans. Foreign Broadcast Information Service, Bratislava, 1206 GMT, June 22, 1997.
64 I. Zvach, "Najlepsim kriteriom je cas," *Slovenska Republika (Slovensko Do Toho!)*, November 13, 1997.
65 FOCUS, "Public Opinion Surveys" (Computer file), Bratislava, 1992–1999.
66 K. Reif and G. Cunningham, "Central and Eastern Euro-Barometer 1–8" (Computer file), Koeln, Germany, Zentralarchiv fuer Empirische Socialforschung, (producer), 1991–1998, Koeln, Germany: Zentralarchiv fuer Empirische Socialforschung/Ann Arbor, MI: Inter-university Consortium for Political and Social Research (distributors).
67 The FOCUS survey conducted in late 1997 shows that HZDS supporters specifically doubted the transparency of EU conditionality and the benefits of EU membership. While few HZDS supporters expected that exclusion from EU structures would be positive for Slovakia, only 27 percent expected the results to be negative. In the population as a whole, the corresponding share exceeded 62 percent (and among supporters of opposition parties, it exceeded 80 percent). In addition, nearly 60 percent of HZDS supporters believed that Slovakia's exclusion resulted from the bias of EU members toward Slovakia rather than from any government action. In the population as a whole the corresponding share was only 23 percent (and among opposition parties less than 10 percent).
68 FOCUS, "Public opinion surveys."
69 P. Demes, "OK '98 Campaign of Slovak NGOs for Free and Fair Elections," Bratislava, SAIA-SCTS, 1998.
70 J. Gould and S. Szomolanyi, "Elite Fragmentation, Industry and the Prospects for Democracy in Slovakia: Insights from New Elite Theory," *Intermarium* 1(2), 1999.

4 The European Union and Romania

The politics of constrained transition

William Crowther

The post-communist political transition in Central Europe has been the subject of nearly continual debate among scholars interested in the process of democratization during the course of the past ten years. Analysts have argued over such issues as the importance of institutional versus cultural factors, the impact of the character of the transition, and the relative weight of internal and external variables in shaping democratization. If anything has become clear through the accumulation of comparative research, it is that the processes involved are highly complex, and that uni-dimensional approaches fail to provide adequate explanation of outcomes. This chapter examines the role of the European Union's (EU) efforts to promote democratization in Romania's post-communist transition. It argues that the European Union, along with other international actors, has in fact exerted substantial influence over the direction of Romanian domestic politics. This influence, however, must be seen as one element among many that have interacted to produce what has been a particularly problematic road toward democratic consolidation. In particular, the circumstances of the immediate post-communist transition, the political configuration that this produced, and Romania's distinctive political culture stand out as key factors in the transition process.

That Romania is in fact a case of difficult democratization is if anything "over-determined." It is often cited as an archetypical example of the problems that beset the post-communist countries. The absence of independent associations; political culture shaped by long-term Ottoman occupation and a predominantly Orthodox religious tradition; a low level of economic development; and a highly repressive communist experience all argue against a smooth democratization process. The country's abrupt and violent overthrow of its communist leadership also predispose it toward an authoritarian successor regime.

Yet counter to these influences are strong impulses in the opposite direction. First, the lodestone of Romania's foreign policy strategy since the early transition period has been integration into Western economic and security structures. Along with this has been the effort to construct a network of international relationships designed to bolster security and advance the country's economic interests. The effort to achieve this goal has constrained the political elite's domestic strategy choices. Second, despite its historic provenance, support for democracy and market capitalism is widespread among both elites and the general population. These factors have served to offset, at least in part, the impact of more negative attributes and provide a context within which the democratizing efforts of external agents might be expected to bear fruit.

This chapter begins by assessing factors prior to the current democratization effort that potentially influence the country's susceptibility to external democratization efforts. It then examines in turn the early democratic opening (1989–1996) and a more mature transition phase (1997–2002). In each of these instances an effort is made to describe key features of the democratization process, and to link these to the hypotheses presented in Chapter 1 regarding the ability of external actors to influence progress toward democratic consolidation.

Romania's pre-transition political legacy

As is the case of many small states, Romania's domestic politics have been inextricably intertwined with its foreign relations. And like most in southeastern Europe, its experience has not generally been a happy one. In essence, the Romanians find themselves in a highly volatile region, with limited domestic resources, and subject to foreign intervention. This condition has shaped the identity, behavior, and political sensibility of Romanian political elites over the course of the past century.

The principalities that predate modern Romania suffered recurrent intervention as a consequence of their geographic position at the crossroads between competing great powers. An already difficult geo-strategic situation was further complicated by the Romanians' self-identification as a "Latin" people situated within a predominantly Slavic demographic zone. Intellectuals reinforced this identification during the nineteenth century. Their efforts to industrialize and modernize the country were bolstered by appeal to the Romanians' "Western" identity. Outsider status, however, intensified Romanian elites' apprehension concerning ethnic threat and spurred their pursuit of a state capable of defending the nation's interests. There was also a strong "indigenist" theme woven through the discourse on Romanian national identity.[1] Appeal to attachment with the ancient Dacian civilization was conjoined with reference to the population's Roman roots. Among a people subject to rapid social change and increased exposure to alien influences this identity became the intellectual focal point for resistance against foreign economic domination and cultural assimilation.[2]

Following achievement of full independence in 1878, Romania's position in the international arena was tenuous and conflict prone.[3] After initially seeking to remain neutral in the First World War, Bucharest entered the conflict on the side of the Allies in 1916. This move was rewarded with the acquisition of territories that approximately doubled Romania's lands. Expansion, however, brought neither peace nor domestic harmony. During the interwar years internal divisions and economic problems plagued the country.[4] Romania's far from perfected democratic institutions were overwhelmed. The dominant National Peasant and the Liberal parties lost ground to right-wing extremists. This context of uncertainty gave rise to a pervasive and deeply rooted nationalist movement. As Irina Livezeanu has shown "The ideal of a unitary, ethnically pure polity informed both mainstream state policies and the programs of oppositional radical nationalist movements."[5] Both the elites associated with the establishment political parties and the younger generation of activists associated with the fascist movement were committed to different variants of the nationalist enterprise.

In its foreign policy, Bucharest initially sought support from Western great power patrons, especially France. When this expedient failed to provide security in the late 1930s, Romanian elites shifted to an increasingly pro-German stance. The concessions of Transylvania, Bessarabia, and northern Bukovina under German pressure were accepted as inevitable. After committing troops to fight with the Axis on the Eastern front in the early war years, Romania belatedly renounced its alliance with Germany and entered the war on the side of the Allies, losing Bessarabia and northern Bukovina once again as a consequence, but regaining Transylvania from the Hungarians.

Impediments to democratic development already evident in interwar Romania were aggravated by the country's communist experience. It has been argued widely that communism failed to resolve the nationalist animosities that characterize much of Central and Eastern Europe. In Romania's case, one can go a step further: the distortions of Romania's communism actively aggravated conditions, promoting xenophobia as a mechanism of regime legitimization. As Katherine Verdery has argued in depth, the promotion of national ideology was in fact an intrinsic element of the socialist regime.[6] The Romanian Communist Partys unresolved internal factionalism during the 1940s retarded efforts to restructure the country's economy, and enabled a "national communist" faction to survive the Stalinist period in place. Avoiding Khrushchev's reforms, the Romanian Communist leader Gheorghiu-Dej undertook an independent "Stalinist" industrialization strategy. This was further reinforced by his successor, Nicolae Ceauçescu, in the second half of the 1960s. After consolidating his control over the country Ceauçescu moved Romania in a more intensely nationalist and more authoritarian direction than his predecessor.

The Ceauçescu regime's totalitarian course also sharpened divisions between Romanian political elites and the rest of the population. Unable to rely on either support from the Soviet Union or the "consumer communism" and political demobilization that was evident elsewhere in Central Europe, the Romanian Communist Party (RCP) resorted to a more traditional authoritarian strategy. The populism and intense nationalism characteristic of pre-communist political culture reemerged, and were enshrined as central elements of RCP ideology.

During its communist period, Romania earned a well-deserved reputation as a foreign policy maverick. Beginning in the early 1960s Gheorghiu-Dej courted conflict with Moscow, ultimately declaring his intention to pursue a "sovereign" communist course. Ceauçescu took an even more extreme position. While remaining within the Soviet bloc, Romania refused to allow Warsaw Pact exercises on its territory and resisted efforts by the Council for Mutual Economic Assistance (CMEA) to integrate regional economies. In the early 1970s, Bucharest traded on its reputation as an "independent" communist state to gain Western economic and diplomatic support, including access to funding from the International Monetary Fund (IMF) and Most Favored Nation Status from the United States. As the disintegration of the Soviet bloc approached, though, so did this foreign policy strategy. The extreme repression of the Ceauçescu regime made it increasingly difficult for Western supporters to maintain positive relations with Bucharest. And with a foreign exchange crisis in the late 1970s, Ceauçescu undertook a policy of intense domestic austerity and national economic autarky that further alienated Western governments. Finally, the Gorbachev reforms in the late 1980s both reduced Romania's value as a player in Cold War international relations, and threw its oppressive character in sharp relief. Thus on the fall of communism, Romania found itself alienated from both East and West and was arguably more isolated than any post-communist regime except Albania.

The 1989 revolution, the international environment, and incomplete democratization

The nature of the revolution of December 1989, which was even more abrupt than others in Central Europe and was marked by significant violence, clearly worked against a smooth democratic transition for Romania. The hurried transfer of power left substantial elements of the communist apparatus intact, and created an environment of intense political distrust. Rapid action by members of the communist regime left no interval in which independent liberal opponents could consolidate sufficiently to play an effective role in negotiating the passage to democracy. The sum effect was a transition situation easily exploitable by an aspiring authoritarian populist leader, such as post-communist Romania's first President, Ion Iliescu.

Two of the hypotheses proposed by Kubicek in Chapter 1 bear directly on Romania's early transition. First, rewards on offer must be real: the incentive must be strong enough for elites to be willing to risk the uncertainty associated with democratization. In Romania's case the issue of rewards is best understood as being twofold. First, there are the instrumental gains of support for economic restructuring, market and financial access, and integration into stabilizing security structures. These instrumental rewards are significant, but became so only at a somewhat later stage in the transition.

Second are the symbolic (yet quite important) and cultural values of "joining Europe." Romania, as has been pointed out by numerous authors over the years, stands out in its almost unanimous enthusiasm for integration into Europe. Despite its history of appalling domestic repression and lack of civil society, public opinion polling shows Romanians' support for democracy to be among the highest levels in the region. The desire to be acknowledged as truly European has become deeply ingrained in the national culture. Thus for political elites to be perceived as shunned from Europe imposes potentially high, if not insurmountable domestic political costs.

Relating to the second hypothesis, if the role of democratic rhetoric was not evident immediately, the stage was set for its appearance. All the central political players in the early transition assumed the rhetoric of reform. Despite any presumed intentions to the contrary, the post-communists as well as the liberal politicians espoused democracy and European integration as valued goals. As the transition progressed, adherence to these goals became a yardstick whereby opposition reformers could measure the success of the regime. In a country where popular attitudes toward democracy were neutral to negative, this assessment might have had no effect or in fact proved to be counterproductive. However, in Romania normative commitment to democracy is widespread and remarkably high. A comparative study of six countries by Evans and Whitefield found 81 percent of Romanians expressing support for democracy; in comparison, in the second highest scoring country in the study (Lithuania) only 57 percent did so.[7]

As Ceauçescu's dictatorship disintegrated, a diverse coalition formed with the intent of gaining control of the popular revolt. It included leaders of the spontaneous uprising, communist leaders who had been marginalized by the ruling clique, and elements that were rapidly abandoning the failing regime. Organized as the National Salvation Front (FSN) and headed by former Politburo member Ion Iliescu, these forces announced their assumption of provisional control over the country on December 22, 1989. Upon coming to power, the FSN announced a program of reform, including a call for elections to be held in April 1990. FSN spokesmen pledged to act as caretakers until elections could be held to select a freely elected democratic successor regime.

Almost immediately, however, both the intentions changed. Rallying to the leadership of Iliescu, former communists joined with representatives of the military to form a dominant core within the FSN. While the RCP itself was abolished in early January 1990, significant elements of the party and state apparatus remained intact and passed into the structure of the successor regime. The FSN announced that contrary to its initial commitments, it would run candidates in the transition elections. Its competitive advantage was obvious. FSN leaders were able to associate themselves successfully with the December revolution. They garnered immediate support by abolishing the most abhorred of Ceauçescu's policies. Furthermore, Romania began the post-communist period with no foreign debt, allowing Iliescu immediately to improve public consumption.

Opposition to the former communists was comparatively weak and badly fragmented. The most significant competition came from the so-called historic parties, the National Liberal Party (PNL), the National Peasant Christian Democratic Party (PNTCD), and the Social Democratic Party (SDP), and the Democratic Magyar Union of Romania (UDMR).[8] The student movement, which played such a critical role in the actual overthrow of the dictator, and other informal organizations also brought pressure on the government, launching public attacks on the Iliescu leadership, which it labeled neo-communist. Street demonstrations in Bucharest demanding resignation of the FSN became increasingly frequent, and were only brought to an end when Iliescu mobilized supportive workers, who rampaged through the capital attacking presumed opponents of the new regime. Coupled with the extension of compromises to the opposition, this orchestrated street violence served to pressure opponents into acceptance of the new political circumstances.

Thus in the May 1990 founding elections for a new bicameral legislature (the Assembly of Deputies and the Senate) and the Presidency, the FSN enjoyed nearly unassailable advantage.[9] While FSN called for measured reform, the traditional parties proposed rapid restructuring and charged the FSN with "hijacking the revolution." In the presidential race, Iliescu won 85.1 percent of the vote. While not as lopsided, returns for the legislature also indicate the FSN's strength. The Front captured 68 percent of the Assembly seats, and 76 percent of those in the Senate races. The elections themselves were subject to widespread criticism centering on intimidation, unequal access to the mass media, and fraud.[10] But despite opposition protests, Iliescu's former communist leadership was able to consolidate its control over the transition.

While not a dominant element in Romanian politics, Romania's extreme nationalists also emerged as a crucial element in the coalition that sustained the Iliescu regime through the early transition. Iliescu relied upon a coalition between his own successor communist followers, reorganized as the Democratic National Salvation Front and then as the Party of Democratic Socialism of Romania (PDSR), along with a coterie of ultra-nationalist parties, including the Party of Romanian National Unity (PUNR) and the Greater Romania Party (RM). Promising a strong guiding hand and "measured" reform, and relying selectively upon the authoritarian-nationalists to counter liberal challenges to his rule, Iliescu was able effectively to control the reigns of power. Under his tutelage, Romania during this period can be characterized as pluralist, but not democratic. Politics became a contest played out between competing elite factions, punctuated periodically by mass mobilization along populist lines. While a substantial improvement over the intense dictatorship of the Ceauçescu period, Romania's early democratic transition was thus imperfect at best.

The FSN government established after the 1990 elections initiated a program of narrow economic reform.[11] Provision was made for 30 percent of the value of state enterprises to be distributed to the population through voucher privatization, and for 70 percent to be distributed by the State

Ownership funds established for this purpose. Private enterprise was legalized. The government called for price controls to be gradually liberalized until market pricing was reached on most goods.[12] Yet, as unemployment and prices both rose as a consequence of the reforms, creating popular unrest, the government responded by indexing wages, which compounded the problem of inflation. The entire process was, in practice, subject to bureaucratic inertia and political intervention, and was fraught with corruption.

Because of the deep political divisions that prevailed at the time, even the limited initiatives undertaken by the government proved destabilizing. Street protests were common, strike activity increased, and consensus within the ruling party broke down. Popular reaction against the FSN and its policies reached a peak in the autumn of 1991, when demonstrations presented a serious threat to public order in Bucharest for a second time since the revolution. Ion Iliescu, however, successfully directed worker's wrath against his chief rival within the ruling party, Prime Minister Petre Roman. Forced from office under threat, Roman became the advocate of party members who favored more thoroughgoing reform. In a classical process of political narrowing, Iliescu's more conservative faction broke from the FSN to form its own organization, the Democratic National Salvation Front (DFSN), which continued to consolidate its hold on power.[13] As an alternative, the FSN shifted in the direction of Romania's coterie of extremist parties: the Socialist Labor Party (PSM), the Party of Romanian National Unity (PUNR), and the Greater Romania Party (RM).

Like the majority of the post-communist regimes, Romania sought to develop relations with the Western powers including the EU as it entered the transition. At least on the rhetorical level, its leaders indicated their commitment to democratic norms and international cooperation. But in the initial transition these goals were severely hampered by the communist links of the regime and its domestic political activities. During the early 1990s Bucharest was unwilling to undertake reform at the pace required to satisfy European leaders. Romania was hobbled in its relations with Europe and the United States by highly publicized instances of violence that characterized Romanian political life, notably the miners' brutal interventions in Bucharest and violence directed toward the country's Hungarian minorities. The attack on Hungarians in Tîrgu Mures in particular was the cause of criticism by the Council of Europe, the European Community, and other bodies. In a clear signal of displeasure, the Iliescu regime was not immediately given access to the European Community's PHARE program, while the United States failed to extend to it Most Favored Nation Status. The Council of Europe was moved to delay action on allowing Romania entry due to its concerns relating to the direction of the country's domestic politics.[14]

While by no means shutting the door on Europe, President Iliescu focused on his relationship with Moscow during this period. This strategy was unsurprising, given the difficulties that Romanian diplomacy encountered in the West, its dependence on Russian raw materials, and the ideological affinities linking Iliescu and Gorbachev. The importance attributed by the regime to its "Eastern strategy" was indicated by the signing of the Romanian–Soviet Treaty of Cooperation, Good Neighborliness and Friendship in April 1991. From the point of view of Western diplomats the Romanian connection with Russia became increasingly problematic in light of growing instability in Yugoslavia. Romania provided a potential source of support for the Milošević regime in the face of Western efforts to isolate the regime. Highlighting the problem, President Iliescu made a high profile visit to Belgrade in September 1990. In succeeding months Romania noticeably lacked enthusiasm for international action against Milošević, expressing support for Yugoslavia and delaying support for sanctions.

The Iliescu leadership thus appears clearly to have pursued a dual foreign policy strategy. At least on the rhetorical level it sought integration into Europe and improved relations with the United States. But given the obstacles that confronted it in the West, it approached Moscow as a key diplomatic ally, and potentially as a primary economic partner.

This orientation proved to be problematic in both the domestic and foreign policy arenas. Contested borders are the historic legacy of Central Europe. Upon independence, Romania's boundaries with Hungary and the USSR (later Ukraine and Moldova) both presented potential disputes.[15] The bilateral treaty with Russia, which seemed to legitimate territorial concessions that occurred as a consequence of the Ribbentrop–Molotov Treaty, touched off a firestorm of opposition from nationalist forces in Romania.[16] Furthermore, far from being limited to the extreme nationalists, opposition to the agreement was expressed by the leaders of the liberal opposition parties as well. This represented a potentially crucial problem for Iliescu, since Romanians of nearly all political stripes hold deep feelings regarding the illegitimacy of the Ribbentrop–Molotov agreement. Like the liberal parties, Western diplomats reacted negatively to the growing accord between Moscow and Bucharest, fearing that the bilateral treaty with Moscow signaled a broader "neo-communist" strategy hostile to the democratic transition. The relationship also presented a growing cause of concern in the context of the emerging Balkan conflict.

The authoritarian character of Romania's government during this period was increasingly evident to foreign and domestic observers alike. Little, however, could be done by the EU and other external actors to influence its activities, in part due to the existence of Russia as an alternative source of support, but also because of the lack of a viable domestic alternative to the regime. The liberal parties, attempt to form a cohesive opposition met with only limited success. In an effort to compete more effectively fourteen democratic parties united to form the Democratic Convention and contest local elections in February 1992. But, as the second post-revolution election drew near, divisions emerged among the main participants of the Democratic Convention: the National Liberals, the National Peasant Christian Democrat Party, the UDMR, and the Civic Alliance Party (PAC). This split among the democratic parties resulted both from leadership competition, and from insertion of the nationalities issue into the electoral campaign. As elections approached, the extremist positions of Iliescu's nationalist party supporters, PUNR and the Greater Romanian Party, ensured that the nationality issue remained central to Romania's political discourse, sowing discord within the opposition

The second post-transition elections, held in September 1992, were significantly improved over the initial contest. While irregularities did occur, less violence accompanied the elections.[17] Most observers agree that fraud played a smaller role, and access to the media for opposition parties was improved. With 47.2 percent of the first round vote and 61.4 percent in the second round of the September 1992 elections, Iliescu dominated the field. The Democratic Convention candidate, Emil Constantinescu, garnered a total vote of 38.6 percent in the second round runoff for the presidency. Voting in the legislative elections was less definitive. FSN support fell to 27.7 percent. PUNR won only slightly more than 2 percent of the 1990 vote, but more than 8 percent in 1992. The parties that constitute the Democratic Convention combined forces captured more than 20 percent of the legislative vote in 1992. This outcome was central to the politics of the succeeding period. Without a legislative majority, the FSN fell back on cooperation with the right-wing nationalist parties to retain its control, which reinforced the party's already evident authoritarian populist tendencies.[18]

In 1992, President Iliescu's post-election strategy relied upon consolidating a base of support among peasants and workers while continuing to pursue limited reform. In the wake of the elections the government of Prime Minister Vacaroiu (supported by President Iliescu), did undertake a more serious effort to restructure the Romanian economy. The government acted to control inflation and initiated a second, more comprehensive program of privatization. The tax system was rationalized, and government deficit was significantly reduced.[19] These partial reforms, however, failed to produced the hoped for benefits of increased investment, and efficiency and growth. Privatization was not allowed to impinge upon the interests of powerful and increasingly imbedded economic interests allied with the regime. Rather than allowing bankruptcies to occur, inefficient state-owned enterprises were kept afloat through transfers from the state budget. The administration, many of whose members remained hostile to market capitalism, erected bureaucratic barriers that hindered the activities of the private sector.

Yet simultaneously with its reforms, the FSN appealed to popular anxiety concerning rapid marketization and social change. It held out the promise of relative stability and continued state protection from the vicissitudes of the market. On the margins, the ruling party also continued to play to the nationalist sentiments that were evident within this segment of the electorate. Following the 1992 elections, President Iliescu formed a tacit legislative alliance with the extreme nationalist parties, whose parliamentary delegations supported Prime Minister Vacaroiu's government.

While politically expedient in the near term, this political configuration proved unworkable from the point of view of policy formation. Much of the political instability and economic stagnation that characterized Romania in the years following the 1992 elections can be traced to the contradictory strains that existed within the ruling party's strategy. Given the character of its leadership and its core constituency, the Democratic National Salvation Front, re-christened the Party of Romanian Social Democracy (PDSR) in 1993, found itself unable to carry out structural reform, or to effectively manage the economy. Prime Minister Vacaroiu's capacity to reform was circumscribed by holdover elements of the communist regime. These included both managers from the state sector enterprises, and the *nomenklatura* class of politically connected individuals who benefited financially from the economy's intermediate stage between market and plan, in essence trading on access to the state. Furthermore, even the limited reforms that were undertaken by Vacaroiu during the 1992–1996 period floundered in the face of popular opposition. While center-right governments (like that of Vaclav Klaus in the Czech Republic) or even more autonomous and consolidated center-left regimes (Poland under Kwasniewski) were able to press forward with economic rationalization, the PDSR was not in a situation to flout opposition. Hence price reforms were often followed by wage increases, defeating their initial purpose. State-controlled financial institutions subsidized non-performing enterprises. Privatization strategies promised decisive action, but implementation was weak, and when serious resistance was encountered, efforts foundered.

A second factor constraining PDSR rule was the party's reliance on its extreme nationalist allies for parliamentary support. An arm's-length relationship in the early 1990s clearly worked to Iliescu's advantage, allowing him to garner support from the nationalist constituency while avoiding direct association with the most extreme statements. But his relationship became both more public and more difficult to manage over time. In 1994 the relationship between PDSR and the extremists was made explicit through the inclusion of two ministers from the PUNR in the Vacaroiu government. This was followed by the conclusion of an open agreement on cooperation with the Greater Romania Party, PUNR, and the Socialist Labor Party in January 1995.

Despite its domestic political benefits, the alliance between the PDSR and the far right ultimately broke down, largely as a consequence of the regime's efforts to reorient its foreign policy. In this sense, the EU's role in shaping President Iliescu's incentive structure was vital. By the mid-1990s, changing conditions in the international environment led to reorientation of the Iliescu leadership's initial foreign policy. In particular, the escalating disintegration in Moscow fundamentally reshaped Bucharest's foreign policy calculus. Political and economic disarray in the Russian Federation limited any diplomatic gains to be achieved through an Eastern strategy. Bucharest's economic relationship with the Soviet Union had suffered steady decline since the late

1980s. In 1991 and 1992, however, it saw a near free fall. Both imports and exports plummeted to approximately half of their 1989 levels by 1993. With little alternative at hand, Bucharest acted to reorient its foreign policy. Thus it became increasingly vital that access to Western markets and sources of funding be assured in order to achieve domestic economic stability.

Romania consequently increased its attention to refurbishing its image and furthering its prospects for European integration. Its efforts in this direction were facilitated by the escalating conflict in the Balkans. Teodor Melescanu, named foreign minister in the Vacaroiu government in 1992, presented Romania as a potential bulwark against the rising tide of Balkan instability that was emerging as a core concern of the Western governments. Political leaders in Bucharest began to campaign persistently to be considered a "Central European" rather than a Balkan state, and to be considered for purposes of integration with countries such as Poland, Hungary, and the Czech Republic. It was clearly recognized by the Romanian leadership that this effort was unlikely to succeed in the absence of action to achieve a better reputation regarding minority rights. Therefore, coupled with its European public relations initiative, steps were taken to improve relations both with Hungary and with Romania's Hungarian minority community.[20] For example in a highly symbolic move Bucharest signed the Charter for the Protection of National Minorities in February 1995, and ratified it almost immediately, in May of the same year.

The same considerations impacted upon the PDSR's attachment to its right-wing allies. Achieving what had now become core foreign policy goals remained problematic in an international community that identified President Iliescu with nationalist extremism. Conversely, it was increasingly difficult to manage the alliance with the right-wing parties while acting to accommodate minorities and improve relations with neighboring states. Hence even as the 1996 round of elections approached, the PDSR was forced to distance itself from its nationalist allies, aggravating already difficult relations with the volatile extremist leaders, and causing a breakdown in the Red–Brown coalition that underpinned the regime.

The effort to achieve acceptance in the West began to meet with limited success even before Iliescu's break with the far right. As suggested by the introductory hypotheses, this was significant in signaling to the regime that potential payoffs were in fact real; e.g. that the Iliescu regime could expect rewards in return for compliance, even given its provenance. An association agreement with the European Union was signed on February 1, 1993. Following two years of discord and hostile discussion of its human rights record, Romania was admitted as a full member of the Council of Europe on October 7, 1993. On January 26, 1994, it became the first country to join the Partnership for Peace program. France, Italy, and Canada supported Romania's bid to become a member of NATO in the first wave of accession. On February 1, 1995, Romania became an associate member of the EU, and in June 1995 it submitted a formal application to become a full member.

Further progress, however, was dependent upon transforming Romania's domestic environment.

The initial phase of Romania's post-communist transition elucidates several questions raised by Kubicek in Chapter 1 regarding the role of the EU in promoting democratization. Clearly, the "novelty of the environment" hypothesis (new leaders in new states will be more open to external prodding than established ones) is directly relevant to conditions in Romania, and did not bode well for democratization. Neither the state itself nor its leadership was new. Far from it, Iliescu himself was a seasoned party leader, and much of the regime that he fashioned in the early 1990s was staffed by personnel drawn from the previous regime. This leadership was thus unlikely to be either without ideas and resources of its own, or to be open to international persuasion. Far from seeking new means of legitimation in the external environment, the FSN acted in a quite skilled way to appropriate traditional mechanisms of legitimation to itself, and to insulate itself from external influence.

A second aspect of the novelty hypothesis, that nationalism will be more of a factor in new states, and will act as a barrier to the EU's democratizing influence, is only partly confirmed. Nationalism did in fact play a highly influential and negative part in the early democratization process. Romania, however, is hardly a new state. National identity has long been, as Verdery shows, "central to Romanian culture and politics" and it continues to be so today.[21] Thus one would have to conclude that this variable is much more particularistic than assumed.

Third, the Romanian case suggests that several of the hypotheses regarding conditionality are interdependent. The relevance of hypothesis 2 (sanctions must be real and believable) appears to be contingent upon hypothesis 3 (if states have alternative sources of support they may withstand pressure). Bucharest was in fact subjected to EU pressure as a consequence of its actions early in the transition. The orchestrated use of violence against regime opponents, questionable (at best) transition elections, and the toleration of attacks upon ethnic minorities led to the country's exclusion from early EU association agreements and restriction of access to external sources of funding. At least initially, however, these facts seemed to have little impact upon the regime. This outcome was not only predictable, but also likely, given the alternative of an Eastern strategy of loose partnership with Russia, a traditional ally whose leadership was ideologically congruent. Once the avenue of development was cut off, however, the salience of exclusion from Western structures was precipitously raised.

Embracing Europe: domestic political realignment in the international context

The contradictions in Romania's foreign and domestic policies were further attenuated as a consequence of the country's decisive 1996 parliamentary and presidential elections. These marked the first definitive regime change since the overthrow of the Ceauçescu dictatorship in 1989. The Democratic Convention emerged as a credible alternative leadership in the mid-1990s. It was clearly less compromised by association with the communist period and more in tune with the EU's ethos of democratic politics and market-capitalist politics. This confronted the FSN with the stark choice of either competing on the terrain of reform and transition, or retreating into a "harder" authoritarian stance, in the mode of neighboring Yugoslavia and several of the former Soviet states. But the demands imposed by the international community on those pursuing this course were manifest, as was the regime's inability to stabilize its economy in the absence of external assistance. One can also conjecture that Romania's leaders, having experienced all too directly and recently the devastating consequences of an intensely authoritarian regime, were themselves unwilling to take the country back in that direction. Thus Iliescu chose to contest the election in 1996 under extremely adverse conditions, and without significantly interfering in the electoral process.

Not surprisingly under the circumstances, the opposition Democratic Convention of Romania (CDR), won decisively in the November 3 parliamentary and first round presidential elections. In the parliamentary race, the CDR took 53 Senate seats and 122 seats in the Chamber of Deputies, in comparison to the PDSR's 41 Senate and 91 Chamber of Deputies victories. In the November 17 second round presidential runoff, reformist forces successfully united behind Emil Constantinescu, displacing Iliescu in a 54 percent to 46 percent victory.[22]

Polling by the International Foundation for Electoral Support (IFES) and the Romanian IRSOP research organization indicated, the breadth of support for change among voters. As Michael Shafir has indicated the factors that most accounted for Iliescu's downfall were loss of the urban workers' vote (32 percent to 21 percent for the CDR), and support of the emerging market-oriented middle class for the opposition. This group overwhelmingly favoured the Democratic Convention, giving it 48 percent of their vote in comparison to 11 percent for the PDSR. Iliescu's support remained strong among those elements of the population most marginalized by reforms. Rural voters in general supported the PDSR over the CDR by 34 percent against 26 percent. Of peasants 53 percent voted for Iliescu and the PDSR, whereas 18 percent opted for the Democratic Convention. The democratic opposition retained the support of the more educated population, gaining 65 percent of the vote from those with higher education.[23]

The transformation of Romania's domestic political landscape that followed the 1996 elections cleared the way for a new wave of domestic reform and the further transformation of the country's foreign policy position. Hopes were high among the population that Prime Minister Victor Ciorbea's coalition government, which included the Democratic Convention, Petre Roman's Democratic Party, and the UDMR, would serve to open the political process, ending the period of paternalism and insider "*nomenklatura capitalism*" that characterized the previous administration. Extensive changes were introduced in the leadership of both the Ministry of Defence and the Security Services.[24] Encouraged by President Constantinescu, the coalition government committed itself to fulfilling a comprehensive economic reform agenda that, they argued, should have been initiated in the immediate wake of the Ceauçescu regime. In the economic realm, state subsidization of non-profitable firms was curtailed, as was permissive financing by the central bank. Romania's currency was allowed to float, and a more aggressive program of privatization was initiated.[25] Constitutional revisions were introduced to address concerns regarding minority rights. Efforts were also undertaken to provide local authorities increased autonomy in relation to the central authorities.[26]

Intersection between external and domestic politics was manifest in the post-1996 reform endeavors. With President Constantinescu and the CDR at the helm of government, Bucharest was determined to make up for lost time in gaining entry into Western political and economic structures. On their part, the EU and other Western actors were committed to aiding in the consolidation of what they saw as a significantly more progressive government. Hence initial Western response to the post-1996 reforms was markedly positive. The IMF provided more than $400 million dollars in credit, and Bucharest's access to PHARE aid was increased. Recognizing that it was unlikely to win immediate admittance into the European Union, Romania focused its efforts on achieving what it considered to be just treatment in the accession process, and an early entry into NATO.[27] After years of dispute, a bilateral agreement was concluded with Ukraine in June 1997 as part of a highly public campaign for inclusion in the first round of NATO expansion at the Madrid Summit in July of 1997.[28] The Ciorbea government also made highly public overtures to Hungary, extending bilateral relations in the cultural, economic, and international fields. The immediate effort failed, as NATO leaders decided to limit initial expansion to Poland, Hungary, and the Czech Republic But Romania's government was reassured that it would receive favorable consideration for later admission. President Clinton reinforced this message during a visit to Bucharest in early July. The United States sought to further soften the blow by promoting a strategic bilateral relationship designed to aid Romania's efforts to achieve NATO membership.

Unfortunately, despite its advantages, the democratic opposition failed in its efforts to fundamentally redirect Romania's politics. The factors that led to the miscarriage of reforms were manifold. Much of the blame can be attributed to the character of the opposition itself. The government coalition, the Democratic Convention, and the UDMR, and the Democratic Party were each themselves politically divided to the extent that Michael Shafir referred to the arrangement as a "coalition of coalitions."[29] Not only did this situation make policy formulation more difficult, it impeded policy implementation as well. As Shafir and others have pointed out, each of the main actors in the coalition supported variants of reform that would have benefited its own supporters, vetoing to the extent possible its partners' initiatives. Hence the reform process devolved into a chaos of particularism, stalemate, and factional bartering.

Second, the Ciorbea government was encumbered with the fallout of its predecessor's failed policies. Increasing debt, fiscal imbalance, and an overvalued exchange rate that were the legacy of the previous government imposed a surplus cost on post-1996 reform efforts.[30] As the Ciorbea government liberalized prices, rationalized the exchange rate, and restricted government spending, Romania experienced a second "transition shock." In 1997 inflation soared once again, to 151 percent, while real wages declined by one-fourth.[31] Prime Minister Ciorbea's replacement and the installation of a new government headed by Radu Vasile in April 1998 did little to improve the situation. Inflation was brought under control, but fundamental divisions remained within the government concerning reform strategy and little further progress occurred. President Constantinescu, clearly aware of the situation, was unable to impose order.

Third, by 1997 practices inimical to democracy had become deeply imbedded in Romanian political life. Clearly, by the time that President Constantinescu and the liberal coalition arrived on the scene, public corruption was rife. While charges were brought against senior officials of the previous administration, it proved difficult to follow through on prosecutions.[32] Neither were the reformers themselves free from culpability. Almost immediately after the change in power charges of insider dealing and influence peddling re-emerged to plague both the Ciorbea and Vasile governments.

It quickly became clear that influential elements of the coalition had little or no interest in authentic reform. This was particularly true of Petre Roman and the USD. The economic consequences of these shortcomings were immediate. In 1999 inflation once again surpassed the 50 percent mark, while 40 percent of the population were reduced to poverty, and unemployment topped 11 percent. Signals that the international community had lost confidence in the regime deepened the crisis. After difficult negotiations the IMF agreed to a $547 million loan in August 1999, but in October Fund officials decided to postpone release of the second tranche because of Romania's failure to comply with the agreed terms. IMF staff criticized the government for failure to meet fiscal deficit targets, to implement civil service cuts, and to restrain spending and wage increases.[33] In a final effort to appease the international community National Bank President Mugur Isarescu was named Prime Minister in December 1999 with a renewed commitment to press home reforms. By then, however, the government's popular mandate had clearly been lost.

Thus as a new round of elections approached in 2000, Romanians were faced with the failure of a second reform bid. Disillusionment with the reformist parties was both deep and widespread. Public opinion surveys entering the elections indicated that while the population generally maintained its commitment to reform, faith in the ability of the liberal parties had been severely eroded by four years of scandal and renewed economic hardship. In polling just before the elections, 75.9 percent of the population favored a market economy, with only 9.2 percent rejecting it. In contrast only 7.6 percent of the population expressed positive attitudes toward political parties in general, and only one of the governing parties (the PNL with 6.6 percent) could claim more that 5 percent popular support. Only 4 percent of the population expressed any level of positive reaction to the government's efforts to deal with corruption.[34]

The internecine factionalism that plagued reform efforts became even more intense in the run-up to the 2000 elections. Conflict within the coalition that had supported President Constantinescu in 1996 totally undermined the ability of the center-right to campaign.[35] Both the political left and the far right were able to exploit these conditions. Former President Iliescu, in contrast to the liberal party leaders, had employed the four years intervening since his 1996 defeat to overhaul the PDSR and to restore his party's internal discipline. In the face of such unremitting economic decline, the party's message of reform moderated by social protection clearly resonated with the population. Finally, many Romanians were won over by the promise of rule by a single party, which, it was hoped, would be able to restore order in the policy arena.[36]

On the far right, the Greater Romania Party and its leader Corneliu Vadim Tudor emerged as the most significant threat to democratic stability since the disorders of the immediate transition. After its poor showing in the 1996 elections (4.5 percent of the vote and nineteen seats in the lower house), most observers felt that the Greater Romania Party would be effectively marginalized in the context of an increasingly stable democratic consensus. Tudor, however, proved to be both a tenacious politician and a skilled agitator. While maintaining his hold on the ethnic extremist base by playing on anti-Roma and anti-Hungarian sentiments, he became the most conspicuous domestic critic of Romania's endemic political corruption. In essence, Tudor established himself as the anti-establishment candidate, and his party as the party of the marginalized outsiders. Benefiting from both the PDSR's shift away from extreme nationalism and from popular disillusionment with the Constantinescu experience the Greater Romania Party became a dominant factor in the 2000 elections, reshaping the Romanian political landscape.

Already disturbed by the failure of the Constantinescu reform effort, Western diplomats clearly signaled growing international concern with the political direction of the country. Just weeks before the voting was to occur, the European Parliament's rapporteur on Romania, Emma Nicholson, commented publicly that "Romania has reached a crossroads in her accession process. Will she accelerate the integration process or will she turn the other way?" Nicholson added that she "would hate to see the Romanian people disappointed."[37]

The results of first round polling in November 2000 saw the moderate parties devastated, sending shockwaves through both Romania and the international community. In the presidential elections Ion Iliescu dominated the field, with 36.4 percent of the vote, followed in second place by Corneliu Vadim Tudor with 28.3 percent, and liberal democratic candidates Teodor Stolojan and Mugur Isarescu with 11.7 and 9.6 percent respectively. Chamber of Deputies results closely mirrored this outcome. The PDSR captured 36.6 percent of the total followed by RM with 19.5 percent. The Democratic Convention was reduced to 5.29 percent, the PNL to 7.49 percent, and Petre Roman's Democratic Party to 7.59 percent. The UDMR's presidential candidate, Gyorgy Frunda won 6.22 percent of the vote, while the party itself gained slightly more, 6.9 percent, in the Chamber of Deputies. Further indicating the electorate's disenchantment with the status quo, turnout in 2000 plummeted by more than 20 percent, and the Democratic Convention failed to maintain its representation in parliament.

Response to this alarming result was immediate. Leaders of the right-wing parties called on their followers to support Iliescu in the second round presidential voting in order to head off a victory by Tudor as the representative of the extreme right. Romanian media commentators decried the damage already done to the country in the first round of the elections, and warned that a second round victory by the Greater Romania Party leader would lead to the country's complete isolation from Western European political and financial institutions.[38] Commentary in both Europe and the United States appeared to bear this out, stating for example that "The election of Corneliu Vadim Tudor . . . would isolate Romania completely from the West and could plunge it into internal conflict or even war with its neighbours."[39] Fears of this result were heightened by EU action to ostracize Austria following the election of Joerg Haider's far-right Freedom Party earlier in the year.

Seizing the opportunity thus provided, the PDSR moved immediately to stake out a position as a moderate and pro-reform force. Iliescu rejected any possibility of forming a government with the Greater Romania Party, denounced "totalitarianism and ethnic extremism," and reasserted his party's commitment to European integration and to accelerated reform.[40] This strategy clearly succeeded in attracting the bulk of the electorate. In second round presidential polling on December 10, 2000, Iliescu's vote nearly doubled, rising to 66.83 percent, while Corneliu Vadim Tudor's share increased by slightly less than 5 percent from his first round total (to 33.17 percent).

The return of the post-communist left and the extreme right's resurgence in Romania's 2000 elections have rightfully been the source of considerable anxiety concerning the country's democratic transition. And while the ballot does stand as an unequivocal indictment of the post-1996 reformers' ability to fulfill the hopes invested in them, it clearly also represents a substantial improvement over the first Iliescu stage in the transition. Rather than being hampered by its association with the extreme right, the post-2000 PDSR (which merged with the Romanian Social Democratic Party and renamed itself the Social Democratic Party (PSD) in June 2001 in a further step to distance itself from its communist heritage) was free to pursue both ethnic accommodation and international reconciliation without fear of alienating its political base. Even more striking, the PSD minority government was supported in parliament by the Hungarian UDMR, whose leaders determined that cooperation with Iliescu was an acceptable price to pay for the exclusion of the Greater Romania Party.

In another positive sign, the formation of a government by Prime Minister Adrian Nastase signaled the dominance of the PSD's more reformist wing. During the period leading up to elections, the former Foreign Minister made a series of statements in support of European integration and accelerated reform. In the context of the elections, however, both domestic and foreign observers questioned whether a revived Iliescu leadership would in fact be any more likely to pursue real change than the first administration.

The European Union's approach to the return of the left to power was cautious. In an April 2001 statement to the parliament during a visit to Bucharest, EU Enlargement Commissioner Guenter Verheugen remarked that the EU wanted to see "clear and unequivocal direction – and proof that substantial reforms can be delivered, already in the short term." Reacting to post-election complaints from the opposition that PSD appointees were interfering with the judicial system Verheugen also pointed out the importance of judicial independence and the rule of law.[41] Prime Minister Nastase's commitment to act on the party's campaign rhetoric and to address issues raised by the EU became evident in the course of 2001 as his government pressed through a series of reforms that had earlier been stalled. Responding to earlier calls by the Council of Europe's parliamentary assembly, in February 2001 President Iliescu signed a property restitution law designed to eliminate shortcomings in the 1995 legislation. When European diplomats raised concerns regarding human rights, Bucharest responded with changes to local administration rules that improved the rights of minorities, including the Roma, and increased access to the communist period security files. When Emma Nicholson, the European Parliament's special envoy for Romania, wrote a report highly critical of the corruption of adoption practices in the country, the Nastase government suspended all foreign adoptions for one year, despite the problems that this caused the country in its relations with the United States.[42]

The hopes of voters that more cohesive government would produce economic progress were, at least in part, fulfilled. In 2000 GDP growth, at 1.6 percent, was positive for the first time in three years. The year 2001 saw growth climb to 5.3 percent, and inflation reduced to 37 percent. These results, and more immediately the reform orientation that produced them, were the source of positive, if somewhat guarded response, by the European Union and other key multinational lenders to Romania. The European Bank for Reconstruction and Development (EBRD) 2001 Transition Report singled Romania out for making significant reform progress under the PSD.[43] Similarly, in their 2001 assistance strategy the World Bank analysts praised the Nastase government for its willingness to undertake serious change, and committed to substantially increased support in 2002–2003 if the effort should be sustained. The EU, while delaying possible accession from 2004 until at least 2007, recognized that the new government was indeed making progress as well.

That the second Iliescu administration has taken a much more affirmative approach to democratization thus appears clear. Its actions with regard to economic reform, openness, and electoral competition, and human and civil rights all point in the same direction. Yet serious cause for concern remains. Primary among the barriers to further reform and democratic consolidation are the corruption and lack of openness that are now imbedded at all levels of the society. In its 2001 accession report the European Commission concluded that corruption was a "widespread and systemic problem that undermined the legal system, the economy, and public confidence in the government."[44] In contrast to other areas, the report found that little progress had been made in dealing with this issue. In other areas throughout the EC report, disquiet over lack of openness and inside dealing was evident. Other international actors have been equally concerned. A World Bank study of the problem indicates that two-thirds of Romanian's believe all or most public officials to be corrupt. The study highlighted the impact of corruption on income inequality, business development, and foreign invest-ment.[45] Similarly, in its 2002 Romanian Economic Assessment, the OECD concluded that corruption was a serious barrier to further progress, and that implementation of anti-corruption measures was lacking.

The reality illuminated by these assessments is not simply that graft is a serious problem. Rather, it is that informal relations of intra-elite bargaining and influence peddling place a range of activities outside the sector of democratic control. Aurelian Craiutu has referred to these phenomena as "perverse institutionalization." He argues that it developed during the first Iliescu administration, and focuses on the broad and ill-defined powers of the executive, the existence of policy domains exempt from the control of elected officials, and the emergence of widespread clientelism.[46] As Craiutu's analysis points out, rather than being understood as an aberration from an otherwise functional economic system, corruption has become integral to the political economy of post-communist Romania. These practices clearly survived the Constantinescu interregnum, and currently stand as the primary obstacle to democratic consolidation.

The extent and significance of the corruption problem highlight the relevance of Kubicek's discussion in Chapter 1 of "gray zone" democracies that exist between open authoritarianism and consolidated democracy. The current Romanian government has indicated both in its rhetoric and in its actions that it is willing to undertake meaningful institutional reforms in order to achieve European integration. On the level of formal democracy, it has met the criteria for inclusion. It has reformed laws regarding minority relations, and made dramatic progress in the domain of regulations regarding privatization and marketization. It is in fact well removed from the extreme of "open authoritarianism."

Further progress toward the pole of "consolidation," however, presents substantial difficulties. First, progress in the "gray zone" is much more difficult to measure. Hence, for the EU and other international actors, it is more difficult to impose hard criteria to which the regime can be held. Second, achieving compliance is likely to be much more difficult, because core interests of the leadership are at stake. Romanian elites have learned to live in the world of pluralism and functioning electoral democracy. But politics is still very much an inside game played between clientelist networks that link major financial interests to particular political leaders. Threatening to destabilize the status quo that provides payoffs in this system would clearly put any political leader at risk. Third, EU decision-makers must consider that under current conditions further pressure may become counterproductive. The PSD is itself internally divided between reformists and conservatives. Pushing reformers to go too far or too quickly may well cause a backlash, and play into the hands of elements less inclined to democratization. Similarly, it must be taken into consideration that, while the overwhelming majority of Romanians are favorably inclined toward EU integration, the main alternative to the PSD in the wake of the 2000 elections is not the center-right, but rather Greater Romania and the radical nationalists, who are anti-democratic and extremely hostile to what they see as external interference.

Conclusion

Andrew Janos noted early in the transitions that the Central European states have historically acted under severe international constraints.[47] During the 1990s this continued reality worked strongly in favor of democratization. In essence, the international environment created a situation in which the benefits to be gained in pursuit of Romania's core goals through cooperation with European actors vastly outweighed any benefits of resistance and confrontation. In that calculus, the European Union played a defining role, rewarding progress and giving clear indications of disapproval when Romanian elites have strayed from adherence to international norms.

President Iliescu's strategy during the first six years of the transition was fairly typical of successor communist (as opposed to liberal reformist) regimes elsewhere in the region. Following the 1989 upheavals, Iliescu appealed to the anxiety that was evident among members of the society, particularly peasants and workers, concerning rapid marketization and social change. He held out the promise of stability and continued state protection. Like Milošević in Serbia and Vladimir Mečiar in Slovakia, his party also played to the nationalist sentiments that were evident within this segment of the electorate, forming a tacit legislative alliance with the extreme nationalist parties. While politically expedient in the near term, this political configuration proved unworkable from the point of view of policy formation in general, and foreign policy in particular. In an international environment dominated by free market-oriented and politically liberal great powers, the ruling Party of Romanian Social Democracy found itself cut off, unable effectively to reform, or to manage competently the country's economy.

The Red–Brown alliance that allowed Iliescu to remain in power despite the PDSR's economic failures became increasingly problematic as efforts to mollify the West took on increased significance. When Iliescu undertook to improve relations with Hungary the PDSR was forced to distance itself from its nationalist allies, aggravating already difficult relations with the volatile extremist leaders, and causing a breakdown in the coalition.

The susceptibly of Romania's domestic policy to the EU and other Western institutions was thus evident even before the 1996 victory of the democratic opposition. The first Iliescu leadership was in fact responding to an internationally determined incentive structure that imposed obvious costs on the authoritarian populist strategy of the early transition period, as well as obvious incentives for reform. While Iliescu was not well placed to take advantage of the reorientation that he himself initiated, Emil Constantinescu's less compromised leadership was clearly seen as a more acceptable partner by European diplomats and was more able to press forward with reform.

It is important to note that the shift in strategy did clearly predate the 1996 electoral transfer. This was in part the result, as argued above, of the foreclosing of alternative external sources of support. It is also evident that, as anticipated by the introductory model, the emergence of a cohesive domestic opposition altered the regime's political calculus. During the heady days of the early transition, the FSN enjoyed a nearly unassailable position. With the center-right weak and fragmented, even in the context of a formally competitive electoral system, the Iliescu leadership had little to fear from its more democratically oriented opponents.

The disappointing performance of President Constantinescu and the reformist parties and the subsequent return to power of the post-communist PSD delineates the immediate effective limits of EU conditionality in Romania. From 1996 onward accession has without question been a core priority of Romanian governments. While Constantinescu and the Democratic Convention failed to provide effective democratic governance during their four years in office, this was clearly as much the result of the reformer's internal divisions and inability adequately to manage the economic fallout left in the wake of the previous regime as it was the result of active resistance to democratization. The CDR did in fact make a great deal of progress in repairing relations with Europe and advancing the reform agenda. Somewhat to the surprise of Western observers, this agenda was embraced by the second Iliescu administration, which in its first two years appears to be as committed to accession as its predecessors and more capable on the level of policy implementation.

Much has been accomplished since 1996 in the way of substantive reform, and the current PSD government is committed to making further changes as necessary to achieve integration into both the EU and NATO. Nine "books" of the EU accession agreement are now provisionally closed. While it is unofficially recognized in Bucharest that a 2007 date for entry into the EU is unattainable, it is also recognized that continued progress in the direction of entry, even at a later date, is essential to the country's long-term development. Significantly, despite the economic hardships experienced in the context of the transition, as of 2001, 70 percent of Romanians continued to hold a positive impression of the EU, and more Romanians than citizens of any other candidate country expressed pride in being European.[48]

Further progress, in essence the "deepening" of the democratic process, however, is likely to take a great deal more time and to be less susceptible to direct external influence. Rather than formal compliance, consolidation requires the internalization of democratic norms by both elites and the broader public. Improvement in this realm is both more difficult to monitor and therefore more difficult to reward or punish without highly intrusive and potentially contra-productive efforts. In essence, over the course of the past decade the European Union and analogous external institutions have done the job of promoting the establishment of domestic democratic structures. Given time, and continued international support, one should have confidence that those new domestic structures themselves will in turn encourage the consolidation of democracy in Romania.

Notes

1 K. Verdery, *National Ideology Under State Socialism: Identity and Cultural Politics in Ceauçescu's Romania*, Los Angeles: University of California Press, 1991, pp. 21–71.

2 S. Tanase, "Changing Societies and Elite Transformation," *East European Politics and Societies*, 13, Spring 1999, pp. 358–364.

3 For a comprehensive account of Romania's place in the Balkan political arena, see B. Jelavich, *History of the Balkans*, Cambridge: Cambridge University Press, 1983.

4 For a thorough treatment of the evolution of Romania's interwar political economy, see H. Roberts, *Rumania: Political Problems of an Agrarian State,* New Haven: Yale University Press, 1951.

5 I. Livezeanu, *Cultural Politics in Greater Romania: Regionalism, Nation Building and Ethnic Struggle, 1918–1930*, Ithaca, NY: Cornell University Press, 1995, p. 4.

6 Verdery, op. cit.

7 G. Evans and S. Whitefield, "The Politics and Economics of Democratic Commitment: Support for Democracy in Transition Societies," *British Journal of Political Science* 25, October 1995, pp. 485–515.

8 For summaries of these parties' programs and political positions, see V. Socor, "Political Parties Emerging," *Radio Free Europe/Radio Liberty Research Reports*, February 16, 1990, pp. 28–35.

9 The Assembly consisted of 396 seats, of which 387 were determined by election, with the remaining posts reserved for representatives of ethnic minorities. In the Senate 119 positions were filled by candidates chosen from 41 multi-member districts. The president was elected simultaneously with the legislature in a two-round runoff election.

10 See, for example, the following accounts: A. Genillard, "Behind Romania's Vote For Ruling Communists," *The Christian Science Monitor*, May 23, 1990, p. 4; "Press Comments on Fairness, Conduct of the Elections," FBIS-EEU-90-107, June 4, 1990, pp. 53–54; V. Socor, "National Salvation Front Produces Electoral Landslide," *Report on Eastern Europe*, July 6, 1990, pp. 24–31.

11 For a more detailed discussion of the early post-communist economic reforms in Romania, see M. Isarescu, "The Prognosis for Economic Recovery," in D. Nelson, ed., *Romania After Tyranny*, Boulder, CO: Westview Press, 1992, pp. 147–165.

12 M. C. Sirbu, "Towards a Market Economy: The Romanian Effort," *East European Quarterly* 28, Winter 1994, pp. 471–519.

13 T. Gallagher, "Romania: Nationalism Defines Democracy," in W. Kostecki, K. Zukorwska, and B. Goralczyk, eds, *Transformations of Post Communist States*, New York: St. Martin's Press, 2000, pp. 188–189.

14 T. Gallagher, *Romania After Ceauçescu – The Politics of Intolerance*, Edinburgh: Edinburgh University Press, 1995, pp. 127–133.

15 In the case of the USSR, four territories were at issue; northern Bukovina and Herta, southern Bessarabia, and Serpent Island were attached to the Ukrainian Soviet Socialist Republic as a consequence of the Ribbentrop–Molotov Pact. Bessarabia proper, also lost to Romania, was established as the Moldovan Soviet Socialist Republic, now the Republic of Moldova.

16 For two views of the 1991 bilateral treaty with the Soviet Union, see W. Bacon, "Security as seen from Bucharest," in Nelson, op. cit., p. 192, and S. M. Botez, "An Alternative Romanian Foreign Policy," in Nelson, op. cit., p. 267.

17 H. Carey, "Irregularities or Rigging: The 1992 Romanian Parliamentary Elections," *East European Quarterly* 29, Spring 1995, pp. 43–68.

18 A. Craiutu, "Light at the End of the Tunnel: Romania 1989–1998," in G. Pridham and T. Gallagher, eds, *Experimenting with Democracy: Regime Change in the Balkans*, London: Routledge, 2000, p. 180.

19 S. D. Roper, *Romania, The Unfinished Revolution*, Amsterdam: Harwood Academic Publishers, 2000, p. 96.

20 D. Phinnemore, "Romania and Euro-Atlantic Integration since 1989: A Decade of Frustration," in D. Light and D. Phinnemore, eds, *Post-Communist Romania: Coming to Terms with Transition*, New York: Palgrave, 2001, pp. 255–256.

21 Verdery, op. cit.

22 For a complete discussion of these elections, see W. Crowther, "Romania," in S. Bergland, F. Aarebrot, and T. Hellen, eds, *Handbook of Political Change in Eastern Europe*, London: Edward Elgar Publishers, 1998, pp. 295–334.

23 On the significance of the transfer of power to the liberal opposition, see M. Shafir, "Romania's Road to Normalcy," *Journal of Democracy*, 8, April 1997, pp. 144–158.

24 See D. Deletant, "Ghosts from the Past: Successors to the Securitate in Post-Communist Romania," in Light and Phinnemore, op. cit., pp. 44–49, and L. Watts, "Reform and Crisis in Romania Civil–Military Relations 1989–1999," *Armed Forces and Society*, Summer 2002, pp. 596–622.

25 M. MacFarlan, J. O. Martins, and P. Paradis, "Romania: Macro-economic Stabilization and Structural Reform," *OECD Observer* 221, April–May 1998, pp. 39–43.

26 R. Weber, "Constitutionalism as a Vehicle for Democratic Consolidation in Romania," in J. Zielonka, ed., *Democratic Consolidation in Eastern Europe, Vol. 1*, New York: Oxford University Press, 2001, pp. 232–234.

27 D. Phinnemore, "Romania and Euro-Atlantic Integration since 1989: A Decade of Frustration," in Light and Phinnemore, op. cit., p. 258.

28 T. M. Leonard, "NATO Expansion: Romania and Bulgaria within the Larger Context," *East European Quarterly* 33, Winter 1999, pp. 517–545.

29 M. Shafir, "The Ciorbea Government and Democratization: A Preliminary Assessment," in Light and Phinnemore, op. cit., pp. 79–103.

30 See the conclusions of N. Budina and S. van Wijnbergen, "Fiscal Deficits, Monetary Reform and Inflations Stabilization in Romania," Vienna: Institut fur Hohere Studies, 1996, available at http://www.inhs.ac.at/publications/eco/publications.htm.

31 A. Smith, "The Transition to a Market Economy in Romania and the Competitiveness of Exports," in Light and Phinnemore, op. cit., pp. 135–136.

32 Tom Gallagher, "Building Democracy in Romania," in Zielonka, op. cit., p. 396.

33 IMF Staff Country Report 00/159, December 2000, p. 18.

34 Open Society Foundation Public Opinion Barometer. Data available at http://www.sfos.ro/.

35 G. Pop-Eleches, "Romania's Political Dejection", *Journal of Democracy* 12, July 2001, pp. 156–169.

36 While support for limited government and democratic norms is apparent in some areas, the same Open Society survey cited above indicates that by 2000, 35 percent of Romanians preferred a party to multi-party democracy. This clearly reflects a reaction to the disorder associated with multi-party rule.

37 Agence France Presse, November 3, 2000.

38 P. Mcaleer and S. Wagstyl, "Rise of Nationalists throws Romania into Uncertainty," *Financial Times*, November 28, 2000, p. 13.

39 J. Blocker, "Western Press Review: EU Summit in Nice; Politics in Iraq And Romania," *Radio Free Europe/Radio Liberty*, December 6, 2000.

40 See Ion Iliescu's statement to the Rompress News Agency, November 27, 2000.

41 "EU presses Romania to Catch Up on Reform," Agence France Presse, April 26, 2001.

42 A. Alexe, "Romania Suspends International Adoptions for One Year," Associated Press, June 21, 2001.

43 "Progress in Transition," *Janet Matthews Information Services*, December 31, 2001.

44 "2001 Regular Report On Romania's Progress Toward Accession," Commission of the European Union, November 11, 2001 (SEC 2001) 1735.

45 *Diagnostic Surveys of Corruption in Romania*, Washington: The World Bank, 2001.

46 Craiutu, op. cit., p. 180.

47 A. Janos, "Continuity and Change in Eastern Europe: Strategies for Post-Communist Politics," *East European Politics and Societies* 8, Winter 1994, p. 131.

48 Candidate Counties Eurobarometer 2001, European Commission, available at http://europa.eu.int/comm/public_opinion.

5   The politics of conditionality

The European Union and human rights reform in Turkey

Thomas W. Smith[1]

This chapter examines EU efforts over the past decade to promote human rights in Turkey through diplomatic pressure and through "conditionality," or making trade, aid, and other forms of association and cooperation contingent on human rights reform. Although deficiencies in human rights have long been an obstacle to Turkey "becoming European," over the years the EU has targeted few resources in this area, and its influence has been modest. This changed markedly after the 1999 Helsinki European Council, where Turkey was named "a candidate state destined to join the Union on the basis of the same criteria applied to the other candidates."[2] Spurred by the credible prospect of membership, Ankara has initiated ambitious reforms in line with the Copenhagen Criteria and the Accession Partnership to strengthen the rule of law, expand basic freedoms, and protect minority rights.

Political conditionality and a culture of human rights

The Turkish case underscores the difficulties of promoting human rights from a distance without clear and significant incentives for target states, as well as the power, under the right conditions, that international norms have in shaping human rights policy and practice. Carrots have mattered more than sticks, but the big carrot – the prospect of EU membership – has mattered most of all. Turkey's reforms, which will entail sweeping constitutional changes and sharp shifts in social norms, have been slow in coming. Before assuming formal candidate status, the pace of liberalization had been glacial. Decades of admonishments had had little effect. Nor had the EC capitalized on conditionality. The 1963 Association Agreement concluded between the EC and Turkey did not mention democracy, human rights, or even politics. Despite abundant human rights rhetoric, it was not until the 1995 Customs Union Treaty that EU association was conditioned on human rights reform, and those provisions were negotiated in political fora not formally attached to the Treaty. Only with the drafting of the Accession Partnership, Turkey's "road map" to membership, were the political requirements of the Copenhagen Criteria clearly articulated.

As a developing country that historically has resisted liberal conceptions of human rights, Turkey represents a hard case to test the normative effects of European foreign policy.[3] While the collapse of the *ancien régimes* in Eastern Europe cleared the way for a new order, this has not happened in Kemalist Turkey. The hard communitarian nationalism invented by Mustafa Kemal Atatürk, while far from monolithic, still commands wide respect. The idea of a secular republic is jealously guarded by the military, but also is imbedded in institutions and ingrained in public life. A modern bureaucracy, a Western legal system, progressive national education, and all the machinery of a modern state are part of that legacy. Skeptics contend, however, that the country's statist institutions are stuck in the 1930s. Hakan Yavuz notes, "Kemalism has been superficially Western in form while remaining rigidly authoritarian and dogmatic in substance. It continues to stress republicanism over democracy, homogeneity over difference, the military over the civilian, and the state over society."[4]

Turkish accession is also unfolding in the shadow of a tumultuous history, marked by geopolitical strife as well as cultural constructions of "the other." When Gladstone swore in 1879 to reform "the unspeakable Turk" through the "coercion by the united authority of Europe," the assumption was that there was something inherently uncivilized about Turkey.[5] Through the more recent ups and down of Turkish–EU relations, many Turks have wondered if the EU today still represents an exclusive "civilizational project," as a number of even centrist European politicians suggest it should. Modern Turkey has also tended to go it alone. "We are like none other," Atatürk often said. Sovereign independence is the leitmotif of the Turkish Revolution, which of course ousted the European powers from Anatolia. But also bound up in Turkish political culture is the idea of an essentialist state. The divided loyalty that a federalist Europe represents is more reminiscent of the *millet*, or "nations" system of the Ottoman Empire than it is of the modern Turkish state. Given the Turkish Republic's understandable desire to avoid the "Ottomanization" of its predecessor, one can appreciate the tension between the new European norms of diminished or shared sovereignty and those of Turkey.

The EU's human rights diplomacy has been tempered by Turkey's pivotal place in the architecture of European security. Membership in NATO and close ties to the USA give Ankara leverage with Brussels. Turkey is a full member of the Organization for Security and Cooperation in Europe (OSCE), and an associate of the Western European Union, and wields an effective veto over the European Security and Defense Identity, the seed of a European army. Hence, Turkey is not merely a supplicant at Europe's doorstep. As *The Independent* of London noted, "like it or not, Turkey occupies too important a place in the geopolitical scheme of things for the West to make human rights the sole yardstick of its relationship with Turkey."[6] Not only does Turkey buffer Europe from the wilds of the Orient, but its modern secularism remains the bright and shining model for democratic development across the Middle East and Central Asia.

The state of human rights in Turkey

That model has not always been a friend of human rights. Despite having decades of democratic experience, competitive elections, and all the trappings of a modern state, Turkey has had an abysmal human rights record. Probably in no other country is this contradiction so pronounced. These failings are the result of constitutional constraints as well as informal abuses of power. Parliamentary elections are vigorously contested and issues dutifully debated – a widely used political science data set ranks Turkish democracy a perfect 10. According to Freedom House data on political rights and liberties, however, Turkey lags some of the most struggling countries in Eastern Europe, virtually all of Latin America, and is on par with the most advanced states of North Africa. Turkey stands out in the survey for having slipped from being "free" across the 1970s to being "partly free" ever since.[7]

While the Turkish military is the guardian of Atatürk's legacy, its harsh rendering of the Kemalist social contract has done that legacy more harm than good. The 1980 coup reinvigorated Kemalism in almost every facet of public life. The laws and institutions ushered in by the "pashas," as the military chiefs are known, remain the greatest obstacles to liberal democracy in Turkey. The 1982 Constitution strictly limited individual rights and expanded the "advisory" role of the National Security Council (NSC) to cover any aspect of society that might conceivably erode the unity of the state.[8] Sami Selçuk, President of the Court of Appeals, has called the document "a set of police regulations" rather than an expression of fundamental rights.[9] According to the Preamble, no protection is afforded "to thoughts or opinions contrary . . . to the nationalism, principles, reforms and modernism of Atatürk; to the principle of secularism." The Penal Code criminalizes publications that "harm the security of the country" or challenge conscription (Art. 155). The mere "allusion or hint" of criticism of the President of the Republic is a crime (Art. 158). A law frequently invoked in political cases targets "those who publicly insult or ridicule the moral personality of Turkishness," the Republic, or organs of government (Art. 159). Kurds as well as Islamists run afoul of "openly inciting people to enmity and hatred by pointing to class, racial, religious, confessional, or regional differences" (Art. 312).[10] Corresponding laws on political parties, freedom of association, the press, broadcasting, video and musical works, language instruction, education, and "crimes against Atatürk" add armature to Kemalism. State corporatist agencies further control public and professional life.

The official ideology has also encouraged a particular definition of human rights. While elites voice support for European-style protections from abuses committed by the state, in Turkish discourse, human rights violations also refer conspicuously to those carried out by separatists and Islamists, and generally neglect group or minority rights. (Some commentators distinguish carefully between "individual rights" and "human rights" to distance themselves from group or cultural claims.) The Kurdish insurgency, urban leftist strife, and Islamic terrorism have fostered a general climate of violence, but one can see how intense civic nationalism might also encourage state violence, as Jacobin authorities shepherd errant citizens back into the fold. There can be little doubt that Kemalist *raison d'état* has contributed to a climate of impunity for those employed by state security organs or acting on their own to suppress treacherous, anti-Turkish voices (as some nationalists have done against leftists and Kurds). Prosecutions have picked up, but lack of accountability remains a chief obstacle to curbing the hundreds of cases of torture reported each year.

Since 1980, Islamists and Kurds have borne the brunt of abuses. Islamists say that the relentless pursuit of Enlightenment ideals has crushed religious freedom. The government Directorate of Religious Affairs has attempted to sever religious life from civil society and nationalize it.[11] In July 1996, Necmettin Erbakan of the *Refah* (Welfare) Party became the first Islamist Prime Minister in Turkish history, only to be squeezed out of office a year later after being presented by the military with an eighteen-point plan to eradicate Islamic influence from government. This "coup-by-memorandum," as it became known, enjoyed the support of many secular Turks who considered Erbakan's often weird tenure in office to be an embarrassment. The Constitutional Court closed *Refah* soon thereafter. In June 2001, the Court closed *Fazilet* (Virtue), the successor party to *Refah*, on grounds that it was a hotbed of "Islamic and anti-secular activities." This was the fourth time since 1970 that the Court had closed an Islamist opposition party and the sixteenth time it had closed a party since the return to civilian rule in 1983.

The Turkish Enlightenment has marginalized Kurds even more than Islamists. The Kurdish predicament is thought by some to be a case of "structural violence," caused by systematic deprivation and social injustice. Incomes in the Kurdish southeast remain about one-tenth of those in the industrial swathe along the Sea of Marmara in western Turkey.[12] For others, it is a question of identity politics. For the first seventy years of the republic any reference to Kurdishness was taboo. Rather, Kurds were referred to euphemistically as "Mountain Turks." The Kurdish language was banned and all but the most folkloric cultural expressions were discouraged. The return to civilian rule in 1983 was accompanied by accelerated efforts to Turkify the Kurdish region.[13] The government refused to register Kurdish names on birth certificates and gave thousands of villages in the region new, Turkish, names. The state continues to stifle Kurdish identity. The Constitutional Court has banned sympathetic political parties. Fearing closure by the government in the run-up to the November 2002 elections, the Kurdish People's Democracy Party (HADEP) changed its name to the Democratic People's Party (DEHAP), but retained its platform. Historically, every other pro-Kurdish party in Turkey has been shuttered by the courts. Kurdish leaders have been jailed; others have been disappeared or killed. Kurdish-leaning newspapers, publishing houses, charitable organizations, and NGOs have been closed. Books about Kurds, Kurdistan, and Kurdish nationalism, including distant historical accounts, have been seized. Yaşar Kemal, Turkey's great Kurdish novelist, was tried for separatism based on his argument that the rich Kurdish language would fade without literary freedom. The taboo surrounding all things Kurdish has lifted in recent years, and there is lively debate about Kurdish cultural rights. But the terms of that discussion are still framed by the contrast between the world history of Turks and the tribal backwardness of Kurds.

The country is in the process of extricating its laws from the war footing laid down during the conflict with the *Partia Karkaren Kürdistan* (Kurdistan Workers' Party), or PKK. Civil liberties were suspended in most of the Kurdish areas beginning in 1987, and while the region remains the site of illegal detentions, torture, disappearances, and extra-judicial killings, these have declined dramatically over the past three years. The provinces of Diyarbakir and Sirnak remain under emergency rule, and the penal code still allows security detainees to be held incommunicado and without charge for extended periods, a practice human rights activists say is tailored for coercing confessions. Having invested so much blood and treasure (more than $100 billion) in the war with the PKK, few Turks are keen to make concessions to Kurdish nationalism. Bitterness from the war, in which about 30,000 have died, runs deep on both sides. According to the Human Rights Foundation of Turkey, an advocate for Kurdish rights, nearly 3,700 Kurdish villages were evacuated, and many burned or razed, between 1990 and 1999, and a million or more people displaced.[14] Vietnam-style "hamletting" was enacted as the war progressed. Turkish officials are now overseeing the return of refugees to their villages. Official permission is required to return. There have been 300,000 applications, half of which have been denied, ostensibly for security reasons. Some of the displaced will be resettled in "consolidated villages" instead of original sites, again for reasons of continued control.[15]

Notwithstanding pressure from business leaders, NGOs, jurists, academics, parliamentarians, and even Turkey's popular president, the constitutional lawyer Ahmet Necdet Sezer, the state maintains its hallowed position. The national security blueprint prepared by the Turkish General Staff in August 2001 retains "fundamentalism" and "separatism" as the chief internal threats. The General Staff has worried that EU membership may harm the "unitary nature" of the Turkish state. Societal attitudes are only slightly more accommodating. There is lingering distrust toward Kurdish and Islamist political ambitions. Many Turks believe that according minority rights to Kurds – or Laz, Assyrians, or Circassians, for that matter – would tempt dissolution, while allowing religious intrusion into the public sphere is seen as backsliding from modernity. Many Turks are simply indifferent to human rights issues.[16]

Turkish–EU relations pre-Helsinki: "declaratory diplomacy"

While EC/EU officials and member states have been quick to condemn Turkish human rights, such admonishments have done little to improve actual conditions.[17] Until recently, this was emblematic of the EU's approach to human rights. Economics, whether in the form of the single market or external trade, remains the Union's *raison d'être*. But human rights is emerging as a dominant theme both in the EU's "Second Pillar," the Common Security and Foreign Policy (CSFP), and in conditionality attached to economic instruments. One is tempted to say that EU's post-Maastricht philosophy of international relations has coalesced around the broad idea of human rights, even if specific policies and practices have left much to be desired or, as in the case of the former Yugoslavia, have failed spectacularly. Civil rights are deeply seated in the European experience and the rhetoric of rights comes naturally to member states. Article 6(2) of the 1992 Treaty of Europe (TEU), or Maastricht Treaty, binds member states to take human rights into account in their external relations. The development of human rights and fundamental freedoms is one of the five objectives of the CSFP. More importantly, the CSFP fuses human rights and international security in the idea of "soft security" related to political and economic chaos, ethnic strife, minority conflicts, border disputes, refugees, and the environment. The "Petersberg Tasks" of rescue, peacekeeping, and crisis management, to be carried out by a EU rapid-reaction force, complete an ambitious human rights agenda. Speaking on behalf of the EU at the Fifty-fifth Session of the UN Commission of Human Rights, German Foreign Minister Joschka Fischer argued that human rights policy was not a "soft topic," but was "tough Realpolitik."[18]

Although basic human rights, as defined by the European Convention on Human Rights (ECHR), are well-settled principles of Community law, the vigorous advocacy of human rights abroad is new. As far back as the Birkelbach Report of 1962, political conditions were enunciated by the Community and in a few cases attached to foreign aid and incorporated in cooperation and trade treaties with third countries. Launched in 1975, the successive Lomé Conventions that govern EC foreign aid have had a checkered history with regard to the promotion of human rights. In several instances, the EC found itself facing treaty obligations to provide aid to governments that were wholesale human rights violators. In 1989 Lomé IV attempted to remedy this by emphasizing social and economic rights and other facets of "good governance" as a condition of continued aid. This was the origin of the so-called human rights clause. The strength of such provisions remains in doubt. Between 1980 and 1995 EC/EU developmental assistance flowed with little distinction to governments good and bad. Among EU member states, only Germany showed much success in attaching rigorous political conditions to foreign aid.[19]

In 1995 the European Council agreed that all general trade and cooperation agreements with third countries (but not sector-specific agreements, on textiles or agricultural products, for example) would stress the "interdependence between human rights, democracy and development."[20] Now written into more than twenty EU foreign aid agreements, the human rights clause has yet to be invoked as reason to suspend or reduce aid. In fact, the treaty language dealing with suspension has softened over time. The so-called "Baltic Clause," which was attached to agreements in 1992 with the Baltic states and Albania, indicated immediate curtailment of cooperation in the event of a serious breach of human rights. Agreements today rely on the more flexible "Bulgarian Clause," which provides for gradations of sanctions short of suspension.[21] EU trade preferences and technical and financial assistance also carry human rights conditions.

Even more recently has the EU begun to spell out human rights expectations for prospective member states.[22] Briefly, Art. 6(1) of the TEU sets the "principles of liberty, democracy, respect for human rights and fundamental freedoms" as principles held in common by the member states. The 1993 Copenhagen Criteria focused on macro-economic stability, but stated also that accession was contingent on "stability of institutions guaranteeing democracy, the rule of law, human rights and respect for and protection of minorities." The 1997 Luxembourg European Council summit called for technical assistance to strengthen human rights through education and training. The 1997 Treaty of Amsterdam asserted that the EU, as an "area of freedom, security and justice," was competent to promote human rights: "The Union is founded on the principles of liberty, democracy, respect for human rights and fundamental freedoms, and the rule of law, principles which are common to Member States." The non-binding Charter of Fundamental Rights of the European Union, adopted at the Nice Council in December 2000, is an avant-garde catalog of rights, including rights to collective bargaining and action, employment placement, fair and just working conditions, health care, and consumer protection.

The principles at stake are thought to be, at a minimum, all the rights and freedoms guaranteed under the European Convention on Human Rights.[23] Nonetheless, the EU has viewed the pursuit of human rights as a chiefly negative task. Its tools have been legal prohibitions on offenses and the threat of severing association or suspending cooperation agreements, blocking accession or, in the case of members, revoking rights of membership. Critics say the approach remains overly legalistic, institutionally jerry-rigged, inconsistent, and generally ineffective, that the EU's human rights talk is nothing *but* rhetoric.[24] A variety of institutions cobble together standards and remedies. Efforts have been fragmented by the individual national interests of the fifteen members. In practice, humanitarian efforts are often overwhelmed by the *force majeure* of security or economic necessity. One critic suggests the EU has been "torn between its moral ambitions and its economic interests."[25]

The Turkish case reflects this evolution from economics leavened with declarations on democracy to concrete human rights criteria attached to formal candidacy.[26] As noted, the 1963 Association Agreement, or Ankara Treaty, was a purely economic instrument. The vast majority of aid to Turkey under the accord was earmarked for economic integration – upgrading export infrastructure, harmonizing weights and measures, according preferential treatment with regard to European tariffs, reducing duties and non-tariff barriers to trade in Turkey, and enhancing the country's appeal to foreign investors. This was probably as much a reflection of European priorities as it was a sign of Ankara's unswerving preference for apolitical, technocratic assistance. Given the Turkish government's aversion toward civil society initiatives, all the better if the lion's share of aid should come in the form of EC-to-Ankara transfers.

This began to change in the mid-1980s. In 1985 the European Parliament passed a resolution calling for normalization of relations with Turkey based on a number of human rights conditions: abolishing the death penalty, ending collective trials, prohibiting torture, abolishing curbs on the freedom of thought, and recognizing the right of Turks to petition the European Court of Human Rights. The EU rejected Ankara's 1987 application for candidate status on grounds that Turkey's economic and political systems were not ready for membership. The decision provided little guidance for improvement, instead pointing to the Customs Union as an alternative form of association. By the end of the 1980s criticism of Turkish human rights practices had intensified, particularly from the EU Council of Ministers and the European Parliament, but there also emerged a clearer sense of what conditionality entailed and which specific reforms would lead to better relations. At the Dublin Council in 1990 the member states explicitly linked closer relations with Turkey to a resolution of the Cyprus impasse.

The early 1990s produced some reforms. In 1990 Ankara recognized the jurisdiction of the European Court of Human Rights. In 1991 Turkey established a Ministry of Human Rights. The same year Kurdish language restrictions were lifted (though only for "non-political" speech) and several offensive sections of the Penal Code dropped. Around the same time Turkish authorities began to prosecute police officers accused of torture. In the run-up to the customs union vote in 1995, the Turkish Grand National Assembly passed scores of legal reforms to bring commercial practices into line with those in Europe. The European Parliament also called on Ankara to release from prison six former parliament members from the pro-Kurdish Democracy Party and to vacate Art. 8 of the Anti-Terror law, which criminalized expressive or political activities aimed at undermining "the indivisible unity of the state." A package of constitutional amendments was passed, slightly modifying the language of Art. 8, while the Supreme Court ordered the release of two of the six lawmakers.[27] These conditions were asserted in political fora rather than formally incorporated into the Customs union Treaty itself. The treaty, concluded in March 1995, does not contain the human rights clause. Indeed, like the 1963 Association Agreement, the Customs Union attaches no political conditions at all. The treaty calls for "effective protection and enforcement of intellectual, industrial and commercial property rights" (Art. 31), but does not once mention human rights.

The Ankara Agreement had envisioned a Customs Union as the penultimate phase before applying for full membership. Even if Europeans did not view the customs pact, which went into effect on January 1, 1996, as a "teleological undertaking" on the march to accession, many Turks did.[28] The Customs Union buoyed political leaders and laymen alike, lubricating additional reforms in civil rights. Optimism was short-lived, however. At the Luxembourg Council in 1997 the European Council rejected Turkey's application for candidate status. Despite a strategically timed package of constitutional reforms, the Council cited continued human rights violations and tensions with Greece. All eleven of the other applications for formal candidacy were successful, although ten of the applicants were Eastern European states whose economies in some cases were in shambles and whose democratic experience was more limited than Turkey's. In a final slap at Ankara, the EU also elevated a divided Cyprus to full candidacy based on a Greek Cypriot application.[29]

It was a crushing blow for Turkey's European vocation. Economic ties seemed to be the extent of integration. Unlike Turkey, none of the eleven successful candidates had entered a Customs Union with the EU. The snub set back reforms and elicited a nationalist backlash, seeming to confirm that the EU was, in the end, a Christian club, and that Turkey was merely a market, to be exploited but not embraced. "Go to Hell, Europe" read the headline of the major liberal Turkish daily, *Hürriyet*.[30] Ankara suspended its political dialogue with Brussels. Liberalization ground to a halt. Then Prime Minister Mesut Yilmaz threatened to withdraw Turkey's application altogether and turn away from Europe, a scenario not lost on EU diplomats when Yilmaz pointedly skipped the European Conference convened in London in March 1998, making a tour of Central Asian capitals instead. Relations hit bottom when Yilmaz accused Germany of pursuing a policy of *Lebensraum* – a reference to Hitler's foreign policy – with regard to the EU's Eastern enlargement. The Luxembourg debacle also energized the *Milliyetçi Hareket Partisi* (MHP), or National Action Party, a far-right party with a sordid history of ethnic and religious chauvinism. Riding resentment toward Europe, the MHP won 16.5 percent of the vote in the April 1999 elections, making it second largest party in parliament and the lynchpin partner in the 1999–2002 coalition government.

Human rights, the Copenhagen criteria, and the Turkish national program

The EU has muddled through enlargement in the past. But with so many candidates now essentially competing for membership, Brussels has had to define clearly its expectations. Beginning in May 1999 Ankara began to craft a detailed pre-accession strategy in line with the Copenhagen Criteria. It was this initiative that led to candidate status being conferred on Turkey at Helsinki in December 1999.

Soon after the Helsinki Summit, the EU and Ankara finalized the Accession Partnership accord. This was the "road map" that hopefully would lead to formal accession talks. From Turkey's standpoint, the Partnership demystified membership and helped alleviate concerns about "fortress Europe" and other "civilizational" issues. At a psychological level, "candidacy status . . . is seen as important because it confirms Turkey's identity as a European state, and because in offering a positive prospect it reinforces the push for domestic change."[31] (Günter Verheugen, EU commissioner for enlargement, cautions that candidacy does not lead inexorably to accession.) To work, incentives should be transparent; only then will conditionality take hold. In the past, political conditions were thought to be merely excuses to bar Turkey from Europe rather than criteria for membership, or even serious attempts to induce reforms. Then Turkish president Turgut Özal claimed in 1989 that "the real purpose behind the long-standing campaign against the Turkish human rights problem was to alienate her from the process of European political and economic integration."[32]

What conditions has the EU placed on membership? [33] Over the short term:

- Address the Cyprus problem;
- Strengthen freedoms of expression, peaceable assembly, and civil society;
- Strengthen efforts to stamp out torture; bring rules on pre-trial detention into compliance with the European Convention on Human Rights and the European Convention for the Prevention of Torture;
- Strengthen opportunities for legal redress against all violations of human rights;
- Intensify human rights training for law enforcement officials;
- Improve the efficiency and independence of the judiciary. Train judges and prosecutors on EU legislation;
- Maintain the moratorium on capital punishment;
- Lift any legal bar to television and radio broadcasts in languages other than Turkish;
- Develop a comprehensive strategy to reduce regional economic disparities.

Over the medium term:

- Make every effort to resolve any outstanding border disputes;
- Guarantee universal enjoyment of all human rights and fundamental freedoms;
- Further develop conditions for freedom of thought, conscience, and religion;
- Review the Turkish Constitution and other laws with a view to guaran-

teeing rights and freedoms for all. Law and practice should conform to
member states;

- Abolish the death penalty. Sign and ratify Protocol No. 6 of the
  European Convention on Human Rights (on capital punishment);
- Ratify the International Covenant on Civil and Political Rights and the
  International Covenant on Economic, Social and Cultural Rights;
- Improve detention conditions in prisons;
- "Align" the constitutional role of the NSC as an advisory body;
- Lift the remaining state of emergency in the southeast;
- Ensure cultural diversity and guarantee cultural rights for all citizens.

Some of these requirements, notably the references to Cyprus and
"outstanding border disputes," fall outside the Copenhagen Criteria. Greek
diplomats insisted that these two provisions head the list of reforms. In
ascending order of difficulty of implementation, the conditions require:
amending the constitution, ratifying international covenants, creating an
independent judiciary, resolving geopolitical conflicts, curbing the military's
role in government, and cultivating a liberal political culture. The requirements are clear enough, though a few – guaranteeing "all human rights and
fundamental freedoms" or ensuring "cultural diversity" – require interpretation. Brussels has put Ankara on notice that it intends to monitor political
development and measure the effectiveness of state agencies, no small matter
given that the political criteria set out at Copenhagen hinge on "stability of
institutions" guaranteeing liberalism. Measuring Turkey's political capacity
will surely entail a greater element of subjectivity than gauging the economic
conditions of accession, which can be more crisply quantified.

   How is Turkey doing? As noted, Helsinki has provided new incentive for
liberalization. Since 1999 there has been a burst of human rights activity
from NGOs as well as more measured efforts on the part of state officials
engaged in the accession process. The most concrete product of this effort
was Ankara's response to the Accession Partnership, the Turkish National
Program for the Adoption of the *Acquis*, unveiled on March 19, 2001. While
political criteria, including human rights, make up only a modest part of the
plan, comprising 7 of 523 pages, the language and timetable are almost
identical to those laid down by Brussels. Each area of improvement is
followed by specific constitutional and other reforms to be undertaken.
Ankara's commitment to a "peace-seeking foreign policy" and its determin-
ation to seek settlement of bilateral problems with Greece as well as its
willingness to work with the UN to break the Cyprus impasse are noted in a
general way in the introduction, but nowhere else. The document's most
delicate language deals with the role of the NSC and the possible lifting of
the state of emergency in several Kurdish provinces.

   Implementation of reforms will come more gradually. In its 2001 progress
report, the European Commission noted that the pre-accession strategy for
Turkey was "well under way."[34] A package of thirty-four amendments to the

1982 constitution was adopted by the Turkish Grand National Assembly in October 2001, though the closure of *Fazilet* in June tempered optimism and to many revealed clear limits on any discussion of Turkish democratization. In February 2002, the Assembly approved a further "mini-democratization" set of amendments, and in August 2002, after an all-night session, it went even further, passing a package of reforms over the opposition of the MHP that would abolish the death penalty and allow for broadcasting, print media, and education in Kurdish. A new judicial bench will review claims by prisoners that their rights have been breached. Training of judges in EU law has gathered speed. State security courts remain an area of concern, though under new legislation all its members will be appointed from the civilian judiciary. Observers noted persistent problems with the independence of the judiciary, affecting military tribunals and also juvenile courts.

The report notes that constitutional amendments are "a significant step toward strengthening guarantees in the field of human rights and fundamental freedoms," including cultural rights and gender equality. Monitors found no improvement in quelling torture and mistreatment of prisoners, especially in the southeast. A number of prison reforms are underway, yet "incommunicado detention" in the provinces under emergency rule remains brutal. The report estimates that 9,000 people are currently in prison in Turkey for crimes connected to freedom of expression. The government's restraint in the case of PKK leader Abdullah Öcalan, and its willingness to place the fate of the separatist leader in the hands of the European Court of Human Rights, portend that Ankara will ratify Protocol 6 of the European Convention on Human Rights abolishing the death penalty. The Commission found "little sign of increased civilian control over the military."

In short, Turkey has adopted a series of half-measures – improvements to be sure, but still short of EU standards. In a controversial rejoinder to the EU's latest progress report, Human Rights Watch charged that Turkey had done little more than "tinsel and varnish" its poor human rights record. "We have seen little but superficial and half-way measures. Yes, there are new human rights commitments and new human rights institutions, but torture remains rampant and free expression is severely limited."[35] The rejoinder went on to suggest that Turkey had installed a Potemkin human rights regime, with a new Human Rights Presidency, a High Human Rights Board, Human Rights Consultation boards, and the Human Rights Investigation Board – all hollow institutions. Human Rights Watch claims further that EU monitors uncritically accepted Turkish claims, and went lightly on Turkey in judging civil liberties where member states are themselves on shaky ground, notably religious freedom and rights of conscientious objectors. Even when progress is achieved, it is often met with skepticism by European officials. One European diplomat noted after the summer 2002 reforms that "there are few signs that Turkey has the collective will to adopt the common practices of the European Union."[36] Skepticism resurfaced in October 2002, when the European Commission announced that ten new members – Estonia, Latvia,

Lithuania, Poland, Czech Republic, Slovakia, Hungary, Slovenia, Malta, and Cyprus – would join the EU in 2004, and that Romania and Bulgaria might sign on as soon as 2007. The Commission deferred a decision on Turkey, citing the country's continued human rights failings.

Finally, there is the question of financial support from Brussels, which will facilitate many of the reforms sought. It is still unclear how much aid the EU will provide for civil society and human rights initiatives. Turkey has often felt short-changed compared to Eastern Europe, which has received EU monies through TACIS and PHARE, the largest of the pre-accession programs. In the entire pre-Helsinki period (1963–1999) the EU made some €4.25 billion in grants and loans to Turkey, about half of which supported the early financial protocols and the Customs Union, and only €4 million of which went to NGOs. Limited funds were devoted to democratization: €8 million for civil society programs, most in grants to municipalities, €120,000 for human rights initiatives, €35,000 for Reporters Sans Frontières work in Turkey, slightly more than €1 million for women's initiatives and work on gender equity, €621,000 to support local media, just over €1 million to strengthen civil society in urban communities, €250,000 to support the Turkish Democracy Foundation, €100,000 for civic education, and €20,000 for the "Hope Bus," a project aimed at inquiring into cases of the disappeared.[37]

EU financial commitments to Turkey have mushroomed on the heels of the Helsinki summit, though those funds, too, are conditional on Turkey's compliance with the Accession Partnership. The European Investment Bank (EIB) has slated €6.425 billion plus additional loans for Turkey for the period January 2000–January 2007. Turkey will also receive a portion of the EIB's pre-accession funds totaling €8.5 billion for the thirteen candidate countries. This is in addition to monies available through the auspices of the Euro-Mediterranean Partnership under MEDA II, which aims to expand trade as well as respect for human rights and democracy across the region. Only a small fraction of the money in each package is geared toward human rights projects. Again, the focus is on economics, with a new interest in high-end services and protection of commercial property rights, particularly intellectual property – the all important "content" of the information age – through the European Digital Content program.

Domestic politics and international linkages

Surveys show that about 70 percent of Turks favor EU membership, and orientation toward the EU has become one of the primary cleavages in Turkish politics. The country's most ardent Europhiles include business elites, liberal "salon" society, the moderate right wing comprising the Motherland (ANAP) and True Path (DYP) parties, and some Islamists, including the ascendant Justice and Development (AK) party, runaway winners of the November 2002 national elections, who see the EU as the path to "de-Kemalization" and hence greater religious freedom. Euroskeptics comprise elements of the army, nationalists in the Democratic Socialist Party (DSP), members of the extreme left as well as the extreme right, including much of the MHP, as well as some Islamists who see the embrace of Europe as an affront to Muslim culture and values. Splits over the EU are also reflected in civil society, where there are both Europhile and Euroskeptic NGOs, although one should note that all the leading Turkish labor unions and business organizations favor membership.[38] The Europhiles in particular have close allies in Europe. Given the importance of such transnational alliances, as hypothesized in Chapter 1, Turkey would appear to be a good target for democracy promotion by the EU.

Much of the conservative establishment in Turkey seems intent on democratizing within the context of the official ideology. While one might expect European identity to lead to European practice with regard to human rights, this has not always happened. Kemalist elites who identify most strongly with the European tradition – the military, the courts, and the civil service – historically have resisted liberal European mores. A number of recent court proceedings, including the case of several Kurdish mayors accused of giving quarter to terrorists, have pitted hardliners against pro-EU reformers. Similar skirmishes are taking place across the government. The military, while supporting EU membership, are deeply wary of the Copenhagen Criteria. Although the "advisory" role of the NSC is constitutionally mandated, its recommendations are not legally binding. Behind the scenes, the group wields coercive influence in virtually every area of public policy. The NSC reportedly has balked at EU measures related to citizenship, Kurdish rights, including language rights, and Turkish–Greek relations. Turkish Chief of Staff, General Huseyin Kivrikoğlu, has denounced EU states for harboring terrorists opposed to Turkey and has dredged up old Turkish fears of dismemberment by outside powers, hinting that the EU may have its sights set on an independent Kurdistan.[39] Turkey's agile Foreign Minister Ismail Cem has been careful to placate the pashas – immediately on return to Turkey from the Helsinki Summit he announced that the NSC retained a legitimate role in national politics. It must also be said that EU calls to curb the prerogatives of the NSC have gotten a mixed reception in Turkey. The military remains one of the most respected institutions in the country, and many Turks sleep better at night knowing that the army is prepared to rein in divisive forces in society.

Although the far-right MHP seems resigned to "becoming European" it hopes to do so without compromising Turkish interests or identity in a sprint for membership. Party leader Devlet Bahçeli sounds increasingly defensive in his claims that Europe is "planting mines" on Turkey's road to membership over Kurdish rights, foreign policy issues related to Cyprus and the Aegean, and even how the Armenian massacres are presented historically.[40] After Mesut Yilmaz, no liberal visionary himself, criticized Turkey's paranoid "National Security Syndrome," Bahçeli responded that according to Yilmaz's "warped mentality, Turkey should accept Greek Cypriot claims, recognize lies about [the Armenian] genocide and pay heed to separatist viewpoints."[41] MHP Deputy Chairman Adnan Uçaş has complained that European demands extend beyond the Copenhagen Criteria, and has called for a popular referendum on reforms. In February 2002, the MHP managed to stall Parliamentary discussion of Art. 312, and also blocked efforts to reform capital punishment laws and to loosen Kurdish language restrictions, although these measures did pass in August 2002.

There are exceptions to this kind of obstructionism. No one has done more to expose Turkey's human rights abuses than Sema Pişkinsüt, a center-left member of the Grand National Assembly, who from 1998–2000 chaired the Parliamentary Human Rights Investigation Committee. Her working group conducted interviews with thousands of prison inmates, finding widespread, routine torture. Snap inspections of police stations turned up an array of sadistic implements of torture. For her good works – which amounted to the first official acknowledgment of torture by the Turkish government – Pişkinsüt was fired and replaced with a more laissez-faire MHP deputy.

Pişkinsüt as well as other reformers inside and outside government have drawn increased support from abroad. There is some evidence of what has been identified as a "boomerang" pattern, in which activists whose efforts are stymied at home call on an international network of fellow travelers who then pressure their governments to intervene with the offending state.[42] Kurdish activists in Turkey are severely hampered, for example, but the large Kurdish diaspora in Western Europe has pressed officials there to take up the cause. Less successful have been visits to Turkey by European delegations to assess reforms (and, often, scold authorities). Such visits bolster dissidents but they also raise nationalist hackles, being seen by many Turks as moralistic and unappreciative of the challenges the country faces, particularly regarding Kurdish separatism.

A different dynamic has spurred Turkey's powerful business lobby to promote human rights. It is often thought that business leaders value political stability whatever the human cost. In Turkey, however, the new entrepreneurial class has become a leading voice for reform.[43] The Turkish Industrialists and Businessmen's Association, or TUSIAD, is by far the most influential pro-EU actor in Turkish politics and a key ally of Brussels, which, of course, is interested in liberal economics as well as liberal politics. The leverage the business community wields is enormous. In 2001, the EU accounted for 51.6 percent of Turkey's exports, and 44.6 percent of its imports.[44] Clout is massed in the hands of a few large family-run firms, almost all of whose top management have trained overseas and imbibed liberal norms. Captains of industry can afford to be free with their criticism, but they too are up against entrenched statists. In 1997 TUSIAD infuriated the NSC when it recommended radical liberalization of policies toward Kurds to allow linguistic and cultural freedom, but also the formation of political parties expressly to pursue Kurdish interests.[45] Even the irrepressible business magnate Sakıp Sabancı has been accused of promoting a dangerous "Basque Model" for Turkey.[46] Since 1999, TUSIAD has stepped up its agitation for reforms in line with the Copenhagen Criteria.[47] In September 2001, the group presented a sweeping package of civil liberties that was more detailed on some issues than the government's National Program. On the question of religious freedom, however, TUSIAD's views closely mirror those of the secular government, and TUSIAD played a behind-the-scenes role in the ouster of Erbakan in 1997.

The process of liberalization remains almost entirely in the hands of elites, who thrust and parry through the tangle of Turkey's bureaucracy. Administrative reforms are distant from institutionalization of norms, and the liberal message has been slow to filter through the apparatus of the state. Parliamentary debate in recent months has centered on freedoms related to the Kurdish language. At the same time, however, Turkish police reportedly have detained hundreds of people pressing for Kurdish to be taught in schools. Similarly, while restrictions on Kurdish-language broadcasting have been lifted, this may not be for the right reasons. The head of Turkish intelligence said that state-run Kurdish-language television broadcasts would be "useful" to counter subversive satellite propaganda.[48] Freedoms of expression are in similar flux. In February 2002, Fatih Taş, the Turkish publisher of Noam Chomsky's essays, was acquitted of charges of distributing anti-Turkish and separatist propaganda. Professor Chomsky, in Turkey to attend the trial, found himself under investigation by a State Security Court after he gave a speech in the southeastern Turkish city of Diyarbakir. Such contradictions are perhaps inevitable during a time of constitutional upheaval, but they also suggest the depth of Kemalist political culture.

Lest Turkish political culture and practice be essentialized into something monolithic and unchanging, one should be clear that important change is afoot. The war is all but over, therefore removing the impetus for the harshest laws and worst abuses. Despite the deep recession, economic liberalization continues. In the national elections of November 2002, the question of whether or not Turkey should join the EU was beyond debate, even if most party election platforms sidestepped concrete human rights issues. Virtually every party, including two new high-profile factions, Ismail Cem's "New Turkey" and Recep Erdoğan's AK Party, were decidedly pro-EU, albeit for many different reasons. The "Islamist-light" AK Party swept to victory, winning 34 percent of the vote, which under Turkey's election law will allow the party to form a government without a coalition partner. This despite the fact that Turkey's chief prosecutor Sabih Kanadoğlu moved to close the party just two weeks before the election – a gambit that prosecutors have used in the past to suppress voting for Kurdish parties. The only other party to cross the 10 percent threshold to gain seats in the Parliament was the center-left Republican People's Party, the staunchly secular, European-nationalist party of Atatürk. For EU democratizers the 2002 election poses an interesting challenge. EU officials met with AK leaders both before and after the elections stressing the virtues of liberal tolerance and respect for Turkey's secular tradition, both of which the Party has pledged to honor. The election may turn out to be a watershed for democratization. With voters roundly rejecting intense nationalists at both ends of the political spectrum, AKP can claim a mandate to liberalize from the center and to Europeanize within the framework of traditional values. Remaining curbs on religious freedom will surely fall. The new government can also be expected to continue liberalization of Kurdish rights. Days after the election, EU officials raised the possibility that, with the MHP no longer in a position to block it, the new government might amnesty many of the country's remaining political prisoners. On a more sober note, however, the European Commission's October 2002 decision to yet again defer setting a timetable for Turkish accession talks may play into the hands of Ankara's old guard and slow implementation of reforms.

On balance, however, the picture is a positive one. While liberal political norms are far from being institutionalized – further still from being "internalized" – the reach of the state over civil liberties is being seriously discussed. An extraordinary 74 percent of Turks are familiar with the Copenhagen Criteria.[49] Moreover, as political economist Ziya Öniş has argued, the accession process itself creates a "virtuous circle," where "the possibility of full membership provides the much needed discipline or the external anchor required to legitimize the reform process."[50] Most important is a growing sense among EU officials and member states that more will be achieved by inclusion than by exclusion. While a firm date remains elusive, a number of EU members favor setting a "conditional" date to open accession talks with Ankara. Greece, too, is edging closer to the idea that an engaged, politically and economically integrated Turkey will be more amenable to solutions over Cyprus and the Aegean than an embittered, excluded Turkey.

The challenge of promoting human rights from a distance

For most of the period under discussion the broad contours of human rights abuses in Turkey were unmoved by European pressure. Turkey has been, to invoke a term used in this volume, a "reluctant democratizer" par excellence. Rising and falling with urban violence, the PKK insurgency, and the extent of Islamic activism, human rights were cast in terms of domestic politics and perceived insecurities. Europe's human rights diplomacy was, until very recently, frankly anemic, relying on little in the way of either negative sanctions or positive inducements. Rhetoric aside, Brussels seemed almost averse to making political demands, perhaps believing that economic liberalization would eventually spur political reform. Before Helsinki, Turkish reform mirrored this half-hearted strategy. Measures taken were often less serious attempts to reform political norms than they were designed to silence specific criticisms or to fulfill minimal treaty obligations. Turkey has been willing to undertake political change in direct proportion to the size of the prize. Ankara made modest accommodations prior to entering the Customs Union, and now is attempting profound reforms on the road to full membership. Joining the EU has become a "national obsession," thus driving reforms.[51] If the credible prospect of membership has provided an anchor for liberalizers, accession itself should bring an enormous boon to civil liberties. Under the European umbrella Ankara may be more tolerant of diversity in its midst.

Notes

1 The author wishes to thank Paul Kubicek of Oakland University and Engin I. Erdem of the University of Virginia for their helpful criticisms.
2 Quoted in the Final Communiqué of the Helsinki European Council, December 1999.
3 For an overview of theoretical issues, see T. Dunne and N. J. Wheeler, eds, *Human Rights in Global Politics*, Cambridge: Cambridge University Press, 1999, and T. Risse, S. Ropp, and K. Sikkink, eds, *The Power of Human Rights*, Cambridge: Cambridge University Press, 1999.
4 M. H. Yavuz, "Turkey's Fault Lines and the Crisis of Kemalism," *Current History*, 99, January 2000, pp. 33–38, p. 34.
5 Quoted in A. Roberts, "Humanitarian War: Military Intervention and Human Rights," *International Affairs*, 69, 1993, pp. 429–449, p. 432.
6 Quoted in W. Hale and G. Avcı, "Turkey and the European Union: The Long Road to Membership," in B. Rubin and K. Kirişci, eds, *Turkey in World Politics: An Emerging Multiregional Power,* Boulder, CO: Lynne Rienner, 2001, pp. 31–47, p. 42.
7 *Freedom in the World Country Ratings, 1972–73 to 2000–01*, London: Freedom House, 2001. Available at [http://www.freedomhouse.org/ratings/index.htm]. There has been no shortage of monitors of human rights in Turkey. The human rights nadir during the war is described in *Turkey: No Security without Human Rights*, New York: Amnesty International, 1996, and US Congress Commission on Security and Cooperation in Europe, *The Continued Use of Torture in Turkey*, Washington, DC: US Government Printing Office, 1997. Recent accounts include *Turkey: Violations of Free Expression in Turkey*, New York: Human Rights Watch, 1999, and US Department of State, Bureau of Democracy, Human Rights, and Labor, *Country Reports on Human Rights Practices: Turkey,* Washington, DC: US Government Printing Office, 2001. The report can be accessed at http://www.state.gov/g/drl/hr/. Detailed monthly updates are available from the Human Rights Foundation of Turkey [http://www.tihv.org.tr].
8 See H. J. Barkey, "The Struggles of a 'Strong' State," *Journal of International Affairs*, 54, Fall 2000, pp. 87–106.
9 *Turkish Daily News*, September 8, 2001.
10 See *Turkey: Violations of Free Expression*, op. cit., pp. 111–122.
11 See C. Houston, *Islam, Kurds and the Turkish Nation State*, New York: Berg Publishers, 2001, p. 90.
12 See K. Kirişci and G. Winrow, *The Kurdish Question and Turkey: An Example of a Trans-State Ethnic Conflict*, London: Frank Cass, 1997; H. J. Barkey, G. Fuller, and M. Abramowitz, *Turkey's Kurdish Question*, London: Rowman & Littlefield,

1998; M. Gunter, *The Kurds and the Future of Turkey*, New York: Palgrave, 1997; and D. Ergil, "The Kurdish Question in Turkey," *Journal of Democracy*, 11, July 2000, pp. 122–135.

13 D. McDowall, *A Modern History of the Kurds*, rev. ed., London: I.B. Tauris, 1997, pp. 424–427.

14 Human Rights Foundation of Turkey (TIHV), Joint Press Release, May 31, 2001. http://www.tihv.org.tr/eindex.html, places the number of displaced at more than 3 million. See also McDowall, op. cit., p. 440.

15 See Houston, op. cit., p. 77; and J. Jongerden, "Resettlement and Reconstruction of Identity: The Case of the Kurds in Turkey," *Global Review of Ethnopolitics*, 1, September 2001, pp. 80–86.

16 See D. Şenol, "Copenhagen Criterion of Minority Rights: Is It Effective in Terms of Political Conditionality? The Case of Turkey," unpublished MSc thesis, London School of Economics, 2001, pp. 17–18.

17 For discussions of this earlier period, see M. Müftüler-Bac, *Turkey's Relations with a Changing Europe*, Manchester: Manchester University Press, 1997, chapter. 6; I. Daği, "Human Rights, Democratization and the European Community in Turkish Politics: The Özal Years, 1983–87," *Middle Eastern Studies*, 37, January 2001, pp. 17–40; and Z. Öniş, "Awkward Partnership: Turkey's Relations with the European Union in Comparative-Historical Perspective," *Journal of European Integration History*, 7, Spring 2001, pp. 105–119.

18 J. Fischer, "Statement on Behalf of the European Union at the 55th Session of the Commission of Human Rights," *Global Ratification Monitor*, April 12, 1999, available at http://www.stm.it/npwj/europe.htm

19 See S. Zanger, "Good Governance and European Aid: The Impact of Political Conditionality," *European Union Politics*, 1, October 2000, pp. 293–317. See also B. Brandtner and A. Rosas, "Human Rights and the External Relations of the European Community: An Analysis of Doctrine and Practice," *European Journal of International Law*, 9, 1998, pp. 468–490; G. Crawford, "Foreign Aid and Political Conditionality: Issues of Effectiveness and Consistency," *Democratization*, 4, Autumn 1997, pp. 69–108; and H. Grabbe, "European Union Conditionality and the Acquis Communautaire," *International Political Science Review/Revue internationale de science politique*, 23, July 2002, pp. 249–268.

20 See "The European Union and the External Dimension of Human Rights Policy: From Rome to Maastricht and Beyond," EU Communication 567 (1995).

21 See E. Riedel and M. Will, "Human Rights Clauses in External Agreements of the EC," in P. Alston, ed., *The EU and Human Rights*, New York: Oxford University Press, 1999, pp. 723–754.

22 See K. Smith, "The EU, Human Rights and Relations with Third Countries: 'Foreign Policy' with an Ethical Dimension," in K. Smith and M. Light, eds, *Ethics and Foreign Policy*, Cambridge: Cambridge University Press, 2001, pp. 185–203. The term "declaratory diplomacy" is Smith's (p. 186). See also K. Smith, "The Use of Political Conditionality in the EU's Relations with Third Countries: How Effective?" *European Foreign Affairs Review*, 3, Summer 1998, pp. 253–274; M. Nowak, "Human Rights 'Conditionality' in Relation to Entry to, and Full Participation in, the EU," in Alston, op. cit., pp. 687–698; D. Liñán Nogueras and L. Hinojosa Martínez, "Human Rights Conditionality in the External Trade of the European Union: Legal and Legitimacy Problems," *Columbia Journal of European Law*, 7, Fall 2001, pp. 307–336; and S. Engert, H. Knobel, and F.

Schimmelfennig, "European Organizations and the Governance of Non-Member States: Domestic Conditions of Success," paper prepared for the 4th IR Conference of the European Standing Group on International Relations, Canterbury, September 8–10, 2001 [www.ifs.tu-darmstadt.de/pg/regorgs/ecpr.doc].

23 Nowak, op. cit., pp. 692–693.

24 See P. Alston and J. H. H. Weiler, "An 'Ever Closer Union' in Need of a Human Rights Policy: The European Union and Human Rights," in Alston, op. cit., pp. 3–66.

25 M. Fowels, "The European Union's Foreign and Security Policy and Human Rights," *Netherlands Quarterly of Human Rights*, 17, 1997, p. 294, quoted in Nowak, op. cit., p. 688.

26 See Z. Öniş "Luxembourg, Helsinki and Beyond: Towards an Interpretation of Recent Turkey–EU Relations," *Government and Opposition*, 35, Autumn 2000, pp. 463–483. See also M. Müftlüler-Bac, "The Impact of the European Union on Turkish Politics," *East European Quarterly*, 34, Summer 2000, pp. 159–179; A. Gunduz, "Human Rights and Turkey's Future in Europe," *Orbis*, 45, Winter 2001, pp. 15–30; B. Duner and E. Deverell, "Country Cousin: Turkey, the European Union and Human Rights," *Turkish Studies*, 2, Spring 2001, pp. 1–24; G. Avcı, "Putting the Turkish EU Candidacy into Context," *European Foreign Affairs Review*, 7, 2002, pp. 91–110; Ersel Aydinli and Dov Waxman, "A Dream Become Nightmare? Turkey's Entry into the European Union," *Current History*, 100, November 2001, pp. 381–388; and Saban Kardas, "Human Rights and Democracy Promotion: The Case of Turkey–EU Relations," *Alternatives: Turkish Journal of International Relations*, 1, Fall 2002 [http://www.alternativesjournal.com/kardas.htm].

27 Hale and Avcı, op. cit., p. 41.

28 See H. Kramer, *A Changing Turkey: The Challenge to Europe and the United States*, Washington, DC: Brookings Institution Press, 2000, p. 192.

29 For a detailed discussion of events at Luxembourg, see W. Park, "Turkey's European Union Candidacy: From Luxembourg to Helsinki – to Ankara?" *Mediterranean Politics*, 5, Autumn 2000, pp. 31–53.

30 Quoted in L. Hockstader, "EU Rejection Provokes Anger, Outrage in Turkey," *Washington Post*, December 14, 1997, p. A28.

31 Park, op. cit., p. 43.

32 Quoted in Müftlüler-Bac, *Turkey's Relations with a Changing Europe*, p. 87.

33 See Decision 2001/235/EC (8 March 2001).

34 See Commission of the European Communities, *2001 Regular Report on Turkey's Progress Towards Accession,* SEC(2001)1756 [www.mfa.gov.tr/grupa/ad/adc/2001.Regular.Report.pdf].

35 See Human Rights Watch, "Human Rights Watch Analysis of the 2001 Regular Report on Turkey," December 2001 [http://hrw.org/backgrounder/eca/turkey-analysis.htm].

36 *New York Times*, August 4, 2002, p. A10.

37 All figures are from the Representation of the European Commission to Turkey.

38 See Duner and Deverell, op. cit., pp. 6–7.

39 A bleak view is S. Ciftci, "Turkey and the European Union: Heading for a Break?," CSIS Turkey Project, March 8, 2002 [http://www.csis.org/turkey/TU020308.htm]. The fear of dismemberment is often traced to the 1920 Treaty of Sèvres, which, had Atatürk not overthrown it, would have resulted in a much

diminished Turkish Republic. This worry that outsiders are plotting to divide the country has been tagged the "Sèvres Syndrome," and is a staple of old-school Turkish nationalist discourse.

40 D. Frantz, "Some Turks See Minefield in Europe," *New York Times*, November 30, 2001, p. A18.

41 *Turkish Daily News*, August 7, 2001.

42 See M. Keck and K. Sikkink, *Activists beyond Borders: Advocacy Networks in International Politics*, Ithaca, NY: Cornell University Press, 1998.

43 See Z. Öniş and U. Türem, "Business, Globalization and Democracy: A Comparative Analysis of Turkish Business," *Journal of Turkish Studies*, 2, Fall 2001, pp. 94–120.

44 Data from the Economist Intelligence Unit [http://www.economist.com].

45 See B. Tanör, *Perspectives on Democratisation in Turkey*, Istanbul: TUSIAD, 1997.

46 See Kirişci and Winrow, *The Kurdish Question and Turkey*, p. 150.

47 TUSIAD, *Turkiye'de Demokratiklesme Perspekrifleri ve AB Kopenhag Siyasal Kriterleri*, Istanbul: TUSIAD, 2001.

48 NTV television broadcast, November 28, 2000.

49 *Turkish Daily News,* August 2, 2000.

50 Z. Öniş, "Turkey, Europe, and the Paradoxes of Identity," *Mediterranean Quarterly*, 10, 1999, pp. 107–136, p. 120.

51 Ü. Özdaş, Center for Eurasian Strategic Studies, quoted in *New York Times*, August 4, 2002, p. A10.

6 The European Union and Croatia

Negotiating "Europeanization" amid national, regional, and international interests

Stephen M. Tull[1]

The 1990s in Europe were marked by the parallel processes of the consolidation and growth of the European Union/Community on the one hand, and the violent breakup and messy succession of the Socialist Federal Republic of Yugoslavia (SFRJ) on the other. The European Union and other regional and international organizations strongly influenced developments in the former SFRJ, but the cost was high and the lessons learned were two-way. Amid all the problems associated with the breakup of Yugoslavia, the democratization agenda of the EU was often lost, and leaders of Yugoslav successor states justified their failure to adhere to democratic norms referring to the exigencies of war and the need to protect the state.

This chapter will focus on Croatia's seeming reluctance to democratize, or more precisely, to embrace European regional and international standards, principles, and timetables of reform. Croatia may stand as the former Yugoslav republic most influenced by the EU, Council of Europe, and OSCE, but it also is clearly torn between the allure of European prosperity and the guardianship of newly gained nation-state sovereignty. During the ten-year rule of President Franjo Tudjman, the assertion of sovereignty clearly manifested itself in a reluctance to democratize. The liberal-coalition government that gained power in 2000 through elections after Tudjman's death in December 1999 has dismantled some of the roadblocks to reform but still is constrained by domestic agendas that do not always correspond with EU objectives. Thus, as in other cases of "reluctant democratizers," the EU has struggled to find a way to insert itself in a positive manner into sensitive domestic matters, hoping that its influence – both moral and, in Croatia's case, with an implicit use of conditionality – would further democratic practices.

Limited IR research on the breakup of Yugoslavia

Most of the scholarly (and non-scholarly) work on the breakup of the SFRJ has been primarily concerned with domestic forces and dynamics rather than the international factors and consequences. The main theme has been to document and account for the "hysteria" of contemporary South Slavic nationalism, juxtaposed at times to the integrationist tendency among the core European actors. Some notable exceptions include the works of Susan Woodward[2] and Richard Ullman,[3] as well as a body of literature mentioning mostly bilateral interventions in the post-Cold War environment. Timothy Garton Ash's work of course also plays out the juxtaposition of Balkan nationalism and other countries' domestic agendas to European integration in a sustained, provocative discourse.[4]

The reason for the initial focus in the literature on the politics of SFRJ and its former constituent republics is clear. The violent breakup of Yugoslavia presented a puzzle. In the euphoria of the times, post-1989, "when people throughout Eastern Europe were still celebrating their unexpected extraction from a failed communism with hope and enthusiasm, it seemed to many that two main tasks lay ahead. These were to create democracy and to marketize the economy."[5] Democratization was a "good thing" and it was easy to be caught up in freedom fever. One possible reason for the relative lack of concern about what would come next was that "nation-building" was considered an unavoidable, usually benign, part of modernization and democratization. Liah Greenfeld's book on "liberal nationalism" describes the functional role nationalism can play toward nation-state consolidation.[6] Her thesis is typical of much conventional thinking about nationalism (especially in late twentieth-century Europe), derived from the historical experience of Western Europe. The violence in former Yugoslavia, however, showed a form of nationalism that impeded democratization and contradicted certain assumptions about modernization. The study of nationalism was re-energized, becoming the main focus for Balkan scholars. At the same time, however, developments on the ground in the region began to make the former Yugoslavia an "outlier" among post-communist states that were moving ahead in a more predictable manner foreseen in the "transitions" literature.[7] Yugoslav "exceptionalism" thus relegated scholars of the region to a different track than those focusing on more "successful" or "normal" cases of democratic transition, a track that was a bit peripherally concerned with how international factors affected domestic developments.

In addition to the intellectual challenge of sorting out the internal dynamics, there may be two other, rather pragmatic explanations for the relative scarcity of international-institutional analyses. First, it has been possible for analysts only to scratch the surface of the international dynamics. The respective roles of regional and international organizations and other actors in former Yugoslavia through the 1990s composed perhaps the most complex international intervention in any conflict area ever. Virtually the whole array of regional and international organizations became and remained active in assistance and diplomatic interventions in this region over this decade. Further, their member states launched bilateral initiatives that were often quite substantive and expansive – this resulted in some confusion during the 1999 Kosovo crisis but also in the Croatian and Bosnian wars. Given this crowded playing field, it will simply take time for scholars to pull together and weigh the conclusions of many lessons-learned studies and a few IR theses that have been undertaken on the activities of specific players.

A second pragmatic issue is that the indigenous scholarship which might be expected to capture best the dynamics of change and give a crucial, contextualized perspective to international involvement has been largely handicapped by the political and economic constraints of the drawn-out transitional period. There have been good articles and books by local scholars, published domestically and in some cases internationally, but they have been neither as prolific nor as critical as one would hope.[8] We should expect a flourishing domestic scholarship as time and relative stability in the region allows a revival of normal academic study.

However, one might note that the lack of focus on the interplay between international and domestic politics is not unique to studies of this region. Geoffrey Pridham suggests that the skewing of literature toward the domestic dynamics is not uncommon.

> The international context is the forgotten dimension of regime transition. . . . This is partly due to the absence of adequate analytical tools and also problems of evidence. . . . Moreover, it cannot avoid the wider problem of different disciplinary approaches and lack of cooperation between them . . . [as well as] the problem of the disciplinary divide between international affairs and comparative politics.[9]

Recognizing the above caveats, this chapter attempts to identify a few areas in which one could delve into the impact of European integration and expansion in the former Yugoslavia, in particular in Croatia. I will touch briefly on other former Yugoslav republics here only to the extent of highlighting common tendencies or indicating what seemingly are fundamentally different relationships to "Europe." Like the other studies in this volume, then, this chapter does not attempt to even recount the whole range of involvement by international and regional organizations. While it may be impossible to test definitively hypotheses about what worked and what did not, some lessons do become clear. For example the Croatian case underscores an important point: how difficult it can be to find a foothold for democratization programs in societies undergoing major upheaval. Moreover, in line with some other works in this volume, it calls into question the effectiveness of relying upon more passive strategies of democratic convergence and therefore recommends the carrot and stick approach when EU democratization assistance is provided.

The Europeanization of Croatia

The EU/EC certainly played an important role in Croatia even beginning before the breakup of the SFRJ, thanks to the hope of a better life "in

Europe" which helped consolidate both the movement for party pluralism and the related independence movement. The nearness of Western Europe gave Yugoslavs a clear vision of what could be – a reminder of what had been in days of Yugoslavia's consumerist glory in the 1970s. An observation by Tonci Kuzmanic about Slovenian politics certainly held true for Croatia and to varying degrees also for the rest of former SFRJ. Kuzmanic writes:

> The Slovene decision to leave the former Yugoslavia was based on the calculation, atmosphere and emotions of rejoining Europe . . . [T]he disintegration of Yugoslavia meant, for Slovenes, "escaping from the Balkans." In this ideological context the East meant totalitarianism, militarism, Stalinism, while the West meant God, democracy, non-violence, freedom. During the 1980s, especially at the end of the decade, "escaping" from the East was perceived as the same as running directly to the West. . . . [When the war began in 1991, the] Slovenes, whose anti-Yugoslav feelings and attitudes were strongest . . . expected concrete help from their "allies," especially those in Western Europe. . . . The "average" Slovene thought that Europeans were simply waiting for their beloved Slovenes to join their democratic and affluent society.[10]

The European dream, however, would prove to be a double-edged sword. Attraction to promises of prosperity unfortunately fueled the ethnic mobilization of nationalist politics throughout SFRJ, and it did not stop the war. However, one could argue that the European vision may also have helped constrain the destructiveness of the conflict as it developed. Perhaps even the most vicious military commanders – at some stage – must have paused to wonder if leveling a city like Vukovar or destroying a cultural monument like Dubrovnik really was in line with their dreams of Europe. Even the official and unofficial security forces that committed war crimes were inclined to hide their crimes from the ever-present reporters and cameras, UN and EC/EU officials, and foreign diplomats. In balance, though, the presence of "Europe," as both an idea and as a political actor, was not enough to prevent monstrous atrocities, let alone push for democratization within most Yugoslav successor states.[11] In general, the performance of the Europeans left much to be desired because it lacked teeth. Again citing Kuzmanic, "the role of Europe in the war in the former Yugoslavia has been improvised, unstudied and modest."[12]

This was not how things were supposed to be. Timothy Garton Ash opens his book *History of the Present* (2000) on the development of "Europeanness" through the 1990s with the following lines: "Even at one minute past midnight on 1 January 1990 we already knew that this would be a formative decade in Europe. A forty-year-old European order had just collapsed with the Berlin Wall. Everything seemed possible. Everyone was hailing a 'new Europe.' But no one knew what it would look like."[13] Even when fighting in the Balkans did break out, there was still palpable optimism: it would be "Europe's hour" in a famous statement by Luxemburg Foreign Minister Jacques Poos.[14] However, that statement would later be ridiculed. In a later chapter on Bosnia and Hercegovina, *circa* November 1995, Ash expresses the bitterness toward Europe felt by many citizens in former Yugoslavia when the European dream evaded (or worse, betrayed) them.[15] He proposes that the idea of progressive Europe, which thrived in Western Europe and largely instigated the popular rejection of communism in Eastern Europe, reached its apogee in 1989. During the 1990s, Europe was thrown back into its "barbaric" past, featuring war and human atrocities in much of former Yugoslavia.

As the wars in Croatia and Bosnia and Hercegovina festered for the first half of the decade, Europe failed. Its "hour" turned into years of disaster for millions of Europeans. The European Community and its member states did not speak with one voice on the original issue of the breakup of Yugoslavia through unilateral secession of constituent republics. As the conflicts progressed, Europe was unable to stop the fighting and its monitors were ridiculed as "ice cream men," thanks to the unfortunate choice of bright white uniforms and their reputation for inefficacy. In both Croatia and Bosnia and Hercegovina, the EU had to cede the leading diplomatic role to the United Nations and the Contact Group (USA, Russian Federation, France, Britain, and Germany).

From the perspective of pro-EU forces, the most important part of the explanation for this failure is that Europe per se was not ready for the challenges of the 1990s. The wars in the former Yugoslavia were not foreseen, and institutionally Europe did not have the capacity or the will to stop them with military forces. The EU was also busy getting ready for the opening of the Common Market in 1992, and working on other intra-EU issues that would be laid out in the Maastricht Treaty. Of course, another element is the domestic side of the equation in the Balkan states. The dominant internal forces in SFRJ were on a collision course by early 1991 (probably at least a year before that), and many were eager for war to have a "settling of accounts." In this environment, incentives to peace and offers to mediate from European (and American) officials could not receive a fair hearing.

However, one would be remiss to focus solely on the negatives. To the credit of the European leaders, the EU weathered the storm. The persistence of the *telos* of the European Union and the pragmatic steps toward this union throughout the 1990s combined to leave a much more capable Europe in the latter half of the decade, and one that does represent a "liberal order" today. Europe and Croatia may have had a troubled relationship through this period, but the relationship continued and developed in important and constructive ways, giving hope that the project of Europeanization in Croatia will now move very quickly.

Material European assistance to Croatia, 1991–2002

In the decade following the 1991 outbreak of the wars for Yugoslavian succession, EU programs allocated over €367 million in emergency and recovery assistance to Croatia alone, of which €292 million was in the form of humanitarian assistance provided through ECHO (the European Community Humanitarian Office). Most of the rest of the EU assistance was reconstruction and technical assistance (mainly through Obnova) intended to relieve suffering and facilitate returns by displaced persons.[16] Other sorts of programs were stunted, generally as a reflection of EU displeasure with the Tudjman/HDZ (Movement for Democratic Croatia) leadership over political and rule-of-law issues. Croatian President Tudjman was seen as unbending in regards to Croatian sovereignty and ethnopolitical rights, and this tainted his relations with the EU and more widely in the international community. Throughout his presidency, Tudjman refused to acknowledge Croatian culpability for ethnic cleansing of Serbs within Croatia, and he denied that Croatia perpetuated or benefited from instability in Bosnia and Hercegovina. He also reneged on promises to guarantee equal treatment to ethnic-minority Croatian citizens. Further, his autocratic style and prioritization of homeland defense over all reform issues left few areas for democratization to take root. He welcomed EU and other international assistance, but he insisted upon taking it on his own terms. True, there were elections, but given all the advantages enjoyed by the HDZ and the tactics of Tudjman and his allies, democracy did not go very deep.

In the mid-1990s, the EU reoriented its assistance strategy to Croatia and its neighbors in order to encourage mutual recognition of states and to remove obstacles to the return of refugees and internally displaced persons (IDPs). Its reasoning was that these would be the preconditions to peace and stability, so real progress in such regional matters would be needed to complement national programs. The EU/EC had always taken a regional approach to the Balkans, but formalized it as the basis of many subsequent EU assistance programs, beginning with a report of the Commission to the Council in 1996.[17] The EU Council of Ministers further endorsed this regional approach in 1997 in conjunction with its plan to place tighter political and economic conditions for the development of relations with the Balkan states to shape them for eventual EU membership.[18]

In line with its regional approach, the European Commission (EC) proposed the Stabilization and Association Agreement (SAA) process for Croatia in May 1999, together with Albania, Bosnia and Hercegovina, the former Yugoslav Republic of Macedonia, and the Federal Republic of Yugoslavia. This was part of a new momentum to achieve stability in the region, and clearly linked to the adoption of the Stability Pact for Southeastern Europe in June 1999. The basic strategic goal of the Stability Pact was/is to bring about stability in the region through drawing the countries of the region closer to the Euro-Atlantic structures and strengthening regional cooperation. Full participation by the governments in the region through ownership of actual projects (and national plans) was a central tenet.

However, not much headway was made on the SAA under Tudjman, who delayed or watered down efforts to liberalize the Croatian political system.

Only after his death in December 1999 and the establishment of the post-Tudjman, social democrat/liberal coalition government were prospects for fulfilling the aims of the SAA bolstered. The new government issued its Working Program in February 2000, which included its new commitment to domestic reform as part of a constructive relationship with the EU. It states:

> Within the process of European integration, the strategic goal of the Republic of Croatia is as soon as possible, to establish contractual relations with the European Union through the Stabilisation and Association Agreement. Pursuant to the Agreement, the Republic of Croatia ought to become an associate member of the European Union, and that would be the most important step towards full membership in the European Union. In order to achieve this goal, political and technical dialogue with the European Union will be intensified at all levels. However, there are still a number of conditions and criteria to be met in the fields of economy, democracy and civil society, and regional stability and cooperation.[19]

Work on the SAA process intensified in spring 2000, and finally Croatia and the European Commission initialed a Stabilization and Association Agreement in Brussels in May 2001.[20] The Agreement was signed and ratified on both sides by December 2001. At the same time, the EU announced its new five-year assistance strategy for Croatia, in line with the Stabilization and Association process. This strategy set forward the following priorities: democratic stabilization, economic and social development, justice and internal affairs, and legal and administrative reform.[21] The bulk of assistance 2002–2006 is to be provided through the CARDS (Community Assistance for Reconstruction, Development, and Stabilization) program. Facilitation of refugee and displaced persons return remains one of the major aspects of the CARDS budget, but this is dwarfed by programs to enable Croatia's institutional reform and economic development needed for European integration.

While these agreements are signal achievements, it is worth noting that the conclusion of this Association Agreement was years after similar agreements had been signed with the more fortunate Central European countries. Had there been no war, there is little doubt that Croatia would join Slovenia at the front of the queue for EU membership. As matters stand, Croatia missed out on the possibility of inclusion in the EU at the 1997 Luxemburg Summit and the 1999 Helsinki Summit, and at present it ranks with Macedonia and Albania as hopeful candidates who have yet to receive an invitation to submit a membership bid. True, such an invitation may be forthcoming, but the fact remains that the failures in the 1990s of both the Croatian leadership and EU diplomacy have set back and protracted Croatia's transition to democratic governance.

European diplomacy during the war

It bears repeating that one of the obvious differences between the case of Croatia and of those countries in the rest of this volume is that Croatia was a republic/country at war, and then recovering from that war, during the time period under consideration. As already mentioned, the whole concept of Europeanization and the package of material assistance offered by the European Union/Community in the 1990s were colored by this fact. It is, therefore, necessary to return to the war and to consider the diplomatic and other interventions by Europe at the beginning. This will lend perspective not only to the evaluation of what was possible by way of outside influence on Croatia, but also as a reminder that this was before the Maastricht Treaty (or "Treaty on the European Union"). Europe was only then negotiating the guidelines for its common foreign and security policy.

To recap, very quickly, here is a timeline of main events:

- Croatia and especially Slovenia become "breakaway republics" already in 1989–1990, taking an increasingly defiant posture against the federal government and Serbia.
- Franjo Tudjman and his HDZ party win the first multiparty elections in Croatia in April 1990; their basic campaign platform is the demand for "the right of the Croatian nation to self-determination and state sovereignty."[22]
- February 1991, Slovenia announces the process of dissolution of SFRJ has begun; Croatia supports the Slovenian proposal for mutually agreed disunion (ostensibly for a new confederation).
- March–June 1991, small-scale conflicts erupt between Serbs and police in Croatia; European Community officials make inconsistent interventions in SFRJ, first defending in principle the right of Yugoslav republics and provinces to self-determination, then attempting to discourage unilateral declarations of independence.
- May–June 1991, EC and USA step up efforts to encourage a last minute compromise between Slovenian/Croatia and SFRJ/Serbia; EC sends a high-level delegation offering SFRJ an association agreement and $4 billion in aid, then in late June, EC foreign ministers and the US Secretary of State deliver the same message that they will recognize only a peaceful agreement as to the future of Yugoslavia and its constituent republics.
- June 25–26, 1991, the parliaments of Croatia and Slovenia declare sovereign and independent republics; the wars begin.
- From July 1991, the European Community and Conference on Security and Cooperation in Europe take the lead in international efforts to contain the conflict; the EC establishes the Conference on Yugoslavia in late August but consistent efforts by the EC and UN to broker a ceasefire fail.

- Fall 1991, the UN imposes an arms embargo on SFRJ; European public opinion strongly supports self-determination for the Yugoslav republics and the EC bends to German pressure to support bids for recognition by the Yugoslav republics.
- November 1991, Vukovar falls to the Yugoslav Army and Dubrovnik remains under siege.
- December 16–18, 1991, an EC summit decides to grant collective recognition to Yugoslav successor states on January 15, 1992 under specified conditions; Germany announces its immediate recognition of Croatia and Slovenia.

The ceasefire that finally fulfilled the conditions for deployment of a United Nations peacekeeping force was signed on January 3, 1992. However, the territory captured by Serb forces and the Yugoslav Army remained out of Croatian state control until 1995 (Croatian offensives against former UN Protected Areas (UNPA) Sectors North, South, and West) and 1997 (UN Transitional Authority for Eastern Slavonia (UNTAES) mission in former Sector East ended). Additionally, the war in Bosnia and Hercegovina, entailing a large Croatian involvement, officially began only in April 1992 and continued through 1995. For these reasons, the Croatian war did not really cease in January 1992, but the primal question of Croatian statehood had been answered.

As can be seen in the timeline of key events of 1991, the European Community and its member states played a central role in the war over Croatian independence. Three days after the Croatian and Slovenian independence declarations in June, the European Council issued a statement calling for a three-month moratorium on further steps to implement their independence. This was formalized in the 8 July common declaration at Brioni that ended the Slovenian war. However, at this stage, the fact that the EC did not completely discredit the declarations of independence was not lost on the Croats and Slovenes, nor on others contemplating secession from SFRJ at that stage. According to one observer:

> The door was left open. . . . The moratorium statement was a compromise provision, behind which lay deep divisions within the EC on the question of recognition of the seceding republics. This division reflected a conflict between international law principles relating to self-determination, on the one hand, and that of territorial integrity of existing states, on the other.[23]

Germany and Belgium leaned toward self-determination while France and Spain favored federal Yugoslavia. This was the beginning of a series of public indications of disagreement within the EC regarding the question of recognition. Rather early in the fall of 1991, it was obvious that the pro-recognition faction led by Germany was winning.

When the EC established the Conference on Yugoslavia in August, the objective was clearly to manage the dissolution of Yugoslavia. British Foreign Secretary Lord Peter Carrington chaired the Conference, and he consistently aimed at facilitating a peacefully agreed settlement acceptable to all republics. He generally favored a loose association among the republics as the ultimate result, and he stressed that there should be no change of borders by force (which effectively ruled out the division of Bosnia between Serbia and Croatia).

One significant initiative of the Conference was to set up the Badinter Commission to arbitrate applications for recognition. When Croatia submitted its application, the Badinter Commission initially recommended against recognition because of insufficient constitutional provisions relating to minorities. The question of minorities, especially ethnic Serbs, was one of the continual litmus tests of Croatia's dedication to democratization and the rule of law. Under pressure from the EC, the Croatian government adopted a draft "Constitutional Law on Human Rights and Liberties, and on the Rights of Ethnic and National Communities or Minorities" in late November 1991. In the Government communique announcing its adoption, however, it was emphasized that the law would come into effect only "from the establishment of a full and lasting peace on the entire territory of the Republic of Croatia." Some of the key officials working on the draft told the media that the purpose of the bill was equally to protect ethnic Croats in areas where they are a local minority as it was to protect Croatian Serbs. There was evidently little that outside pressure could do to fundamentally change the perspective of Tudjman's top officials when it came to questions of the independence and ethno-national character of the Croatian state.[24] The Badinter Commission's reactions to Croatia's application for independence turned out to be irrelevant when Germany forced the issue of recognition without conditions.

Referring not only to Croatia, but to Slovenia and especially Bosnia and Hercegovina as well, Stanley Hoffmann gives the Europeans rather bad marks for their performance in managing the crisis of Yugoslav succession. He sees: (a) very little preventive diplomacy to stop the first fissiparous tendencies; (b) they were split by the choice of principles between maintaining territorial integrity and recognizing the right to self-determination; (c) they were split on the question of recognition and the conditions allowing it; and (d) no European country was ready to use force.[25] While his scorecard is essentially sound, it is only fair to recall the circumstances. To start with, the EC members' attention in early 1991 was focused on negotiations of the Maastricht Treaty, and only in the course of the year did they work out the most elemental foundation to the common foreign and security policy. Moreover, the war in Croatia and violent collapse of SFRJ, once it began, left little room for outside intervention aside from damage control or conflict management/containment. The European Community's hesitancy to commit itself to more robust intervention might have been prudent. Richard Ullman argues just this point, taking the reluctance of statesmen in the 1990s as an improvement over the great-power rivalries over the Balkans as recently as the 1970s. He writes:

> If the EU had been able to speak with one voice in dealing with non-member states, if the goal of a common foreign and security policy had become reality, and above all if that policy were one that diverted large quantities of resources into an economic program for Yugoslavia, dissolution and disaster might have been averted. . . . To assume such behavior [including threatening military intervention] on the part of the west Europeans or the Americans is to underline just how improbable anything like it would have been. This is especially true regarding measures that might have averted the disintegration of the Yugoslav federation. Given all the other demands on the separate European governments and publics, and on the common institution of the European Community (EC) – as it then was – why should they have made significant concessions to Yugoslavia?[26]

Ullman goes on to say that hindsight on the calamitous wars resulting from the collapse of Yugoslavia indeed does justify paying almost any price to avert it. But his point is that the decision-makers of the time were being pragmatic and responding with reasoned measures under imperfect knowledge of how things would develop.

Another observation to bear in mind is that it was much more difficult in 1990–1991 to know on which side to intervene in the Croatian independence struggle. Certainly the hindsight of today, when the leading proponent of the federal option (Milošević) is indicted and on trial in The Hague, makes it easier to support Croatia. However, it should not be forgotten that Tudjman's nationalist ideology and authoritarian leadership style raised concerns at the time among many within Yugoslavia and abroad. Warren Zimmermann directly compares the two, Milošević and Tudjman, and gives only a backhanded compliment to Tudjman:

> Tudjman is obsessed by nationalism. His devotion to Croatia is of the most narrow-minded sort, and he has never shown much understanding of or interest in democratic values. . . . Tudjman's saving grace, which distinguishes him from Milošević, is that he really wants to be a Western statesman. He therefore listens to Western expressions of concern and criticism and often does something about them.[27]

While Tudjman was explicit and unapologetic about his nationalism, Milošević called out his nationalist banners only for instrumental purposes. In fact, in stark contrast to the HDZ program in Croatia, the November 1990 election platform of Milošević's Socialist Party of Serbia was the European dream:

The Socialist Party is the right choice for those: 1) who want to live in peace and not in national hatred and national conflicts; 2) who want a brighter tomorrow for their children, instead of uncertainty and the threat of a fratricidal war; 3) who want to live well on the fruits of their labor; 4) who in the freedom of others find the condition for their own freedom; 5) who are for democratic dialogue and tolerance; 6) who expect their society to help them when they need it; 7) who are for the values of the progressive Europe, for joining the most progressive socialist forces.[28]

In this milieu and with such Balkan leaders as Milošević and Tudjman, it was an unenviable challenge to the leadership in the European Community and the wider international community to pick the champion of – or put forth the best strategy to assist – democratization. Perhaps, this is why the United States took the prerogative of leaving the Yugoslav crisis to the Europeans (and the United Nations) at precisely the crucial period for deciding on the question of recognition of Croatia and Slovenia.[29]

The balance on EU performance

In Chapter 1, Kubicek poses the question of "Have EU efforts paid off?" He observes that on balance the literature credits the EU (then the EC) with some success in democratic transition and consolidation in Southern Europe (Greece, Portugal, and Spain), but then qualifies this with questions of causality.[30] The counterpoint is that many factors (internal and external) converged to affect democratization in those countries. One could echo his contention that the "EC served as a guardrail for states that were already intent upon traveling the road of democratization."[31] This point is perhaps even more pertinent to the study of the EU's influence on "reluctant democratizers," such as Croatia in the 1990s, where the stakes of state politics may have been exaggerated by extraordinary conditions. The main question in such cases is what are the potential and limits of external agents and international norms in contributing to democratization efforts? There are two issues that must be addressed to answer this question. The first is whether the EU has the capacity and will to project its influence and thus assist in democratization. The second is what other forces (internal/domestic to the democratizing country and from other external actors) are at work and how.

So far as the capacity and will of the EU goes in the case of Croatia, this has evolved from a very low starting point to quite a strong array of options in the past decade. A recent International Crisis Group report details the progress made in these ten years since Maastricht.[32] Nina Graeger similarly highlights EU institutional practices during the 1990s that have now set the stage for the EU to play a greater role in conflict prevention and management (citing, e.g., conditioned assistance deals such as the Stabilization and

Association Agreements, the EU Monitoring Mission, civilian police, and the idea of a European Rapid Reaction Force).[33] One might also add the various EC/EU negotiators and representatives who played a crucial role during and after the wars in Croatia and Bosnia and Hercegovina, and more recently in the former Yugoslav Republic of Macedonia. The EU (through the EC, European Bank for Reconstruction and Development, the European Agency for Reconstruction, and in Kosovo as the head of a pillar in the integrated UN mission) also has demonstrated its competence for leading reconstruction planning and material support.

One must not, however, forget the other side of the coin. I believe that as important as the international forces were in Croatia, domestic factors related to political interests and values (including elite leadership and salient cleavages and alliances) were more crucial in determining the pace of the country's "Europeanization."

In weighing domestic responsiveness to external forces in the case of a reluctant democratizer, one must be careful to give due credit to the real political calculations domestic leaders must make. In the case of Croatia under President Tudjman, the rejection of some of the demands and conditions placed by the EU and international community was not solely for ideological reasons. Even though he was driven by his nationalist vision, Tudjman considered his project one of democratization and Europeanization, and he was consequently receptive to suggestions and even more to forceful inputs.[34] However, there were often too many high-cost demands (e.g. guaranteed rights to non-ethnic Croats) by the EU, the UN, and other external actors. Certainly according to his calculation of the risks facing his regime, ethnic nation, and new state, Tudjman could not uncritically follow every proposed step to democratization. Given his vision, therefore, one wonders what the EU could have done to set up incentives to change his mind and push forward a democratic, liberalizing agenda.

Strictly in terms of applicability of the ideal mechanisms for EU influence cited by Kubicek, contagion and convergence hold some meaning so far as the almost mythical attraction of "Europe" (or Western Europe) for the region's population. Public opinion surveys conducted for the Croatian Ministry for European Integration over the past two and a half years find a rather strong knowledge of the EU and a generally positive disposition toward it.[35] However, in not-yet-democratic societies, the sentiment affected by these mechanisms is often marginalized from the key political processes. Moreover, one could argue that average citizens as well as state leaders could not (or did not want to) connect the dots between domestic democratization and EU assistance and/or membership. That is, convergence would not occur given the conflicts Europe had with a nationalizing agenda – an agenda which would always have priority in the HDZ leadership. Rather than relying upon more passive notions of contagion or convergence, it was clear that Croatia would have to be prodded if there would be any hope of domestic political liberalization.

Therefore, I would find conditionality to be a much more promising tool in principle. To return to Kubicek's "guardrail" metaphor, EU conditionality places a very high and strong guardrail along the bumpy, winding road facing the new Balkan states. The carrot and stick (both very big, please) approach has been the only consistent tactic for getting compliance with European standards of democratization in former Yugoslavia. But because of circumstances in much of the region (namely that carrying a big stick requires substantial resources and runs high risks), it has sometimes been hard to apply this approach. It seems that only in recent years, particularly after the 1995 Dayton Accord that ended fighting in Bosnia and hostilities between Croatia and Serbia, has conditionality become a practical tool that can be applied in the context of normal EU relations with Croatia, Serbia and Montenegro, Bosnia and Hercegovina, and the other states of the region that will one day vie for EU membership.

Kubicek notes that the EU can only "underwrite" democracy but cannot impose it on non-member states.[36] However, the institutional experiments by the EU in supporting transitional administrations and broad international peace and stabilization initiatives in the Balkans have provided some models for greater direct EU control on democratization/conditionality. This is particularly the case in the EU pillar in the integrated UN mission in Kosovo, in the EC's co-sponsorship with the World Bank of major recovery and development assistance coordination region wide, and in various EU-supported functions in post-Dayton Bosnia and Hercegovina. Classifying and evaluating these various instruments will be a fruitful area for policy development and academic research in the future.

Notwithstanding the credence I place on conditionality for influence in the Balkans of the 1990s, the EU and other organizations have pursued some softer, lower profile, less risky policies more in line with expectations of contagion/convergence. In particular, the European Commission has had large programs in support of opposition political and non-governmental civil society actors. The Royaumont Process, for example, was explicitly launched to tap into these bodies. In Croatia, and throughout the region, however, it would seem that large obstacles remained in the way of the effectiveness of this approach to democratization. Most of the alternative actors remained marginalized and frustrated in the domestic political scene. This could be partially explained by the hold over the entire population of the ideology of the nationalist project, or it may be simply that the benefits will pay off only indirectly and subtly in the future.

I believe the pervasiveness and strength of a basic nationalist (i.e. state-building) ideal has been a firm limit to the EU's tapping into alternative fountains of liberal democracy. Even now, in the post-Tudjman era in Croatia, one senior UN political officer has characterized the limitation thus: on the one hand, Croatia's economic agenda has been written more or less completely by the EU; but on the other hand, its political agenda is still largely written with Serbia/Federal Republic of Yugoslavia in mind. It is political suicide in Croatia to speak in more than passing reference to a reestablishment of full, friendly relations with all the other former Yugoslavian states. Notwithstanding some progress in inter-state relations and regional cooperation, this is the lasting inheritance from Tudjman, Milošević, and the war of independence, and its influence on domestic politics should not be underestimated.

Postscript

I would like to make two closing remarks to qualify the lessons learned from Croatia. First, the use of conditionality for assistance by the EU or any other "donor" is discussed in this chapter only in relation to non-essential democratization and capacity-building assistance. There is unanimity in the humanitarian community that humanitarian assistance should never be subject to political conditionality. This raises a problem for the case study of Croatia as an indicator of what works because, as has been noted above, 80 percent of the material assistance to Croatia through EU programs has been strictly humanitarian. The argument about the limits of contagion through unconditioned assistance programs, however, still holds.

The second qualification is a reminder that the EU approach and actual interventions in the former Yugoslavia have evolved through many manifestations (and many mistakes) since 1991. In fact, the saving grace for the EU in the face of the major challenges to its interests and its image has been its flexibility and adaptability over time. Andrew Moravesik makes a strong argument to this effect, presenting the EU as first and foremost a pragmatic political union.[37] In looking at Croatia for lessons about EU success or failure, then, it is important to keep this adaptability foremost in mind rather than to latch onto a model assistance program that could simply be replicated elsewhere. There are those who disagree with the assessment of the EU as flexible, adaptable, or pragmatic.[38] I leave this as an open question, but one that may give some hope to EU efforts to prod "reluctant democratizers."

Notes

1 This chapter was written in a private capacity. The views expressed herein do not reflect any official view of the United Nations.
2 S. Woodward, *Balkan Tragedy: Chaos and Dissolution After the Cold War*, Washington, DC: The Brookings Institution, 1995. See also Woodward, *Socialist Unemployment: The Political Economy of Yugoslavia, 1945–1990*, Princeton, NJ: Princeton University Press, 1995.
3 R. Ullman, ed., *The World and Yugoslavia's Wars*, New York: Council on Foreign Relations, 1996.
4 See in particular T. G. Ash, *History of the Present: Essays, Sketches and Despatches from Europe in the 1990s*, London: Penguin, 2000.
5 G. Stokes, *The Walls Came Tumbling Down: The Collapse of Communism in Eastern Europe*, New York: Oxford University Press, 1993, p. 203. See, as an

example of the perspective Stokes describes, Ash's stories of "blissful ignorance" in *The Magic Lantern: The Revolution of 1989 Witnessed in Warsaw, Budapest, Berlin, and Prague*, New York: Random House, 1990.

6 L. Greenfeld, *Nationalism: Five Roads to Modernity*, Cambridge, MA: Harvard University Press, 1992.

7 The *locus classicus* for this genre remains P. Schmitter, G. O'Donnell, and L. Whitehead, *Transitions from Authoritarian Rule* (four volumes), Baltimore: Johns Hopkins University Press, 1986.

8 For an idea of some of the work that has been done, the reader is recommended to begin with the Political Science Faculty in Zagreb (especially publications by Ivan Grdesic, Ivan Siber, and Nenad Zakosek), and to see the work of Vladimir Goati in Belgrade.

9 G. Pridham, "Democratic Transition and the International Environment: A Research Agenda," CMS-Occasional Paper No. 1, February 1991, reprinted in Pridham, ed., *Transitions to Democracy: Comparative Perspectives from Southern Europe, Latin America and Eastern Europe*, Aldershot: Dartmouth Publishing Company, 1995, pp. 445–446. Pridham's chapter explores the literature for explanations.

10 T. Kuzmanic, "Slovenia: From Yugoslavia to the Middle of Nowhere?" in M. Kaldor and I. Vejvoda, eds, *Democratization in Central and Eastern Europe*, London: Pinter, 1999, p. 132. See Kaldor and Vejvoda in the same volume, pp. 1–2.

11 One could argue for a more positive role for the EU in Slovenia, a state that escaped almost all the fighting, enjoyed a relatively prosperous economy and ethnic homogeneity, and now stands among those post-communist states likely to be included in the first round of EU expansion.

12 Kuzmanic, op. cit., p. 133.

13 Ash, *History of the Present*, p. xv.

14 Ibid., p. 211.

15 Ibid, pp. 208ff. See also his chapter in the same volume, "The Case for Liberal Order," pp. 316–334.

16 Source of these figures is an EC brochure "Croatia – The European Contribution," available on the "Europa" website (http://www.europa.eu.int) and cited on the Croatian Ministry for European Integration's website (http://www.mei.hr). For the Obnova Program, the official document is Council Regulation (EC) No. 1628/96, July 25, 1996 "Relating to Aid for Bosnia and Hercegovina, Croatia, the Federal Republic of Yugoslavia, and the former Yugoslav Republic of Macedonia" (on http://www.seerecon.org).

17 SEC/96/2525. See O. Kovac, "Regional Approach of the European Union to Co-operation among Countries of the Former Yugoslavia," *Review of International Affairs* 47, December 1996, pp. 1–5.

18 Croatia in particular was under significant EU and UN scrutiny and pressure during 1997 over its compliance with the Dayton and Erdut agreements, its lack of cooperation with the International Tribunal in the Hague, half measures to enable refugee and IDP return, and other political and human rights issues. The EU Council of Ministers put Croatia's President Tudjman on notice that continuing problems in these areas were contrary to Croatia's expressed ambition of EU accession. Croatia's relations with the EU remained difficult until the death of President Tudjman in December 1999 and the election of a new government and president in early 2000.

19 "Working Programme of the Government of the Republic of Croatia for the Period 2000–2004," February 8, 2000, found on the website of the Ministry for European Integration, op. cit.

20 Plus an Interim Agreement governing trade matters. See "Stabilization and Association Agreement Between the EC and Croatia Signed Today," IP/01/1503, Luxemburg, October 29, 2001 on Europa website, op. cit.

21 See "Croatia: Commission Adopts New Strategic Framework for Assistance" (EC five-year strategy for financial assistance to Croatia), IP/01/1864, Brussels, December 19, 2001.

22 The minimum objective was greater Croatian independence in a new Yugoslav confederation, but with new internal borders allowing integration of all regions inhabited by ethnic Croats. Tudjman is firmly committed to the ethno-national revolution. He believes that "the fall of Yugoslavia was, from the start, predestined" because of a "clash of civilizations"; and that Croatian independence follows from the "natural right to a Croatian nation-state." (These quotes are from an address to a joint session of the Croatian parliament, March 23, 1993. However, the same sentiments are strewn throughout his writings, speeches, and interviews.)

23 P. Radan, "Secessionist Self-Determination: The Cases of Slovenia and Croatia," paper presented at a conference on National Self-Determination Today: Problems and Prospects, Macquarie University, November 6–7, 1993, p. 11.

24 For a sustained, comparative evaluation of the HDZ leadership in the overall context of Croatia's fledgling multiparty system, see my PhD dissertation, "Ethnopolitics and Conflict in the breakup of Yugoslavia: A Theory of Ethnic Mobilization," Department of Political Science, University of Michigan, 1995. Of particular note here is the response I received in elite interviews to the following statement: "Croatia should never sacrifice its national sovereignty, even if this means staying out of the European Community." HDZ leaders "strongly agreed" in 71 percent of the cases, as compared to 58 percent strongly agreed overall (still high), 38 percent of the liberal opposition (that took power in 2000), and 83 percent of the ultra-nationalist far right.

25 S. Hoffmann, "Yugoslavia: Implications for Europe and for European Institutions," in Ullman, op. cit., pp. 102–109.

26 Ullman, op. cit., pp. 14–15.

27 W. Zimmermann, "The Last Ambassador: A Memoir of the Collapse of Yugoslavia," *Foreign Affairs* 74, March/April 1995, pp. 7–8.

28 *Vreme* (Belgrade), No. 11, December 9, 1991.

29 As Zimmermann writes, "Yugoslavia had become a tar baby in Washington. Nobody wanted to touch it." Op. cit., 1995, p. 15.

30 Kubicek, "International Norms, the EU, and Democratization: Tentative Theory and Evidence," Chapter 1 of this volume.

31 Ibid., p. 9.

32 "EU Response Capability: Institutions and Processes for Conflict Prevention and Management," ICG Issues Report, No. 2, Brussels, June 26, 2001.

33 N. Graeger, "Regional Organisations and Peace Operations: Exploring the Roles of the EU and the OSCE," draft paper presented in first working group on "Cooperation Between the UN, NATO, and Other Regional Organisations in Preventing and Managing Conflict in Europe," The International Peace Academy, April 20–21, 2001.

34 Zimmermann, op. cit., pp. 7–8.
35 In the fourth semi-annual survey of December 2001, 97 percent had heard of the EU, and 78 percent had a generally positive orientation toward it. Seventy-seven percent favored Croatia's joining the EU while 13 percent were against. Positive benefits expected from the Stabilization and Association Agreement are led by "a common market and open borders" (85 percent). Negative impacts feared from the Agreement include, unfortunately still, the highest percentage (68 percent of all respondents) citing "the need for collaboration with countries in the region" ("*nuznost suradnje sa zemljama u regiji*"); others (60 percent) feared economic problems and a loss of Croatian autonomy/independence ("*samostalnost*") (42 percent). These levels hold in the fifth survey, summer 2002. See the Ministry for European Integration website, op. cit.
36 Kubicek, op. cit., p. 10.
37 A. Moravesik, "Despotism in Brussels? Misreading the European Union," *Foreign Affairs*, May/June 2001.
38 Ibid. Also see the interesting proposal by M. Barnett and M. Finnemore in "The Politics, Power, and Pathologies of International Organizations," *International Organization* 53, Autumn 1999, 699–732.

7 The European Union and Ukraine

Real partners or relationship of convenience?

Paul J. Kubicek

Since gaining independence in 1991, Ukraine has been confronted with a variety of challenges on both domestic and international fronts. One primary task was state-building, as Ukrainians had to craft institutions befitting a sovereign state from the wreckage of the Soviet Union. Economic and political reforms were also top priorities, and Ukrainian leaders committed themselves, at least rhetorically, to construction of market and democratic institutions. Nation-building was also on the agenda, as there was a perceived need to form some sort of common Ukrainian identity among a populace that heretofore had not imagined themselves to be part of a meaningful political community. Obviously, meeting all the requirements of this "quadruple transition" would be difficult, and much remains to be done on all fronts.[1]

The foreign policy challenges were no less daunting. Ukraine had to secure its independence vis-à-vis a Russia with uncertain imperial ambitions. Separatist threats in Crimea, backed by numerous Russian political actors, would have to be managed. Ukraine would have to find a way to negotiate the division of spoils from the USSR with Russia (e.g. the Black Sea Fleet), while trying to overcome dependence on Russia in critical areas such as energy.[2] Meanwhile, Ukraine would also need to look westward for crucial political and economic support, both for domestic development and for international security. Overarching these specific concerns and policies was the question of Ukraine's international affiliation: was it part of the East, the West, or a bridge between the two, an actor that would pursue "active neutrality"? Reflecting in part this ambiguity in the country's basic foreign policy orientation, Ukraine developed a "multi-vector" foreign policy, directed chiefly toward Moscow, Brussels, Warsaw, and Washington.

By 1998, however, one vector – Europe – had superceded all others, as Ukraine's "European choice" was announced as a necessary decision, a reflection of strategic realities, and the country's desire to "return to Europe." Chief among Ukraine's foreign policy goals is eventual ascension to the EU, a move towards integration that stands in stark contrast to its reticence to participate in the Russian-led Commonwealth of Independent States (CIS). For its part, after some hesitation, the EU has become the largest bilateral provider of technical and financial assistance to Ukraine. Ukraine and the EU have signed a Partnership and Cooperation Agreement (PCA) and the EU announced in 1999 a Common Strategy on Ukraine that acknowledged Ukraine's "European aspirations."[3]

While Ukraine can count some successes in the past decade, suffice to say that the country still has a ways to go before it can hope to join the family of consolidated democratic states in the EU. Ukraine and Moldova are the only states that have formally expressed a desire to join the EU that are not in the current membership queue, as no invitation has been extended from Brussels. Surely, part of the reason is economic, as the Ukrainian economy is nothing short of a disaster. However, well-documented failures on the political front, particularly in pushing ahead with democratization, are also important, and have become more apparent since 1999. Sherman Garnett suggests that the foreign policy aspirations of joining with the West and the domestic reality of political and economic stagnation mix like "oil and water."[4] In our terms, Ukraine surely ranks among the most reluctant of the "reluctant democratizers" in Europe.

This chapter seeks to understand the interplay between the EU and Ukraine's domestic political agenda. Clearly, Ukraine's "European choice" has not been accompanied by a similar "democratic choice" at home. Why is there such a disjuncture? Can the EU do anything to blend together the "oil and water"? With membership off the table at present, does the EU hold a strong enough hand to encourage political change? Does it really care? These are some of the questions that this chapter hopes to answer.

Ukraine the reluctant democratizer

In the decade since independence, Ukraine can list some noteworthy accomplishments: the country's independence is secure; it has concluded important treaties with Russia and its other neighbors; after signing the Non-Proliferation Treaty (NPT), it became a major recipient of Western aid; Crimean separatism is no longer a major threat; unlike in Russia, disagreements between the President and the Parliament (*Verkhovna Rada*) have been handled peacefully; there is a new Constitution; regional and/or ethnic divisions have not led to chaos or civil war; and the worst period of hyperinflation and economic decline (1992–1994) appears to be over. One author even went so far as to claim Ukraine as a "relative success."[5]

That being said, it is clear that all is not right with the country, a fact acknowledged by Ukrainians themselves. When asked in June 2001, only 11 percent of respondents in one survey thought the country was headed in the right direction.[6] It is not hard to ascertain why. Despite recording 6 percent economic growth in 2000 (the first year of positive growth since independence), the economy remains in shambles. The GNP per capita is a paltry $840,[7] and 70 percent of workers have wages below the government-established living minimum.[8] Hundreds of thousands of workers suffer from wage arrears and "hidden unemployment." Total foreign investment from 1991 to 2000 has been a measly $75 per person.[9] Privatization has benefited the few, and corruption is rampant.[10]

These serious problems are compounded by and perhaps caused by incomplete democratization in the country. True, elections are held, there are numerous parties, voters have choices, and the results of the vote have been respected by political actors. Ukraine even has seen the electoral defeat of a sitting president, a relatively rare event in the post-Soviet space. However, these merely add up to "electoral democracy,"[11] and the real practice of the country is better described as that of "super-presidentialism" or "delegative democracy,"[12] as there is little to check the power of an executive branch that has catered to the oligarchic elements often referred to as the "party of power."

This is really nothing new. Ukraine's first president, Leonid Kravchuk (1991–1994), made every effort to concentrate executive power in his hands. He would impugn his critics by questioning their patriotism and justify his political moves as acts of Ukrainian state-building. He ran roughshod over parliament, using his power to issue executive decrees. Parties and non-governmental organizations that might transmit citizens" demands and force political accountability remained weak, shut out by state corporatist structures that favored the former communist political and economic elite.[13] Meanwhile, the economy tanked and corruption flourished. His play toward *derzhavnist"* (statehood) won him some support among nationalists, but even the leader of the national democratic Rukh party acknowledged that the country was run by leaders who were indifferent or hostile to democratic ideals.[14]

The election of Leonid Kuchma as President in 1994 brought some grounds for hope. There was a peaceful transfer of power, Kuchma spoke in favor of radical economic reform, and he pushed forward a pro-Western foreign policy. In 1995–1996, however, efforts to write a new constitution for the country degenerated into a power struggle between Kuchma and a more leftward-leaning *Verkhovna Rada*. The impasse was settled peacefully (with Kuchma threatening to call a referendum on the issue), but the constitution did confirm a strong presidential system. With Parliament defeated, the emergence of various regional "clans" has become a theme in Ukrainian politics, with Kuchma being the ultimate arbiter and often backing the "Dnieprpetrovsk" clan from his hometown. His pick for Prime Minister, Pavlo Lazarenko (1996–1997), was eventually arrested in Switzerland for money laundering, as he and his cronies had pillaged the state's energy sector. Parliamentary elections in 1998 did meet international democratic standards, but results failed to produce any coalition to challenge the President. In any event, one should not have expected these or any elections to engender much change. Oleksandr Pavliuk notes:

> Ukraine's political process is not transparent: politics are defined not by the competition between ideologies and party programmes, but by behind-the-scenes squabbling of powerful financial and political groups

or clans. Ukraine has yet to establish the vibrant rule of law and strengthen its civil society. Major components – political parties, NGOs, independent media, etc. – remain weak, have little influence on the domestic political process, and are often controlled and dominated by vested shadow interests or – as they are often referred to – oligarchs.[15]

Matters would get worse. The 1999 presidential elections, which Kuchma won, were marred by a host of problems, including a clampdown on independent media, financial irregularities, pressure on state employees to campaign for Kuchma and on local officials to deliver him the vote, and vote-rigging. The Council of Europe called the campaign "a disgrace," and the election itself failed to receive a passing grade from international observers.[16] Serhei Holovaty, a Kuchma critic on the right, noted that the elections signaled a "creeping coup" and that people are now more "cynical" and "hopeless" and "don't feel that their voting makes any difference anymore."[17] An April 2000 referendum, designed to increase presidential powers vis-à-vis Parliament even further,[18] passed, albeit amid widespread allegations of fraud from international and Ukrainian observers and the fact that its legal standing was at best dubious.

The most debilitating event for democracy and for the country overall, however, would be the scandal of "Kuchmagate," which broke in November 2000. The general story is rather well known: a member of the presidential security service, Mykola Melnychenko, taped alleged conversations involving Kuchma, in which, among other things, he acknowledges money laundering and other financial shenanigans, implicates himself in the grenade attack on an opponent in the 1999 campaign, and, most notoriously, suggests presidential involvement in the murder of an outspoken journalist, Georgii Gongadze.[19] The tapes were broadcast in Parliament, and Melnychenko went into hiding abroad. In the words of one journalist, this "makes Watergate look pretty harmless."[20] Kuchma at first denied the voice was his, then acknowledged that it was his voice but it had been spliced together on the digital tape. Some independent analysts assert the tape has not been doctored, and one Ukraine watcher from Freedom House acknowledges that "the sheer volume of data suggest that the source is authentic."[21] However, rather than try to prove his innocence, Kuchma has shut down parliamentary investigations while blaming the incident on those foreign and domestic elements that seek to undermine Ukraine's sovereignty.[22]

The revelations on the tapes led to an effort in the *Verkhovna Rada* to impeach Kuchma, protests by a "Ukraine Without Kuchma" movement, and a signature campaign to force a referendum to remove the President. None of this went anywhere, as the protesters were forcibly dispersed by the police, "Ukraine Without Kuchma" leaders were intimidated by security officials, and the requisite votes and signatures failed to materialize. Notably, polls reveal an overwhelming majority of Ukrainians – 86 percent in one October 2001 query – believe the tapes to be authentic.[23] The fact that they are still saddled with Kuchma – whereas Serbs got rid of Milošević – speaks volumes about the weaknesses of civil society and on going regional schisms in the country that make it difficult for any one leader or movement to unite Ukrainians.[24] Ukraine now is on the brink of "Belarusification" – open authoritarian rule by a President shown to be willing to use violence to maintain his hold on power.

Ironically, the largest casualty was the popular and reformist Prime Minister Viktor Yushchenko, who was appointed by Kuchma at the end of 1999 and was generally credited for Ukraine's economic recovery in 2000. By 2001, however, he was seen by Kuchma (and his opponents on the left) as dispensable and was voted out in April. Meanwhile, Kuchma has blocked foreign radio broadcasts of additional Melnychenko tapes, issued a decree to strengthen his control over the Cabinet of Ministers, approved state security oversight of the .ua domain on the Internet, and has appointed an old ally in the oligarchic mold, Anatoliy Kinakh, former head of the Union of Industrialists and Entrepreneurs, as new Prime Minister. He and his allies spearheaded creation of a new electoral bloc, an oligarch-dominated "For United Ukraine," for the 2002 parliamentary elections. Many believe he is even thinking about running for a third term, something prohibited by the current constitution.[25] He is secure, having cowed the press and his political opponents and taking advantage of a "passive Ukrainian public largely resigned to being ruled by corrupt politicians."[26]

Many still hoped for the best, however. By 2002, attention turned to parliamentary elections and the return to politics of Yushchenko, who launched the pro-reform "Our Ukraine" bloc, considered the primary democratic force in the country and the best chance to reinvigorate a perpetually stalled reform process. Yushchenko, however, has refused to adopt a strident anti-Kuchma position, and has eschewed an open alliance with Yulia Tymoshenko or Oleksandr Moroz, Kuchma's most vociferous opponents. Moreover, over a month before the election, observers noted that Kuchma and his allies among the oligarchs and regional leaders were busy applying "administrative measures" (a euphemism for fraud) to ensure a compliant media.[27]

The results of the March 31, 2002 vote were equivocal. Yushchenko's "Our Ukraine" did win more votes than any other party (24 percent), but Kuchma's bloc did better in the single member districts, so that it ultimately won more seats (182 of 450) than "Our Ukraine" (117).[28] Many Ukrainian and international observers alleged electoral irregularities, ranging from dirty tricks and restrictions on the opposition (Tymoshenko, after surviving a car crash, was restricted by authorities to campaigning only in Kyiv), inaccurate lists of voters, limited media access to the opposition, and state-led efforts to wring pro-Kuchma votes out of prisons, the armed forces, the civil service, and state-owned factories. Yushchenko himself contended, "Democracy is the loser. That is the main defeat of these elections."[29] While it remains to be seen if the new *Verkhovna Rada* will be able to challenge

Kuchma (many parties, including the Communists, claim to support impeach-ment, and new tapes allege Kuchma's involvement in arms smuggling to Iraq), some are already sounding alarmist bells, noting that "gloom prevails," that Ukraine "may slip closer to becoming an international pariah state," and, in Tymoshenko's words, Ukraine will "no longer be a viable partner for Europe."[30] One poor sign is that the head of the presidential administration was appointed parliamentary speaker, giving Kuchma additional leverage over the legislature. Kuchma himself, however, continues to insist that the victors in the election will help chart "the European choice of Ukraine, whose components are further market and democratic transformations."[31] Rhetoric of this sort aside, disappointment reigns among reformers, who are left hoping for better results in 2004 presidential elections.

Ukraine's European choice

Despite Kuchma's political shenanigans at home, he is credited by many with steering Ukraine away from Russia and toward the West. He inherited a state that was nearly an international pariah because it continued to hold nuclear weapons inherited from the Soviet Union and had delayed rudimentary elements of economic reform. Russian pressure – particularly on energy deliveries – also threatened Ukrainian independence. Thus, Kuchma quickly embarked upon a "multi-vector" foreign policy, aiming to gain Western support by announcing "radical" economic reforms in October 1994 and pushing ratification of the NPT through the *Verkhovna Rada* later that fall.

Casting himself as the "reformer," Kuchma was thus able to win political and economic support for Ukraine from the West, which in turn strength-ened his hand in dealing with Moscow. Ukraine has been an enthusiastic member of NATO's Partnership for Peace (PfP), joined the Council of Europe in 1995, has a "strategic partnership with the US," supported NATO expansion, enjoys (along with Russia) a Charter of Distinctive Partnership with NATO, and has spearheaded the GUUAM group (i.e. Georgia, Ukraine, Uzbekistan, Azerbaijan, Muldova) that seeks to balance Russian dominance in the post-Soviet space.[32] Ukraine's strategic position as a bridge between West and East has also helped win backing from the West, with one analyst famously dubbing the country the "keystone in the arch" of European security.[33] Events in 2000–2001 have tested Ukraine's overall relationship with the West, but both sides appear to be committed to strengthening ties for the long term. Chief among Ukrainian priorities at present is its relationship with the European Union.

The foundation for Kyiv's current relationship with the EU dates from 1994. In June 1994, Ukraine concluded a Partnership and Cooperation Agreement (PCA) with the EU, the first CIS state to do so. This agreement, however, fully came into force only in March 1998 due to ratification problems in EU member countries. The PCA establishes an institutional framework for relations, including an annual Ukraine–EU summit, ministerial level meetings, and exchanges between the *Verkhovna Rada* and the European Parliament. Working committees have been established to tackle issues such as trade and investment, customs, energy, nuclear issues, crime, technology, education, and economic development. The PCA includes a provision allowing for a free trade area in the future, and includes a number of specific provisions regulating trade. The PCA helped open the door further to EU assistance through the TACIS (Technical Assistance to CIS) program, which will be discussed below.

The PCA, however, is essentially an arrangement to facilitate trade by helping to bring Ukraine up to World Trade Organization (WTO) standards. While it does specify twenty-seven areas of cooperation, it is best viewed as a "roadmap" to assist in the economic reform process, particularly on opening the Ukrainian economy to the world.[34] Technical economic questions are pre-eminent among its provisions, and while it does allow for the relationship between the two parties to evolve to a more advanced stage, it falls far short of the Association Agreements concluded with states in the queue for EU membership. Moreover, many of its provisions have yet to implemented, with both sides accusing the other of not sticking to the Agreement, particularly on trade and investment barriers. One official with the European Commission lamented that Ukraine's compliance was "at most hesitant and at times even ebbing," as Ukraine was "in breach of virtually all key provisions on trade in goods."[35] Examples include preferential treatment of the Ukrainian auto industry, fees for imports of medicine, and export restrictions on scrap metal. Ukrainians, for their part, felt that restrictions on the importation of Ukrainian steel and textile products (which are covered under special protocols), undermined the notions of fairness and partnership in the PCA.

Frustration with the PCA, however, did not lead either side to abandon the relationship. On the Ukrainian side, despite the admission that much needed to be done to fulfill the PCA, the rhetoric vis-à-vis Europe began to be ratcheted up by 1996. It was during this time that the "European choice" became a cornerstone of policy. In February of that year, Kuchma sought to link his country with Europe, claiming that "the cradle of Ukrainian culture is European Christian civilization. That is why our home is, above all, Europe."[36] In April, in front of the Parliamentary Assembly of the Council of Europe, Kuchma announced that its strategic goal was integration in European structures, with priority on full membership in the EU.[37] Despite the fact that the EU did not even entertain the prospect of Ukrainian membership, a European and Transatlantic Integration Department was set up in the Ministry of Foreign Affairs, and the National Agency of Ukraine for Reconstruction and Development became the National Agency for Development and European Integration.[38] In 1998, prior presidential statements became manifest in state policy with the issuance of the presidential decree "Strategy of Ukraine's Integration in the European Union." In August 2000, another presidential decree created a National Council on the

Issues of Adapting Ukraine's Legislation to the Legislation of the European Union, a body to be chaired by Kuchma himself.

Ukrainian officials are emphatic today about the importance of the European vector in Ukrainian foreign policy. The head of the Presidential Administration opined that there is a "clear consensus in Ukraine today that our development must be linked to European structures. No other alternative is being considered."[39] Then-Foreign Minister Borys Tarasiuk proclaimed in 1999 that the "European idea has become Ukraine's national idea and a consolidating factor for its society."[40] Ukrainians also began to classify their country as "Central European," suggesting its similarity with countries such as Poland and leaving the moniker "Eastern Europe" (with its various negative connotations) to Russia.

The motives behind this "European Choice" are fairly easy to discern. The EU is seen as a guarantor of political stability and economic prosperity, and membership in this exclusive "club" would be proof of Ukrainian success in the post-Soviet period. Moroney notes that "in 'choosing' the European path Ukraine is opting for a proven way to modernize the country, bridge existing technological gaps, create new jobs, attract foreign investment, and improve domestic producer's [*sic*] competitiveness in EU and global markets."[41] The EU would also be a source of aid, and membership in the EU would prevent a new "Eurocurtain" being drawn along the Polish–Ukrainian frontier, a fear of many Ukrainians today. Ties to the EU may also provide additional security against possible Russian threats to Ukrainian independence. Many might note that closer ties with the EU would promote democracy and the rule of law, but given the actions of state authorities, one must wonder if this is an important goal for the current cast of Ukrainian political leaders.

While Ukraine's "European Choice" is prominent in the rhetoric of state officials, what can one say about the views of the public? The evidence on this score is mixed. True, surveys do indicate that the idea of entering the EU is supported by the majority of the population.[42] In fact, according to these sources, pro-integration opinions in Ukraine are currently higher than they are in several Central European countries.[43] However, this does not mean that Ukrainians are unequivocally pro-Western: Eurobarometer surveys from throughout the 1990s found more Ukrainians thinking ties with Russia or the CIS are more important than ties to Europe or the USA.[44] An April 2001 survey found similar results, with over 60 percent of respondents endorsing closer ties to Russia or the CIS, whereas 25 percent put priority on developing ties with Western states.[45] Fraser Cameron of the European Commission reports other surveys noting that a Western/EU orientation is favored by only 15 percent of the population, and that Kuchma's victory in 1999 should not be interpreted as a popular endorsement for the "European Choice."[46] Most important, perhaps, is the fact that the mass public and organized interests appear to know little about the EU and do not constitute an active force in Ukrainian foreign policy.[47] This point will be developed further in the chapter, but for now suffice to say that the "European Choice" has been more a reflection of a segment of the Ukrainian political elite, driven to the West in part, at least, due to an uncertain geopolitical environment.

Moreover, one should stress that the "multi-vector" approach of Ukrainian foreign policy has not given way to a uni-directional focus on Brussels. Russia remains very important for Ukraine: it is still its largest trading partner (despite a 50 percent fall in the volume of trade from 1996 to 1999), it is the source of most Ukrainian energy, and for cultural and historical reasons a source of attraction to many in Ukraine. While pursuing ties with Europe, Kyiv has tried to improve relations with Moscow as well, concluding a treaty on friendship and cooperation in 1997. The fact that the EU has yet to open the door of membership to Ukraine is also making some question the wisdom of putting most energies and hopes in the EU, and many Ukrainian officials are not happy with what they see as the EU's "throwing European CIS countries out of the framework of integration processes in Europe."[48] In September 2000, Tarasiuk, who was unabashedly pro-European and a symbol of the country's Western orientation, was sacked. This was interpreted by some as a "major concession to Russia and a slap to the West."[49] More recently, in wake of the Gongadze affair, the ouster of Yushchenko, and the granting of political asylum in the USA to Mykola Melnychenko, Kuchma has noticeably turned toward Moscow, since Putin does not treat him as a pariah or criminal.[50] Viktor Chernomyrdin, named ambassador to Kyiv in May 2001, also promises to bring greater prospects of Russian–Ukrainian economic integration (especially in energy), and Kuchma in turn has let Putin know that Russia will be the "top priority," even as his foreign minister assures Brussels that Ukraine will "stick to a European course."[51] Many are concerned that Western pressure on Ukraine would do little but drive the country further into the embrace of Russia, although some do question the extent of Moscow's interest in Ukraine.[52] The EU, as well as other Western actors, has thus been put in a difficult position about how to respond to Ukraine's democratic shortcomings. It is to EU policy toward Ukraine that we now turn.

Europe's response

Although the stated European concerns in Ukraine – implementation of meaningful economic reform, political and economic transparency, and creation of democracy and the rule of law – have been a constant since Ukraine gained independence, European policy has evolved over time. Pavliuk divides the policies into four phases: neglect (1991–1993); support (1994–1996); frustration and fatigue (1997–1999); and disengagement (2000–present).[53] At present, the questions are if and how the West (and the EU more specifically) can re-engage with Ukraine and further processes of political and economic reform.

From 1991 to 1993, Ukraine received scant attention from Western capitals. Some were skeptical about the viability of the Ukrainian state, but the bigger problem was that Western policy was focused on Russia and Ukraine was viewed as uncooperative on nuclear disarmament issues. Kuchma, then Prime Minister, suggested, "On the map of world leaders, Ukraine does not even exist. They are indifferent to whether Ukraine is independent or not."[54]

Instability in Russia in 1993 and a change in leadership in Kyiv in 1994 helped break Ukraine's isolation. As mentioned, Ukraine joined the PfP and eventually signed the NPT, and Kuchma announced a package of "radical" economic reforms and won support from international financial institutions. The PCA represented a marked strengthening of the European "vector" in Ukrainian foreign policy, and over the years this has been supplemented by other agreements, notably a Common Strategy on Ukraine, announced in December 1999.

The EU's motives for engaging Ukraine are also not hard to identify. Instability or protracted economic difficulties in Ukraine – a state that will border the EU with Polish accession – would be a threat to the EU. Ukraine is also a large potential market for European trade and investment. Ukraine independence is also seen by some as a guarantor against a revival of Russian imperialism, although Moroney notes that US policymakers have been quicker to recognize Ukraine's strategic importance than their European counterparts.[55] However, since Ukraine is not in queue for membership, the European investment in Ukraine is not nearly the same as in Poland, Hungary, or other candidates for membership. As Pavliuk notes, "The EU's stake in Ukraine is certainly not as high as Ukraine's stake in the EU," as well as the fact that relations with Ukraine are not a "self-sufficient goal" for the West but instead a means for pursuing other goals: nuclear disarmament, NATO enlargement, good relations with Russia, and the closure of Chernobyl.[56] This fact does much to explain shortcomings in EU policy.

What have been the general results of EU engagement with Ukraine? Aid has been dispersed primarily through the TACIS program. From 1991 to 1999 (with most of this after 1994), total EU assistance to Ukraine totaled €4 billion, 1.5 billion from the EU itself and 2.5 billion from member states.[57] This includes technical, macroeconomic, and humanitarian assistance, and considerable emphasis has been given to nuclear safety and assistance to Ukraine in the closing of the Chernobyl power station. As a whole, TACIS in Ukraine manages nearly sixty programs, many of which are designed to enhance transportation, border control, the natural environment, legal reform, and education.[58] While much of the money is dispersed to the government, there are some programs that seek to foster non-governmental organizations, and of late there has been an emphasis on using TACIS to help Ukraine fulfill its commitments under the PCA. Of the many TACIS programs, some are more relevant to our concerns of democratization. One is the Democratizing Society by Improving the Professionalism of Journalists and Media Project. This is listed as a three-year project, with funding of €209,000. The project aims to improve training of journalists and an independent media center backed by TACIS has also set up a website to track censorship and violence against journalists.[59] Taking note of problems in this area, the EU has also sponsored a seminar on the media. This is all fine, but does it get to the problem of blatant state interference in the media? Does training of journalists overcome this problem? Is the website really reaching the people and making a difference? While one should not be overly pessimistic and conclude that nothing can be done and therefore nothing should be done, one might wonder how effective programs like this can be. One could mention others as well – for example a TACIS project to foster civic education in grades 9–11 – that may make a difference over the long term, but hardly meets criteria of a hard-nosed program of conditionality.

What has been the general assessment of the TACIS programs? Fraser Cameron of the European Commission contends that the results have been "mixed." While praising efforts in the financial and energy sectors, he is less impressed with progress on enterprise development and legal and administrative reform. Part of the problem, he asserts, is that resources have been spread too thin in a variety of sectors.[60] Moreover, one could add that many of TACIS's aims and tactics – particularly in Western-style education, professional training, and NGO development – will take time to pay off and can reach only a small fraction of Ukrainian society. Moreover, studies have shown that foreign assistance in the post-Soviet region has had mixed results, as NGOs gear their programs more toward donor needs than the needs of their constituents and can become "ghettoized" in their own little world, detached from their own societies.[61] Suffice to say that civil society in Ukraine today remains very marginalized.

Obviously, TACIS programs need not fall into these sort of problems and can be re-targeted to emphasize certain areas – the legal sector appears to be the top priority at present – but their ability to address the most politically sensitive questions (as opposed to ensuring compliance with technical elements of the PCA) may be limited. More to the point, perhaps, the EU has a limited capability to change the general structure of the overall political economy of the state. That is, one does not have to be an orthodox Marxist to argue that as long as the economy is dominated by an oligarchy that the odds are against a genuine democratic breakthrough or a shift in behavior of the existing elite. TACIS and other programs may be able to provide some basic training or rudimentary institutions, but they may have only marginal impact on how the Ukrainian polity really operates. Finally, one should note that the TACIS program does not operate under conditions of conditionality or with well-defined incentives for the Ukrainian state. Programs that are judged a failure are unlikely to be renewed, but the overall consequences to the state are not clearly laid out. Thus, unlike in Central Europe, where the Copenhagen Criteria and adoption of the *acquis communalltaire* provide an easy scorecard for progress with high incentives for compliance, aid to Ukraine operates within a far more ambiguous environment. This may limit the effectiveness of EU engagement with Ukraine.

On another front, there has been growth in EU–Ukraine trade, with the EU being Ukraine's main trading partner outside of the CIS, accounting for 22.5 percent of Ukraine's total trade flows. From 1994 to 1998, the total volume of trade nearly doubled (reaching about €5.75 billion in 1998), but EU exports have fallen in the wake of the 1998 fallout from the Russian crisis and increasing protectionist measures. Still, the EU has managed to enjoy a trade surplus with Ukraine, a fact well recognized by Ukrainian critics of engagement with the West.[62] However, trade with Ukraine represents under 1 percent of total EU trade and is far less than trade with Central European countries, yet another indication that ties with Ukraine are on an entirely different level than the EU's ties with its immediate eastern neighbors.

Perhaps sensitive to some Ukrainian concerns and looking to push reforms ahead in Ukraine, Brussels upgraded its relationship with Kyiv in 1999 by promulgating a Common Strategy on Ukraine in December 1999. Notably, this was a "consolation prize," given in lieu of offering membership to Ukraine, whose candidacy had not been entertained in either EU decisions on enlargement in 1997 in Luxemburg or in December 1999 at the Helsinki Summit. This document also falls short of offering Ukraine Associate Membership, a halfway-house measure that Kyiv considered a realistic alternative to an invitation to full membership. Overall, the Common Strategy pays homage to the "shared values and common interests" of the EU and Ukraine while outlining several broad goals for the EU (e.g. furtherance of democratic and economic transition, ensuring peace and stability). It "acknowledges Ukraine's European aspirations and welcomes Ukraine's pro-European choice," while noting that full implementation of the PCA is a "prerequisite for Ukraine's successful integration into the European economy."[63] For our purposes, one should note that the Strategy (in addition to a host of economic, environmental, and security concerns) specifically notes EU support for the "consolidation of democracy and good governance." While the document is often high on rhetoric and short on detail, it does list some specific democratization efforts, including supporting Ukraine's efforts to sign and observe international human rights obligations, encouraging an ombudsman institution in Ukraine, and contributing to the development of free media in the country. However, the Strategy duly notes "the main responsibility for Ukraine's future lies with Ukraine itself."

What have been the results of this Strategy? Are there signs of progress? While a typical scholarly assessment is that "internal stagnation threatens to unravel the hard-fought gains of Ukrainian foreign policy,"[64] some official EU statements present a far brighter picture. Javier Solana, the EU's High Representative for its Common Foreign and Security Policy, wrote in a Ukrainian paper in 2000 – just before the Kuchmagate scandal broke – that "over the years, Ukraine has committed itself to moving towards a fully functioning democracy, and the results are already very clear to see." Furthermore, he looked forward to "the results of the recent referendum being implemented," despite the widely documented evidence of fraud associated with the referendum.[65] A joint statement from the EU–Ukraine Summit in September 2001 did not mention Gongadze by name, while noting Kuchma's own commitments to the rule of law, human rights, and democracy.[66] A report from the Council of the EU in December 2001 was worded a bit stronger, with the EU emphasizing "profound concerns" about violence against journalists, and noted that Ukraine also needed to make more efforts to ensure judicial independence. However, the EU also noted it was "encouraged by Ukraine's resolve to pursue its policy of reform and to comply with European standards."[67]

This is not to say that the EU has refused to criticize Ukraine in more specific ways. In 2001, the EU issued two declarations that revealed clear concerns. One was on the Gongadze case and other was on Yushchenko's dismissal. The statement on Gongadze expressed concern about the media environment, called for a full investigation into Gongadze's disappearance and an independent analysis of the tapes, and reminded Ukraine of its commitment to broader democratic freedoms. There was, however, no implicit or explicit threat of sanctions if the case was not resolved to the EU's satisfaction. The statement on Yushchenko was a bit stronger, as the EU stressed that progress with the reforms adopted by the Yushchenko government are "a prerequisite for a deeper relationship with the EU."[68] Chris Patten, the EU Commissioner for External Relations, also noted in March 2001 that

> Ukraine wants to draw closer to the EU and its neighbours. We welcome that. But for that to happen, Ukraine must be able to demonstrate its willingness and ability to live up to basic values, European values, values which are also set out in our Partnership and Co-operation Agreement. That means strengthening the rule of law, making progress in the fight against corruption and adopting market-oriented legislation . . . [However] Ukraine has lost a lot of time.[69]

Actions, of course, may speak louder than highfalutin diplomatese, and it is no doubt true that many European states view Ukraine as a state on the fringe of Europe (like Turkey, at least prior to 1999), with little or no chance of really joining Europe. Garnett opines, "In the chancelleries of Europe, little thought is given to Ukraine, except perhaps in regards to Chernobyl."[70] In 2000, in a move that some considered quite ominous for Ukraine, Germany, Italy, and France began discussions with Russia on a gas pipeline that would bypass Ukraine (the Russians are upset at apparent siphoning of gas from the existing pipelines that traverse Ukraine). One author insisted, "Western Europe has handed an old hegemonic power a hammer, and stood by as Moscow announced that it would bring down that hammer."[71] The fact that the IMF has been withholding credits from Ukraine, as well as the general Western embrace of Russia after September 11, 2001, also may signal in general Western disengagement from Ukraine.

Despite tensions in the relationship, however, the EU seems eager not to alienate Ukraine and continues to stress the importance of "strategic partnership." Notably, a recommendation by the Parliamentary Assembly of the Council of Europe to expel Ukraine from the Council of Europe – adopted in April 2001 in the wake of Kuchmagate – was never adopted. Instead, in 2001 at its Gothenburg Summit, the EU offered to include Ukraine in the European Conference, an informal gathering of European states. While one cannot say for sure what was discussed behind the scenes, members of the EU delegation in Kyiv informed me in the summer of 2001 that there had been no discussion of a cut-off or curtailment in aid to Ukraine. Moreover, they noted one should not look only at the most public or visible programs, pointing to progress on a host of technical issues relating to the PCA that had been made by the Yushchenko government. Trying to put a good face on what they acknowledge can be a trying environment, they stated that they were cautiously optimistic about prospects for reform after the 2002 elections.

Thinking theoretically about EU–Ukrainian relations

What is to be made of EU–Ukrainian relations? Despite words on both sides to turn rhetoric of cooperation into concrete steps, skeptics suggest that little has been accomplished. One Ukrainian report noted that the European idea has become "mythologized in the Ukrainian political discourse and turned into a substitute of the late communist myth, with no firm connection with the reality [*sic*]."[72] Another observer went further, noting not only that Western influence "does not go very far," but also that "Ukraine's previous talk about integrating with the West was never matched by real action. Kiev has been happy to take Western money, but it was equally happy to take free Russian gas. Beyond that, it has never had much of a foreign policy."[73]

This is not say that nothing has been accomplished. In 1997, Ukraine adopted a moratorium on the death penalty – a requirement for membership in the Council of Europe – and finally banned it in May 2001. Checkel notes how the Council of Europe and other external actors were instrumental in encouraging Ukraine to adopt an inclusive, non-ethnic definition of citizenship, a decision that contributed to relative inter-ethnic harmony in the country.[74] Due in part to EU pressure and promises of compensation, Ukraine closed the reactors at Chernobyl at the end of 2000.

However, disappointment has been marked on both sides. Ukraine has not been invited to join the European club, and the EU, despite using strained language not to sound too harsh, sees precious little progress on basic elements of political and economic reform. By 2002, eight years after the signing of the PCA, EU–Ukrainian relations are ambiguous as ever, and Ukraine continues to muddle along, still proclaiming its "European choice" but with more real action occurring on the Russian vector of its foreign policy.

Why have relations with Europe reached this point? Obviously, one can point fingers to Kuchma and his entourage, and no doubt the tape scandal has been a serious disappointment to foreign friends of Ukraine. Problems in EU–Ukraine ties, however, were evident before November 2000. Some can be attributed to unrealistic expectations and simple misunderstandings. Writing in 1999, Pavliuk noted the "frustration" on the Ukrainian side and "fatigue" on the part of Europe. He notes

> much misunderstanding, disappointment, and even frustration over-shadow the EU–Ukraine relationship at present. Despite several years of political dialogue and cooperation, each side still has little knowledge of the other, and the two see the future of their relationship quite differently. While Ukraine has declared its intention to become a EU associate member and its ambition to attain full EU membership in the future, the EU does not include it in either the "fast track" or "slow track" group of future members.[75]

In particular, one might note that Ukraine's elites have yet to understand that the EU is much more interested in democratic development and economic performance than Ukraine's geopolitical significance or its "European" heritage and that membership in the EU is qualitatively different from membership in the OSCE or Council of Europe. Moreover, one is often struck by the fact that while the mantra "return to Europe" flows freely from the lips of Ukrainian policymakers and academics, there is little recognition that the Europe of today is far different than the one when Ukraine supposedly established its "European roots."

Certainly, by 2001–2002, the situation was made even worse. While much of the blame is commonly put on Kuchma and the "Party of Power" in Ukraine that has dragged its feet on fundamental reforms, Ukrainians point to a lack of clear and inclusive strategy and perhaps even discriminatory treatment by Brussels. While the EU has provided much technical assistance to the country, one wonders – the Common Strategy not withstanding – if there really is a sound strategy behind EU efforts. Chris Patten, pointing to both inherent EU limitations and mistakes in actual policy conceded, "we cannot supply the clear, unambiguous political will that is needed [to push forward reform in Ukraine]. There has been too much insistence in the past on the forms of our partnership, and too little on the groundwork to make that partnership a reality."[76]

In order to understand better why EU–Ukrainian relations have reached a sort of impasse, and, in particular, why Ukraine remains a "reluctant demo-cratizer," let us examine the hypotheses put forward in Chapter 1 concerning convergence and conditionality. Some undoubtedly "fit" better than others. Let us examine each in turn.

Six notions were proffered regarding the likelihood of democratic convergence. The first was that of "cultural match," the idea that the norms being promoted by external agents must resonate with some domestic norms. While this hypothesis can run close to being a tautology (democratic norms will take hold in countries with democratic norms), one can better understand how it would function in cases of cultural disjuncture (e.g. think of debates over "Western" versus "Asian" or "Islamic" values). While Ukrainian leaders certainly give lip-service to democracy and its component parts (openness, rule of law, competition), declarations ring hollow when the practice has become increasingly authoritarian. The key point is that democratic norms have at best shallow roots and are being germinated in post-communist soil. In other words, much of the Ukrainian elite was, until recently, part of the Soviet/communist elite, and "Soviet" values and practice still reign. Whether or not one chooses to classify this as a "cultural disjuncture," I would venture to say that when European leaders sit down to talk with Kuchma and his appointees they recognize they are not talking to "one of their own." Taking this argument beyond Ukraine, the implication would be that old communists (at least in the Soviet Union) cannot be turned into liberal democrats, a proposition that appears to ring true in a variety of countries.

The second set of hypotheses concern the novelty of the environment, meaning new states or new elites. Checkel, who examined the Ukrainian decision to adopt inclusive citizenship laws, supports the notion that "novelty" matters; that is, new elites or those in an entirely new setting will be more willing to consider outside ideas and advice. His evidence on this particular issue is compelling, but that does not mean the argument applies across the board and on the wider issue of political liberalization. Moreover, it ignores the fact that no setting is really "new." Ukraine is a new state, but its elite has a distinctly non-democratic past. Since Ukraine has yet to have a "democratic breakthrough," this communist past continues to exist as a "residue" in the post-communist period.[77]

What of the counter-hypothesis, which argues that the need to foster nationalism in new states will work against outside efforts to shape domestic political decisions? While it can hold in some cases (as Stephen M. Tull suggests with respect to Croatia in Chapter 6), it does not work very well in the Ukrainian case. While there are some extreme nationalist groups that are resistant to any effort to usurp Ukrainian sovereignty, the more mainstream national democrats, represented in the Rukh party and the former *Derzhavnist'* faction in the *Verkhovna Rada*, tend to be pro-Western, not only viewing the West as a source of security against Russia but also because they largely endorse a liberal political and economic system for Ukraine. Indeed, it is the Communists, not the nationalists, who are the most anti-Western group in the country, but even they have yet to issue an objection to the idea that Ukraine should seek EU membership.

As for the status of the persuader, one can only note that most important political players in Ukraine hold the EU in very high esteem. There is, of course, criticism of the EU, but mostly on the grounds that the EU is not doing all it should for Europe or moving fast enough to facilitate Ukraine's ambitions to join Europe. Few would argue that the EU represents a "bad" role model or that the EU has no moral authority. One may wonder then how come Ukraine has not hurried to fulfill EU demands, but no doubt the general unwillingness of the EU to bear down harshly on Ukraine is a factor. EU "permissiveness" thus may undermine some of its authority.

Another hypothesis was that of how rhetoric or lip-service to norms is important and can potentially "spill over," leading to real policy changes. Obviously, Ukrainian leaders have been willing to repeat the rhetoric coming from Europe, and every EU–Ukraine joint declaration dutifully notes the commitment of each to "common values." This, however, continues to ring a bit hollow. One reason there has yet to be any spillover is the relative weakness of domestic actors seeking a genuine reform agenda. Not being in a strong position to "use" the rhetoric of the elite against the elite, would-be Ukrainian democrats have not been able to produce pressure for change. Coupled with the lack of firm pressure from the EU (which will be addressed more below), the incentive or need to move beyond rhetoric has been low.

This same idea bears on the notion of the role of transnational networks in generating real activity beyond just rhetoric. In other words, the EU must engage more than just governments by working with actors in civil society. In Ukraine, this is problematic because civil society is so weak. Political parties are poorly organized, trade unions are crippled, professional organizations play a limited role, and small business organizations have failed to grow in the shadow of government–oligarch networks. Although Rukh and some other national democratic forces are unequivocally pro-EU, they have never constituted anywhere near a majority in the Parliament. Pavliuk notes that the problem is that "real power" in the country is held by economic pressure groups that "have so far dictated the need for protectionism and preservation of the existing political and economic systems in Ukraine rather than their adaptation to European norms and principles." He adds that "no large Ukrainian businesses have a strong stake in the EU market,"[78] which further limits the ability of the EU to team up with agents "from below" to pressure the government to change course. This is not to say that the EU has no cards at all to play. However, it plays them very conservatively, backing away from supporting the "Ukraine without Kuchma" movement and other opposition groups. As for the current elite, it is hard to pinpoint how they would benefit from making reforms (e.g. economic transparency) sought by the EU. As a consequence, the government machinery "on the whole is largely ambivalent or even suspicious of the country's European integration."[79] The result has been rhetoric with the hope of receiving some type of assistance, but foot-dragging on many basic political and economic issues.

Finally, we come to the hypothesis on convergence: that soft tactics (e.g. persuasion, engagement) will bring more results than hard tactics (e.g. threat of sanctions). To date the EU has relied upon softer tactics, and has yet to apply conditionality in an explicit manner. For example rather than demand full implementation of the PCA before moving EU–Ukrainian relations to a higher level, the EU instead put forth its Common Strategy. True, the Strategy does note the need to fulfill the PCA, but this is an obvious effort to lay out a new framework to allay some Ukrainian concerns and give the appearance that relations are moving forward. In discussions with EU officials in Kyiv, they put much more stock in engagement, dialogue, and policy change in small, incremental steps than in pushing a policy of "take it or leave it" conditionality (e.g. fulfill the PCA now or else face this punishment). Their reasoning was that EU–Ukrainian relations had to be handled gingerly, and that Ukraine was, in essence, not far enough down the path to membership for the EU to make strong demands. Of course, one might wonder if current policy holds enough promise to get Ukraine moving down that path. Off the record, they conceded not only frustration with Ukraine but also a recognition that the hopes behind current policy may have been too high. While advocates of the current policy can point to progress in some more technical, "low politics" areas, there is scant evidence that soft tactics have helped push forward democratization.

Turning now to the hypotheses on conditionality, one factor stands out: conditionality has yet to be applied rigorously to Ukraine. The carrot of membership – the variable that has been assumed to help push reforms through potential bottlenecks in Central Europe – is not on the table. In 1999, when the EU announced its list of candidates for membership, Ukraine was not among the "Helsinki 13," although some of the other candidates, notably Turkey, significantly fell short of the Copenhagen Criteria. Without an endpoint, a target with clear rewards, the incentive to follow EU dictates or preferences may be low. This is already a problem for some countries farther down the membership queue, who may question when (if ever) the EU will expand to include them. Obviously, with Ukraine not even in the queue, the question of "What do we get out of this?" may have more resonance.

This problem is compounded by the lack of sticks employed by the EU. Sanctions have not been employed or considered by the EU. Declarations are made on some issues, but these are not followed up by any actions. For example it is been almost two years since the tape scandal broke, and there has yet to be a full, impartial investigation demanded by the EU. Nonetheless, there were no consequences. Ukraine is not a pariah, and since November 2000 Kuchma has welcomed leading EU political figures in Kyiv. Even the Council of Europe backed away from a recommendation to expel Ukraine for its failures to respect basic elements of democracy. Ukraine may be experiencing political "Belarusification," but one would not know this from EU policy.

Of course, this begs the question of why Ukraine has been treated so gingerly, in contrast to Belarus. One possible reason, as Pavliuk has suggested, is that the EU really does not care that much or have a really large stake in Ukraine, so it is willing to turn a blind eye to some developments and is reticent to risk conflict. Another reason is that the EU (and the West more generally) does not want to risk "losing" Ukraine. True, Ukrainian leaders will argue that the country has no other choice but Europe, but they do not always act as if this is the case. Russia remains by far a more important economic partner, and Kuchma, after directing some accusatory barbs at Moscow in the wake of the tape scandal, quickly made overtures to bolster Ukrainian–Russian cooperation. This is done not only for its own merits, but also with an eye to the West, playing a "Russia" card to extract concessions and aid from the West, where acolytes of geopolitics fret about a possible Russia–Ukraine reunion. Cynics might therefore suggest that the billions in aid from the USA and the EU is used more to buy off Ukrainian elites than to promote political or economic change. The point is thus not that the West cares nothing for Ukraine, but cares only that it remain outside Russia's sphere of control. Ukraine's "exit" option thus gives it the capacity to escape harsh demands of conditionality and, knowing this, the West chooses to "ride softly" with Kyiv while forgetting about any "big stick."

Much of the preceding points to a final problem: the ambiguous nature of "gray zone" democracies as identified by Pridham. The truth is that Ukraine is no Belarus, meaning that it suffers from a "soft" authoritarianism rather than outright repression. Elections are held; competition is allowed; civic freedoms do exist and are respected at least part of the time. True, there are significant lapses, but EU leaders can draft documents noting Ukraine's "democratic progress," something impossible in the case of Belarus. Moreover, Kuchma at least continues to invoke the rhetoric of reform and moving towards Europe, thus making it harder perhaps for the EU to pull away entirely. In short, I would suggest that the quasi-democratic nature of the Ukrainian state allows each side to play a game. The EU (and other actors, to be sure), not willing to throw in the towel and admit, among other things, that years of effort and billions in aid have done little to produce democracy, can cling to the notion that Ukraine possesses some democratic elements, is not as bad as some of its neighbors, and could, with new elections, make a real breakthrough. Ukrainian elites, for their part, are able to present a democratic face to the world, while engaging in manipulation and behind the scenes maneuvers (occasionally not well hidden) to ensure they remain in power. It is better for both sides to act as if the emperor has clothes.

This argument is meant to be provocative and would be criticized by those who point to Ukraine's accomplishments. I have acknowledged a number of them, but it does appear that from 1999 to 2002 democracy has regressed, not progressed. At the same time, the EU (and other actors who are looking to encourage democracy in Ukraine) has stuck with previous policies that have paid limited dividends. If and how the EU can help transform Ukraine's "gray zone" democracy are questions without any clear answer, although one imagines that Brussels may be tired of asking them.

Envisioning progress in the EU–Ukrainian relationship

There is ample reason to be pessimistic, not only about Ukraine but about EU policy. True, the EU could turn away from Ukraine, cut off aid and suspend agreements pending progress toward democracy, but this would be highly risky and may jeopardize some hard-won agreements on some issues. Some would argue that the EU should not employ sticks but instead add to its pile of carrots for Ukraine. Kuzio, for example, asks how the stated EU desire "to help Ukraine achieve its goals of consolidating democracy, protection of human rights, reform of the economy, and full integration into the international community can be fulfilled by excluding Ukraine from EU membership."[80] To date, membership has been offered only to those well on the path to meeting its criteria. One wonders if dangling such a carrot in front of a state with so far to go would bring any result.

In all likelihood, the EU will avoid any radical change in approach. It does not honestly know if it would even want Ukraine as a member, but knows that it does not want to risk antagonism. Current policy, while not producing immediate results, does at least aspire to deepen the EU–Ukrainian relationship and allow the EU to exercise some influence in some issue areas. Many Ukrainians will be disappointed with only "partnership" or a "common strategy" that falls short of membership. One might also ask how long European officials can come to Kyiv with "empty hands" repeating the same messages on human and civil rights and economic reform?[81]

While some may clamor for a shift in EU policy, one might note that the current, limited approach does bow to one inescapable reality: the impetus for change will have to come from within Ukraine itself. Ukraine's European prospects hinge less upon what Brussels offers than on what Kyiv actually does. Obviously, much remains to be done on the democratization front, and only the most intrusive (and therefore impolitic and unworkable) outside intervention could hope to dismantle the oligarchic political and economic structure of the state that is the prime obstacle to democracy. However, this need not mean that the EU give up and simply wait. As one EU official argued with a note of hope, pushing issues such as economic transparency, legal training, civic education, and product standardization is not going to bring about wholesale political change overnight.[82] However, if the EU stays committed to a process that will be inevitably rather bumpy, it can make a difference over the long term. Engagement with non-governmental actors will be ever more important, as they are likely to be the source for positive change. Over time, European standards, not Soviet ones, will become the norm, at least the norm to which one aspires, even if in practice matters fall short. Looking down the road, "convergence" is still possible, even if one cannot see much tangible progress at present.

This conclusion, in contrast to some of what was argued above, will strike some as far too optimistic. However, it is very much the case that Ukraine is a "work in progress." Both sides do have much to learn from the shortcomings of current approaches. The EU may have to offer greater incentives as well as prod more with deft uses of some sticks, and the Ukrainian elite could undertake a number of moves to smooth relations with Europe. It will take work on both sides, and progress may not be immediately obvious. Both sides have the rhetoric down fairly well. Europe cannot force change in Ukraine, but it can offer support to those elements in Ukraine eager for change and working to turn the discourse of "European choice" into real and lasting reforms.

Notes

1 Good general sources on post-Soviet Ukrainian domestic politics include A. Wilson, *Ukrainian Nationalism in the 1990s: A Minority Faith*, Cambridge: Cambridge University Press, 1997; T. Kuzio, *State and Nation Building in Ukraine*, London: Routledge, 1998; Kuzio, P. D"Anieri, and R. Kravchuk, eds, *State and Institution Building in Ukraine*, New York: St. Martin's, 1999; and M. Dyczok, *Ukraine: Movement without Change, Change without Movement*, Reading: Harwood Academic, 2000.

2 Works on Ukrainian–Russian relations include R. Solchanyk, *Ukraine and Russia: The Post-Soviet Transition*, Latham, MD: Rowman & Littlefield, 2001, and P. D'Anieri, *Economic Interdependence in Ukrainian–Russian Relations*, New York: SUNY Press, 1999.

3 O. Pavliuk, "Ukraine and the EU: The Risk of Being Excluded," in I. Kempe, ed., *Beyond EU Enlargement*, Gutersloh: Bertelsmann Foundation, 2001, p. 69.

4 S. Garnett, "Like Oil and Water: Ukraine's External Westernization and Internal Stagnation," in T. Kuzio *et al.*, op. cit., pp. 107–133.

5 Solchanyk, op. cit., p. 81.

6 Survey of 1,200 Ukrainians conducted by Democratic Initiatives. The work of this organization, which is regularly updated with new material, can be found at http://www.dif.com.ua (accessed July 17, 2001).

7 *Zerkalo nedeli* (Kyiv), July 4, 2001.

8 Oleksandr Stoian, head of the Ukrainian Federation of Trade Unions, in *Profspilkovy visti* (Kyiv), April 13, 2001.

9 *Kyiv Post*, June 29, 2001.

10 Transparency International ranked Ukraine 83 out of 91 countries surveyed in 2000. Only Azerbaijan among ex-Soviet states ranked lower. From *Kyiv Post*, July 5, 2001.

11 P. Kubicek, "The Limits of Electoral Democracy in Ukraine," *Democratization* 8, Summer 2001, 117–139.

12 N. Diuk, "Sovereignty and Uncertainty in Ukraine," *Journal of Democracy* 12, October 2001, 57–64, and Kubicek, "Delegative Democracy in Russia and Ukraine," *Communist and Post-Communist Studies* 27, December 1994, 443–461.

13 Kubicek, *Unbroken Ties: The State, Interest Associations, and Corporatism in Post-Soviet Ukraine*, Ann Arbor, MI: University of Michigan Press, 2000.

14 Viadcheslav Chornovil in *Vysoky Zamok* (Lviv), December 8, 1992.

15 Pavliuk, op. cit., p. 74.

16 Report of Commission for Security and Cooperation in Europe (CSCE), "Ukraine's Presidential Elections," December 1999, at http://www.house.gov/csce/UkraineElections1999.pdf (accessed August 3, 2002).

17 *Toronto Globe and Mail*, July 12, 2000.

18 The measures would strip parliamentarians of immunity and allow the President to dismiss Parliament if the body failed to establish a parliamentary majority or pass the budget in a specified time.

19 A voice resembling Kuchma's is heard to suggest handing him over to the Chechens and "grab him, strip him, leave him without his pants, let him sit there." Gongadze's headless corpse was found in September 2001. The best source of materials is *Ukrainska Pravda*, Gongadze's former employer. It can be found at http://www.pravda.com.ua

20 J. Steele, "Kuchmagate," *The Guardian*, February 27, 2001.

21 Adrian Karatnycky, President of Freedom House, testimony at US House Hearing, "Ukraine at the Crossroads," May 2, 2001, found at http://www.brama.com/survey/ 11567.html (accessed February 1, 2002). A Ukrainian parliamentary commission in February 2002 also concluded that the tapes were unedited. See *Kyiv Post*, February 14, 2002. However, one "independent" investigation by Kroll Associates, undertaken at the bequest of the pro-presidential party Labour Ukraine exonerated Kuchma in the case, but few observers in Ukraine put much stock in its findings.

22 See Kuchma's letter to the *Financial Times*, February 27, 2001.

23 Kuzio, "Ukraine One Year After 'Kuchmagate'," *RFE/RL Newsline*, November 28, 2001, available at http://www.rferl.org/newline/2001/11/281101.asp (accessed August 3, 2002).

24 T. Kuzio, "National Identity and Civil Society in Ukraine: Explaining the Yushchenko Phenomenon," *RFE/RL Newsline*, January 30, 2002, available at http://www.rferl.org/newsline/2002/01/300102/asp (accessed August 3, 2002).

25 Since the constitution came into effect in 1996, Kuchma could claim that the two-term limit does not apply to him since he was first elected in 1994, but the constitution clearly states that no person shall be president for more than two terms in a row, which he will have served by 2004.

26 I. Lozowy, "Kuchma's Comeback," *Ukraine Insider* 1, September 20, 2001.

27 Tammy Lynch, "Getting the Media Ready," *NIS Observed* 7, February 13, 2002.

28 Electoral results from *The Economist*, April 6, 2002. Half the seats are determined by party-list proportional representation and half are from a single member district plurality system. The figures above may include some "independents" who are in fact allied with one or another electoral bloc.

29 *New York Times*, April 2, 2002.

30 *The Economist*, op. cit., and *The Times* (London), April 1, 2002.

31 *New York Times*, op. cit.

32 The best overall view on Ukrainian foreign policy is Solchanyk, op. cit.

33 S. Garnett, *Keystone in the Arch: Ukraine in the Emerging Security Environment of Central and Eastern Europe*, Washington, DC: Carnegie Endowment, 1997.

34 J. P. Moroney, "Ukraine's European Choice," in T. Kis, I. Makaryk, and R. Weretelnyk, eds, *Towards a New Ukraine III: Geopolitical Imperatives of Ukraine: Regional Contexts*, Ottawa: Ottawa University Ukrainian Studies, 2001.

35 K. Schneider, "The Partnership and Co-operation Agreement (PCA) between Ukraine and the EU – Idea and Reality," in L. Hoffman and F. Mollers, *Ukraine on the Road to Europe*, Heidelberg: Physica-Verlag, 2001, p. 71. See also F. Cameron, "Relations between the European Union and Ukraine," in J. Clem and N. Popson, eds, *Ukraine and Its Western Neighbors*, Washington, DC: Woodrow Wilson Center, 2000, pp. 80–81.

36 Quoted in Solchanyk, op. cit., p. 92.
37 Pavliuk, op. cit., p. 66.
38 Solchanyk, op. cit., p. 93.
39 Volodymyr Lytvyn in the *Washington Times*, June 19, 2001.
40 Quoted in Solchanyk, op. cit., p. 94.
41 Moroney, op. cit., p. 2 of manuscript.
42 Pavliuk, op. cit., p. 71, cites an April 2000 poll that put support for joining the EU at 57 percent, with only 20 percent opposed.
43 See figures in H. Grabbe and K. Hughes, "Central and East European Views on EU Enlargement: Political Debates and Public Opinion," in K. Henderson, ed., *Back to Europe: Central and Eastern Europe and the European Union*, London: UCL Press, 1999, pp. 186–187.
44 Kubicek, "Regional Polarisation in Ukraine: Public Opinion, Voting, and Legislative Behavior Over Time," *Europe-Asia Studies* 52, March 2000, 273–294. See also Garnett, 1999, op. cit., pp. 120–122.
45 Poll by SOCIS Center of 1,200 Ukrainians, reported in Center for Peace, Conversion, and Foreign Policy of Ukraine, *Monitoring Foreign and Security Policy of Ukraine*, April–June 2001, p. 76.
46 Cameron, op. cit., p. 88.
47 Garnett, 1999, op. cit., and Pavliuk, op. cit.
48 Borys Tarasiuk in *Uriadovyi Kur'ier*, April 18, 1998.
49 J. Sherr, "The Dismissal of Borys Tarasyuk," Occasional Brief 79, Conflict Studies Research Centre, RMA Sandhurst, October 6, 2000.
50 Although Kuchma has met with some Western officials, and John Paul II, since November 2000, Putin was the most prominent and honored guest at the celebration of ten years of Ukrainian independence in August 2001, a proposition that would have been unthinkable ten years ago. For more on Kuchma's turn to Russia, see D. Arel, "Kuchmagate and the Demise of Ukraine's 'Geopolitical Bluff'," *East European Constitutional Review* 10, Spring/Summer 2001, 54–59.
51 For these contrasting reports, see the *Financial Times*, June 1, 2001, and *Agence France Presse*, May 30, 2001.
52 T. Bukkvoll, "Off the Cuff Politics: Explaining Russia's Lack of a Ukraine Strategy," *Europe-Asia Studies* 53, December 2001, 1,141–1,157.
53 Pavliuk, "Unfulfilling Partnership: Ukraine and the West, 1991–2001," unpublished manuscript, Kyiv, East-West Institute, 2001.
54 *The Economist*, May 15, 1993.
55 Moroney, op. cit.
56 Pavliuk, "Ukraine and the EU," p. 81, and "Unfulfilling Partnership," p. 15.
57 The European Commission, "The EU and Ukraine," at http://europa.eu.int/comm./external_relations/Ukraine/intro/index.htm (accessed July 11, 2001). From 1991 to 1998, approximately 60 percent of the EU assistance was grants through TACIS for various projects, with most of the remaining aid in the form of loans for macroeconomic stabilization and development. See Cameron, op. cit., p. 82.
58 For more on TACIS and other EU activities, see data from the EU Delegation in Kyiv at http://www.delukr.cec.eu.int/en/eu_and_country/data.htm (accessed February 14, 2002).
59 See the website of the institute of Mass Information at http://www.imi.org.ua (accessed August 3, 2002).
60 Cameron, op. cit., p. 83.

61 S. Mendelson and J. Glenn, eds, *The Power and Limits of* NGOs, New York: Columbia University Press, 2002.

62 Website "The EU and Ukraine," op. cit.

63 European Council Common Strategy of December 11, 1999 on Ukraine, Document 1999/877/CFSP, found in *Official Journal of the European Communities*, December 23, 1999.

64 Garnett, 1999, op. cit., p. 124.

65 *Zerkalo nedeli*, September 19, 2000.

66 Joint Statement of EU–Ukraine Summit, 11 September 2001, obtained from http://www.europexxi.ua/english/index.html (accessed February 14, 2002).

67 Council Report to the European Council on the Implementation of the Common Strategy of the European Union on Ukraine, 15195/01, December 11, 2001.

68 See Declarations of the EU presidency, "About Working Conditions for Media and to Remind About Concerns Regarding the Gongadze Case," 5922/01, February 5, 2001, and "On Developments in Ukraine," 8082/1/01, April 27, 2001, available at http://europa.eu.int/abc/doc/off/bull/en/200101/p106046.htm and http://europa.eu.int/abc/doc/off/bull/en/200104/p106023.htm (accessed August 3, 2002).

69 Speech at the European Parliament, March 14, 2001, found at http://europa.eu.int/comm./external_relations/news/patten/speech_01_121.htm (accessed July 11, 2001).

70 Garnett, 1999, op. cit., p. 128.

71 T. Lynch, "Ukraine: A New Territorial Pact for Europe?" *NIS Observed* 5, October 25, 2000.

72 "The Problem of Changing the Non-Integration Status of Ukraine in its Relations with the European Union," Occasional Report No. 31, Center for Peace, Conversion, and Foreign Policy of Ukraine (Kyiv), September 2001.

73 J. Bush, "Whither Ukraine?" *Business Central Europe Magazine*, June 2001, available at http://www.artukraine.com/buildukraine/whitherukr.htm (accessed August 3, 2002).

74 J. Checkel, "Why Comply? Social Learning and European Identity Change," *International Organization* 55, Summer 2001, 553–588.

75 Pavliuk, *The European Union and Ukraine: The Need for New Vision*, Kyiv, East-West Institute, 1999, p. 4.

76 Patten, op. cit.

77 For more on this notion that borrows from the idea of "path dependency," see Kubicek, *Unbroken Ties*, op. cit.

78 Pavliuk, "Ukraine and the EU," op. cit., p. 72.

79 Ibid., p. 73.

80 Kuzio, "The EU and Ukraine: A Troubled Relationship," in J. Gower and J. Redmond, eds, *Enlarging the European Union*, Aldershot: Ashgate, 2000, p. 156.

81 A. Lobjakas, "Ukraine: European Union Expected to Keep Kyiv on Hold," *RFE/RL Newsline*, February 13, 2001, online at http://www.rferl.org.nca/features/2001/02/13022001105430.asp (accessed August 3, 2002).

82 Off-the-record discussion with official in Kyiv, July 2001.

8 The European Union and democratization in Morocco

Bradford Dillman

Morocco is a political exception in North Africa and in the wider Arab world. Resting only a few kilometers away from the Rock of Gibraltar, it is geographically closer to the European Union than any other Arab country. It has a long historical relationship with Europe through colonialism and trade, and more than a million people of Moroccan descent live in the European Union. In 1987 Morocco was the first Arab country to formally seek membership in the European Economic Community. No other Arab country has since followed this example. While Egypt and Tunisia witnessed a reinvigorated authoritarianism in the 1990s aimed at crushing Islamists, and Algeria plunged into a civil war after a brief political opening from 1989 to 1991, Morocco in the last decade has experienced a steady political liberalization characterized by dramatically improved human rights protections, pluralistic elections with significant competition, and the installation of an opposition-led government in 1997. The most recent parliamentary elections in September 2002 were the most honest in Morocco's history, with a moderate Islamist party tripling the number of seats it holds in the Assembly of Representatives. In Freedom House's 2001–2002 survey of freedom in the world, Morocco received a score of "5" for political rights and "5" for civil liberties, tying Jordan as the freest country in the Arab world after Kuwait.[1]

Despite measurable progress in political liberalization, Morocco has yet to make a democratic transition and begin the process of democratic consolidation. The monarchy remains the dominant political institution, unwilling to cede key decision-making powers to the elected parliament. Like his father, King Hassan II, since his accession in 1999 King Mohammed VI has been reluctant to transform his regime into a constitutional monarchy. Like the other "reluctant democratizers" examined in this book, Morocco can be seen as a country in political transit subject to considerable political and economic pressures from Europe, but averse to accepting the full package of political reforms proffered by Brussels. Morocco provides an important case for assessing the influence of EU democracy promotion efforts in countries that have little chance of ever joining the Union. As a non-European country, it lacks the cultural and geographic attributes of would-be EU countries such as Latvia, Slovakia, Romania, and Croatia. Absent any realistic prospect of joining the EU, Morocco has yet to experience the domestic transformative effect of diffusion of European norms and expectations that other applicants to the EU experienced. Moreover, Morocco has not been subject to the package of institutions, conditions, and programs embodied in PHARE and TACIS, the EU's pre-accession packages for EU applicants in Central Europe and the former Soviet Union. Instead, its relations with Europe have been embedded in the Euro-Mediterranean Partnership (EMP, launched in 1995), which has a different set of goals, resources, and conditionality for countries in the southern Mediterranean.

This chapter seeks to assess the influence of the European Union on democratization in Morocco. The Moroccan case is significant in that the country's domestic configuration differs significantly from that of other "reluctant" democratizers, but also because the incentives and constraints the EU can bring to bear on the country diverge from those available on Europe's eastern front. Moroccan "exceptionalism" provides important lessons about the limits of European influence on political change in the southern Mediterranean. This study argues that the effects of European policies are contingent on the nature of the Moroccan regime and the country's domestic political economy. In other words, the manner in which political and economic elites in Morocco adapt to external factors has a significant impact on whether or not democratization advances. While Europe has consistently promoted the goals of democratization since the early 1990s, its actual policies have been tenuous regarding political change in Morocco. The EU's political and economic policies have had contradictory effects, and assessing their causal importance requires attention to the independent effects of primarily domestic Moroccan factors. The chapter provides an overview of recent political developments in Morocco, assesses alternative explanations for Moroccan exceptionalism, and shows how the responses of key Moroccan actors to specific European political and economic constraints have influenced the democratization process.

The limits of Moroccan democratization

Morocco is a reluctant democratizer, taking significant steps to liberalize politics but failing to adopt the key institutional and electoral changes that would allow for a full democratic transition. A brief examination of domestic political trends since the early 1990s reveals a tension between support for change and an effort to maintain monarchical domination. This tension partly results from the intersection of top-down and bottom-up strategies for liberalization.

Fiscal crises in the 1980s prompted economic reforms that have bolstered the private sector, whose members have sometimes challenged government policies and filled a number of seats in the parliament. The emergence of an indigenous human rights movement, spearheaded by the *Organisation*

Marocaine des Droits de l'Homme (OMDH), and urban riots during the 1991 Gulf War put pressure on the King to free a number of political prisoners in 1991 and amend the Constitution in 1992. In the following years, King Hassan II progressively reformed the political system by releasing more political prisoners, creating a human rights council, and again amending the Constitution. The reforms have made the country more pluralistic and representative than other Arab countries. These changes, like others in the following ten years, can be seen as a response to pressures from the European Commission and the European Parliament, as well as to demands from domestic opposition parties that had begun to cooperate together under the umbrella of the "Koutla" bloc. However, these changes can also be seen as a preemptive strategy on the part of King Hassan II designed to co-opt opposition parties and therefore divert credit for reforms to the monarch. King Hassan II had historically pursued a similar strategy of segmenting the opposition and placing himself above the political fray in order to preserve his legitimacy and his pivotal political role.[2]

In the lead-up to the 1993 parliamentary elections, the first since 1984, major political parties were allowed to give advice to the government on the application of the electoral code. The major opposition parties (the Socialist Union of Popular Forces [USFP], the *Istiqlal* Party, and the Party of Progress and Socialism [PPS]) were able to bring about some changes in electoral districts and revision of voter lists, but had little effect on the overall electoral process. Of the 333 parliamentary seats, 222 were chosen through direct elections and 111 were chosen through indirect elections. Manipulation of the elections ensured the dominance of the parliament by a center-right coalition of parties (*Wifaq*) loyal to the monarchy.[3] The opposition "Koutla" parties, which won 45 percent of the directly elected seats but gained few indirectly elected seats, refused to accept a large number of cabinet positions following the elections, and a largely technocratic government was appointed. Although the Koutla bloc refused to participate in a new government, their new discourse on human rights persuaded the King to create a Ministry of Human Rights.

By 1996, King Hassan II began to stress the importance of consensus and *alternance*. Also in 1996, two new NGOs, Maroc 2020 and Transparency Maroc, launched advocacy campaigns against corruption. Koutla opposition political parties campaigned for a new constitution and a new electoral code. Following negotiations between the palace and political parties, a constitutional revision was formulated creating a new upper house and a 325-seat lower house elected on the basis of a simply majority voting system. Voters approved a referendum on the constitutional revision in September 1996. Before the 1997 parliamentary elections, the major political parties signed a national pact with the Interior Minister Driss Basri, pledging to respect the new electoral code in exchange for the administration's impartiality and fairness in the elections. The 1997 elections for the lower house gave equivalent percentages of seats to three blocs: the reconfigured Koutla; the pro-monarchy

Wifaq; and a pro-establishment centrist grouping. With 34 percent of the popular vote, the Koutla was allowed to form a government of *alternance* under the leadership of Prime Minister Abderrahmane Youssoufi, whose USFP held 17.5 percent of the lower house's seats. An Islamist group, *Al Islah*, won a handful of seats running under a proxy party later renamed the Party of Justice and Development.

The 1997 elections, leading to Islamist participation in the parliament and leadership of the government by an opposition coalition, marked a significant degree of liberalization. However, *alternance* was not synonymous with democratic transition. Turnout in the elections was only 58 percent, while in the less-contested elections in 1993 it had been 63 percent. Political parties issued complaints about administrative manipulation, gerrymandering, and vote buying. The indirectly elected upper house could and did block legislation from the lower house. The King still controlled appointments of his loyalists to the key ministries of the interior, justice, Islamic affairs, and foreign affairs. Moreover, the 1996 Constitution did not reduce the dominant decision-making powers of the monarch. A relatively fair election and USFP-led government did little to change the political prerogatives of the King; pluralism was more cooptation of the opposition than the beginning of political power transition. The monarch's power was untouched because it is not subject to political party composition. The King still controlled a vast network of personnel, patronage, and arbitration (the central administration traditionally called the *Makhzen*) that was not subject to control by or even accountability to political parties, the judiciary, or the legislature.

Before his death in 1999, King Hassan II had released most political prisoners, institutionalized a discourse on human rights protection and anti-corruption, and allowed the opposition significant influence on budget prioritization. Upon assuming the throne in 1999, his son, Mohammed VI, started to talk of the importance of administrative reform, individual liberties, and the rule of law. He sacked the powerful Interior Minister Driss Basri and made a number of moves to liberalize, although he has back-tracked in some areas such as media freedom. The new King faced a slew of new civil society organizations that joined political parties in broadening demands for political reform. The framework of political discourse has changed in the country, but open questioning of the institutional role of the monarchy is still rare.

Reflecting the new perspective of Mohammed VI, the September 27, 2002 parliamentary elections were the freest and fairest in Moroccan history. The Party of Justice and Development, an Islamist party, won 42 seats in the 325-seat lower house.[4] The USFP was the best performing opposition party with 50 seats, followed by the *Istiqlal* with 48 seats. The conservative National Rally of Independents (RNI) gained 41 seats while the conservative, Berber-based Popular Movement (MP), gained 27 seats. Twenty-two parties won at least one seat in the legislature. For the first time, women were guaranteed 30 seats.

The themes of the elections were "transparency" and "credibility." Despite several minor irregularities, there was a general perception that the elections were the most transparent in Moroccan history. Nevertheless, they did not herald a democratic transition. Turnout was only 51.6 percent, and 15 percent of cast ballots were declared void, both indications of lack of voter enthusiasm. The adoption of a new electoral code based on a party list system had encouraged the proliferation of political parties. The results show a high degree of party fragmentation, reducing the cohesiveness of any grouping able to form a government and allowing King Mohammed VI to manipulate parties as his father had done. In early October 2002, the King named his loyal Interior Minister, Driss Jettou, as the new Prime Minister. By November, Jettou had put together an unwieldy, ideologically diverse, coalition government with the USFP, *Istiqlal*, RNI, MP, and a former communist party. A democratic transition is still elusive without basic changes in the constitutional and informal power of the monarch and without an opposition capacity to promote a transformative agenda.

Moroccan democratization from a theoretical perspective

In seeking to account for the "reluctance" of many Arab countries in the Middle East and North Africa to democratize, analysts often cite the importance of domestic variables whose influence on the prospects for political change is much more significant than that of international variables. These domestic variables are a combination of cultural, political, and economic impulses, many of which have deep historical roots and are not easily altered by self-willed "democratizers." Among the political variables that may inhibit democratization are: the structural weakness of civil society;[5] the inability of political parties to present credible alternatives to existing powerholders; the institutional predominance of the military; and, simply, the reluctance of existing elites to exit. Presumed cultural barriers include: Islam as a historical legacy;[6] a political culture of authoritarianism; patriarchy;[7] a culture of conspiracy theories;[8] and an opposition dominated by Islamists with anti-modern and anti-democratic world views. Socio-economic variables are also presumed to have profound structuring effects: low levels of per capita gross domestic product;[9] poor educational standards; and the lack of a vibrant private sector. In their simplest form, these *internalist* arguments stress that, regardless of external pressures, Arab countries in the Middle East/North Africa (MENA) region have a set of domestic characteristics that mitigate against successful adaptation to global norms of economic liberalism and participatory democracy.

In contrast, a number of authors have presented *externalist* arguments for why MENA countries have yet to transition toward democracy. Geopolitical factors often rank prominently. The necessity for MENA states to prepare for possible war and the frequency of interstate conflict in the region have produced dominant military institutions and justified the suppression of demands for popular representation. Transnational ideological rivalries, coupled with repeated, mutual infringements on states' sovereign rights, have complicated the task of establishing legitimate institutions of government. Moreover, the security interests of Western powers in the region have served as an excuse for the European Union and the United States to indulge friendly authoritarian rulers. External economic factors also have a role. To the extent that MENA countries are inserted in the international economy primarily as exporters of hydrocarbons and labor or as recipients of official aid and strategic rents, the result has been the emergence of *rentier states* that tend to redistribute externally generated resources rather than to tax their own citizens directly.[10] The potential liberalizing effects of economic globalization have been muted by the region's slow pace of structural adjustment, maintenance of high levels of protectionism, and inability to foster regional integration.

The conventional *internalist* arguments have limited utility in explaining the lack of democratic transition in Morocco. Morocco's civil society is one of the most vibrant in the Arab world, as evidenced by a historically important labor movement and a relatively open press.[11] Political parties have significant historical roots, represent distinct social strata, and have participated in pluralistic elections for decades. Despite significant military spending of 4–5 percent of GDP since the takeover of the Western Sahara in 1976, the Moroccan armed forces have not had a predominant role in politics in contrast to the *Makhzen*. Culturally, Morocco has a strong patrimonial-monarchist tradition and an Islamic political culture. However, unlike many other Arab countries, the Islamist credentials of the monarchy are strong and the opposition Islamist movement is divided. The largest Islamist party, *al-Adl wal-Ihsan* (Justice and Charity), which did not participate in the September 2002 elections, is popular yet lacks the same degree of deep-rootedness, obscurantism, and violence found in some Islamist parties elsewhere in the Middle East. Economically, Morocco has high illiteracy and the lowest per capita GDP in North Africa, yet still manages to have the highest rankings for political freedom in North Africa according to Freedom House. Unlike many of its Arab counterparts, it has no rents from hydrocarbons. Instead, it has a vibrant private sector with significant "structural power."[12]

Similarly, many of the standard *externalist* arguments fail to provide much guidance in the Moroccan case. While King Hassan II was strongly supported by Western governments, his country was not militarily involved in many of the MENA region's key conflicts. The occupation of the Western Sahara has caused tension with Algeria, yet, far from being a pretext for domestic repression, the Green March has been extremely popular with Moroccan political parties. Morocco has a diversified economy in which phosphate rents are no longer high, and it has significantly lowered tariff barriers.

Despite lacking a number of characteristics of Middle Eastern "exception-alism" that have been identified as democracy inhibitors, Morocco has been subject to a number of domestic and international pressures that the democratization and globalization literature posit have accelerated democratic transitions elsewhere in the world. And yet Morocco has yet to make a democratic transition. In the third wave of democratization, Paul Drake argues, "international forces created an international democratic conjuncture."[13] The international forces were economic, technological, and ideational. Paolo Aliboni notes that from 1991 to 1993, the EU's share in the total trade of the Maghrib was over 65 percent, much higher than its share for Latin America, Eastern Europe, or any other world region.[14] Morocco's heavy trade reliance on a major bloc of democratic countries in close proximity to its borders did not seem to have the same transformative effects as proximity and trade dependence in other regions.

Morocco has also faced economic pressures resulting from changes in European policies and demands for structural adjustment. With the shift in European Mediterranean policy in 1995 away from a series of Cooperation Agreements to the Euro-Mediterranean Partnership (EMP), pressures for structural adjustment and political development have increased, at least in the long term.[15] The creation of a unified European market has also restricted access for North African labor and, indirectly, for industrial goods in a more competitive European market. Beginning in 1996, the EU switched from a reference price system for agricultural imports to quotas, putting pressure on Moroccan, Tunisian, and Egyptian agricultural exporters. The European switch to the EMP and the Barcelona Process, focusing on free trade, openness to foreign direct investment, and more generous (but conditional) aid, created pressures on Morocco to adopt a range of policy changes associated with "good governance." Moreover, since 1985 Morocco has faced a variety of economic crises that required bailouts from the International Monetary Fund and the World Bank, and associated conditionality. Aid from the European Union and the United States since that time has increasingly been conditioned on political reform, greater protection of human rights, and expansion of the role of the private sector.

On a more general level, Morocco has been profoundly exposed to globalization. Exposure to Western media through satellite dishes and the Internet is quite substantial. Diffusion of Western culture and norms has also been significant through extensive cross-border exchange, education of Moroccan elites in French institutions, and the presence of a huge expatriate Moroccan community in Europe which frequently travels back to Morocco, presumably diffusing European norms in their country of birth. At a minimum, Morocco has faced pressures from the rise of new economic actors, changes in communications technology, and demands from leading capitalist states. If we are to believe some globalization theorists, deeper integration in a globalized capitalist system – via multinational corporations, free trade organizations, and capital inflows – creates pressures for economic policy reforms that enhance transparency, accountability, the rule of law, and, ostensibly, the prospects for democratization.

Moroccan "exceptionalism" is not well accounted for by either *externalist* or *internalist* propositions. Despite a range of pressures from Europe, including historic ties, geographical proximity, and diffusion of new norms and expansion of trade, there has not been a fundamental regime transition that one would have expected if *externalist* explanations had causal explanatory power. Moreover, political changes in Morocco in the last decade suggest that domestic impediments to democratization have not been as significant as many *internalists* have suggested and that Morocco has some domestic characteristics that could facilitate its joining the much-heralded "Third Wave" of democratizing states.

There are several key reasons for the limitations in *internalist* and *externalist* theories when applied to the Moroccan case. Much of the democratization literature focuses on the dependent variable, i.e. it looks at countries that have already undergone a successful transition and seeks to explain why, based on those cases. The danger, pointed out above, is that presumed "causes" of success can also be found in non-transition cases like Morocco. A parallel methodological problem in the social sciences is to look for the absence of a phenomenon (in this case democratization) rather than its presence.[16] Many comparativists writing on democratization have tended to ignore that significant political change (short of democratization) has been occurring in the MENA region, a fact not overlooked by many Middle East specialists in the 1990s.[17] The problem is in positing universal causes of democratization based on historical waves without assessing their explanatory power in non-democratized cases where there has been significant political reform.

Another problem is sorting through the multiple variables, both domestic and international, that may have a causal influence on "reluctantness," given the change in variables over time and their mutually constitutive relationship. As will be suggested later in this chapter, some variables can have contradictory effects on the likelihood of democracy, depending on how they affect specific institutions in Morocco. A related problem is that of time-bound tests of the impact of variables seemingly inhibiting or facilitating democratization. It might be argued, for example, that the impact of European pressures for democratization in Morocco can only be measured in the long term, and thus one's failure to find an impact after only several years is not evidence of the lack of significance of these pressures. If pressures have not "played themselves out" yet, it is hard to dismiss them. Still, without a theory of how long variables need to play out, we have no way of knowing when to test their significance. Finally, as is clear from much of the literature on democratic consolidation, having procedural democracy does not necessarily mean having "real" or "liberal" democracy. When the multiple ingredients of "democracy" are measured, Morocco, in comparison with other transitional cases variously labeled "delegative democracies" or "unconsolidated democracies," is not as "reluctant" a democratizer as it would seem. One could argue that the prerogatives of the Moroccan *Makhzen* are roughly equivalent to the executive powers of some new presidential democracies.

Moroccan "exceptionalism" (lack of democratic transition but significant political liberalization) can best be explained by a focus on the mutually causal role of internal and external influences. Reluctance to fully democratize cannot be entirely attributed to either international or domestic variables, but to the interaction of both. Moreover, it is important not to reify concepts such as "state" and "civil society" or "public" and "private," because in North Africa the boundaries between these units are often difficult to define. Important economic and political actors frequently straddle assumed independent domains, and thus it is more useful to focus on the pattern of relations between actors than on nominal institutions.

A useful point of departure is an analysis of Morocco's elite political economy, defined as a set of individuals, institutions, rules, and relationships that distribute decision making and material resources amongst a group of relevant elites. This elite political economy is not necessarily synonymous with a specific type of political regime or economic system. The same type of political regime (e.g. a monarchy) can be based on different political economies that reflect a country's history and social relations. The assumption is that a system of political economy determines who makes decisions and how decisions are made, and creates incentives for actors either to support or resist democratization. Assuming one can understand the "rules" and relationships governing key elites in Morocco's political economy, one can gain an understanding of how members respond to pressures for political change.

The norms and institutions embedded in a system of political and economic relationships can evolve with the entry of new actors into the network or the ejection of old actors. They can also break down completely, potentially opening the way for rapid democratization. Given the characteristics of an elite political economy (based on specific criteria indicated below), one can hope to explain how its members respond to external incentives and constraints (specifically from the European Union), and the implication of those responses for the possibility or likelihood of political reform. Depending on their structures, rules, and relationships, different systems in southern Mediterranean states may respond to similar external pressures and opportunities in different ways. Whether a country is more or less susceptible to democratization is seen as a function not of strictly internal characteristics or strictly international variables, but of the way in which international forces affect the dynamics of an existing distributional framework. The relative impact of EU forces on democratization depends on the specific nature of the Moroccan political economy and its contingent responses to variable EU policies. EU policies often have had contradictory, if not paradoxical, effects on the incentives Moroccan have to support deep political reform.

There are five characteristics of a political economy that have an important influence on how it responds to external constraints and opportunities: (1)

the major sources of resources; (2) the key members; (3) its relative porousness, i.e. its openness to new members; (4) the stability of rules and norms which govern interactions; and (5) the level of contestation over state institutions.

In Morocco, elite income, profits, and rents come from diversified sources, unlike in the case of Algeria where oil and gas revenues are the lynchpin of actors' interactions. Some of the key Moroccan sources include: phosphate exports; rents from property ownership and banking activities; revenues from exports of manufactured goods (especially textiles); income from *Makhzen*-controlled holding companies; foreign loans and grants; and taxes on imports. The overall resources of the network are variable, partly due to the impact of fluctuations in the weather affecting agricultural production and growth rates, swings in foreign direct investment, variability in the stock market, and changes in government regulations. Given this relative diversity, one would predict less vulnerability of elites to external pressures, but also a greater capacity to accommodate declines in specific resources.

Key powerholders in Morocco's political economy include the *Makhzen*, landed elites, and several dozen merchant/financial families. Other significant, but not dominant actors compared to some other MENA countries, are military elites, party elites, public sector managers, and organized labor. The regime has been relatively porous to a variety of actors through a well-institutionalized system of cooptation, incorporation, and patronage orchestrated by the King.[18] Dominant landowners and commercial and industrial families tend to be loyal to the monarchy in exchange for important positions and the capacity to accumulate wealth.[19] Orchestrated factionalism has meant that individuals can move in and out of favor with the monarchy, but generally are not permanently denied its patronage or prestige. In other words, penalties for "defection" from the regime are relatively low and often temporary.

Since his ascendance to the throne in 1999, Mohammed VI has accelerated the entrance of new entrepreneurs and technocrats into the governing circle, and the incorporation of opposition party elites into important legislative functions. Between August 1999 and October 2001, the King made some 150 key appointments within the monarchy, government, and provincial administration.[20] More than 60 percent have studied in France, the majority are trained bureaucrats with no political party experience, and most have roots in Rabat and Casablanca as opposed to Fez where many traditional elites came from. Despite the presence of many newcomers, the socio-economic background of most new appointees and the retention of many of King Hassan II's councilors indicate a process of elite "recycling" rather than renewal.[21]

The rules governing elite interactions have had comparatively high stability since the early 1990s, resting on a generally accepted consensus about the role of the *Makhzen* in the political system. Patron–client ties, cronyism, and oligopolistic behavior are important historical patterns. Moreover, the legitimacy of authoritarianism rests on a "master–disciple dialectic" embedded in Moroccan Islamism and cultural history.[22] *Makhzen* favoritism, however, tends to be market enhancing rather than market destroying. Compared to Egypt and Algeria, there is relatively low violence in elite exchanges. Contestation over state institutions is muted, although there are incremental pressures for economic change from loyalists who recognize the importance of preserving a significant, institutionalized role for the Monarchy. One sees a process of ideological convergence in favors of economic liberalism since the 1990s. Agreement over the need for economic restructuring and adaptation to European free trade has "depoliticized" the public sphere by deflecting discussion by political parties and administrative elites away from fundamental questions about how power is distributed in the political realm.[23]

The Euro-Mediterranean partnership

In order to assess the impact of EU policies on the Moroccan elite political economy and its receptivity to democratization, it is necessary to look at the overall package of EU policies embodied in the EMP. Since 1995, the EMP has been the primary vehicle for the European Union to influence political and economic developments in the country. This is followed by an examination of the specific political pressures emanating from the EU as a whole and some of its member states. Finally, the impact of European economic policies on Morocco will be analyzed.

The Euro-Mediterranean Partnership, also known as the Barcelona Process, has been Europe's primary mechanism to influence political, economic, and security trends in the southern Mediterranean since 1995. Central to the process is a European effort to create a free trade zone in the Mediterranean by 2010, provide financial aid for economic development, establish a security dialogue, and promote political stability in the "arc of crisis" from Morocco to Turkey. The Partnership is partly a response to American hegemony, or Pax Americana, in the Middle East. To the extent that geopolitical rivalry with the United States is a strong motivating principle, particularly for France, democracy promotion has been a minor goal compared to promotion of regional integration. Moreover, the EMP has effectively been held hostage to the halt in the Arab–Israeli peace process. If the Barcelona Process was designed to bolster European influence in the region, it has met with limited success. European governments have different priorities vis-à-vis the southern Mediterranean, and EU institutions have conflicting interests.

Many of the limitations of the Barcelona Process stem from its overall conceptualization. It often tends to be viewed by Europe as a defensive policy against drugs, immigration, and violence coming from the South. As an economic policy, it is often viewed as offensive, in that Europe wants to open up the southern Mediterranean to European investment and exports without reciprocating on issues that matter to the South like textile quotas, agricultural exports, and fishing rights. An underlying assumption of the EMP is that accelerated economic development will help resolve some of the underlying factors that produce security threats in the region, such as poverty and socio-economic disparities. It is an article of faith, according to Leon Hadar, that "free trade and more aid will enhance stability and prosperity on the southern and eastern Mediterranean rim, foster cross-border trade within that region, underpin the Middle East peace process, and help advance pluralism."[24] However, it is not certain that the Partnership will foster economic development or that economic change will lead to greater stability and security in the region. Free market reforms, backed by EU aid and investment, may have illiberal effects on southern Mediterranean economies, leading to a re-concentration of economic power.[25]

Another problematic assumption of the Barcelona Process is that economic development will lead to more political liberalization, and eventually democratization. Like the United States, the EU has an incrementalist-developmentalist approach to democracy-building that unwittingly can play into the hands of authoritarian rulers. The EMP's economic dimension has overshadowed its proclaimed goal of promoting the rule of law and human rights through development. The democratization deficit in Europe's Mediterranean policies stems to a significant degree from European fears that democratic elections would lead to Islamists gaining significant power in political systems. Rather than focusing on the freeness and fairness of elections, the European Council, in its June 2000 Common Strategy on the Mediterranean Region, pledged to "promote the strengthening of democratic institutions and the rule of law," "support and encourage efforts to promote good governance," and "stress the importance of promoting and protecting human rights." Promotion of "good governance" and "transparency" is not necessarily the same policy as democracy promotion.

EU political initiatives in Morocco

It should be noted that a number of issues in EU–Moroccan political relations are separate from the EMP but have had the capacity to complicate EU political initiatives for democratization. EU demands that Morocco take effective steps to halt immigration and stem drug trafficking have repeatedly soured relations. Fishing rights for Europeans in Moroccan territorial waters have been a contentious issue, and King Hassan II briefly refused to renegotiate a new accord in 1992 when the European Parliament, citing human rights violations, voted against a four-year aid program worth $600 million. Since 1999, Mohammed VI has refused to renew a fisheries accord, thereby straining relations with Brussels but earning wide support from Moroccan society. Although the EU has sometimes criticized Moroccan policy in the Western Sahara, it has allowed Morocco to stonewall on holding a UN-sponsored referendum in the Sahara and seems willing to accept Morocco's autonomy plan as a substitute for independence. Perhaps most contentious has been the issue of the Spanish enclaves of Ceuta and Melilla. The monarchy's championing of their return to Moroccan sovereignty has been widely popular. Relations with Spain and the EU were strained in 2002 when Spain forcibly retook Parsley Island from a handful of Moroccan troops who had laid claim to it.

Within the framework of the Barcelona Process, the EU has promoted a host of political changes in Morocco and in the southern Mediterranean as a whole. Some of the more important areas the EU has given attention to are democratic norms, human rights, civil society, Islamism, and elections. While norms of respect for democracy had been included in EU policies toward the Mediterranean before 1995, the importance of political pluralism was stressed in the 1995 Barcelona Declaration. In signing association agreements with the EU as part of the EMP, southern Mediterranean countries like Morocco (in 1996) formally pledged their commitment to respecting political pluralism, liberalization, and basic liberties. These "background" norms were, to a large extent, minimal standards towards which regimes should aspire even if they failed in the short or medium term to introduce substantive democratic procedures and institutions. In practice, avoiding destabilization of incumbent regimes has been a high priority. Socialization into democratic norms was deemed much more important than attaching specific political conditionality to economic aid.[26]

The tepidness of EU norm enforcement is partially attributable to the reluctance of southern European states (unlike northern EU states) to push the democracy agenda too far. France in particular has been an ardent supporter of the monarchy and an important advocate for Moroccan interests in Brussels.[27] Moreover, given that investments of European private companies in the southern Mediterranean (compared to East Asia and Latin America) are limited, pressure for fundamental political reforms is muted. EU private sector actors tend to be more interested in reducing trade barriers, liberalizing public sector procurement, and increasing the transparency of customs procedures, which are rooted in norms of good governance.[28]

Human rights promotion has been important in Morocco, especially when the European Parliament voted to withhold aid to Morocco in 1992 over human rights violations. Morocco's human rights violations in the Western Sahara, as well as its stonewalling in the face of UN efforts to organize a referendum in this vast territory, have generated criticism in some European capitals. King Hassan II responded to the discourse on human rights by adopting it as his own and by creating institutions to show his credibility on this issue. He created a Ministry of Human Rights and released virtually all political prisoners before he died. The notorious prison of Tazmamart was shut down and exiles encouraged to return. The government even went so far as to set up a system for compensating the families of those who had suffered severe human rights violations. European governments and NGOs have been quite vocal about specific human rights cases, in a sense as a substitute for their unwillingness to deal with broader political issues. While European pressure may have affected the King, more importantly the human rights agenda was utilized as a sort of insurance policy by the monarchy. Exiles could be reintegrated into the political elite. In a sense, "defectors" and potential agitators were co-opted into the elite political economy in return for accepting limits on the contestation over state institutions, specifically the role of the *Makhzen* in the political system.

The EU has devoted some resources to building civil society institutions in the southern Mediterranean, based on a belief that this would enhance prospects for civil politics and democratization. The main funding programs of the EMP have been MEDA I (1996–1999) and MEDA II (2000–2006).[29] One of the civil society promotion programs funded by MEDA I was the MEDA Democracy Program (MDP). From 1996 to 2000, forty-six projects funded by the EU's MDP involved Morocco. Among other things, the money was designed to: develop civil society organizations and NGOs; put human rights education into school curricula; empower women; and promote a rule of law. However, the MDP funding was minuscule, amounting to only 0.3 percent of MEDA I funds sent to Morocco from 1996 to 1999.[30] Moreover, three-fourths of the projects were managed by European NGOs, and those Moroccan civil society associations that got money tended to be elitist and unrepresentative.[31] Beginning in 2000, control of the EMP's democracy programs was shifted to the European Commission's Democracy and Human Rights Department. The EU effort did little to promote democratic socialization from the bottom up.

What is striking about EU political initiatives is the effort to ignore or marginalize Islamist political parties and NGOs. This stems from what Europe tends to perceive as the paradox of Arab democratization. In a number of countries, Islamist parties are capable of attracting mass votes and could win parliamentary majorities in competitive and genuinely free elections. If the perception is correct that Islamists believe in "one man, one vote, one time," then once they are in power through a democratic process, they will prevent future democratic elections and destroy democracy. Society and opposition political parties will not be able to prevent, legally or through resistance, the halting of subsequent fair elections. Many EU policy-makers, like their authoritarian counterparts in the southern Mediterranean, believe that the only way to prevent this presumed paradox is to prevent Islamist electoral participation or delay it until secularist parties are sufficient competitors. One of the clear aims of the EMP is to resolve the paradox by fostering economic development that would alleviate the social problems that often propel young people to vote for Islamist parties.

Morocco is something of a unique case in North Africa, in that Islamists have not proven capable of getting a majority or even plurality of votes. The presumed paradox does not seem to hold, given the Islamic legitimacy of the King, relative weakness of the Islamists, and the willingness of the regime to accept Islamist participation in the parliament. Morocco's elites have partially co-opted moderate Islamists in a way consistent with general EU demands for pluralism (with stability), even though Europe itself has shunned moderate Islamists in Morocco and the entire southern Mediterranean. The Party of Justice and Development did gain a respectable forty-two parliamentary seats in 2002, while the more radical Justice and Charity refused to participate in elections. There are many secular and pro-monarchy parties that are capable of rivaling these parties successfully. It is not clear that even with a plurality Moroccan Islamists could enforce a legal or constitutional end to fair elections, assuming they would even want to do so.

Gudrun Kramer argues that there is no inherent anti-pluralist essence to Islamist beliefs and that the positions of Islamists "depend on the balance of forces within the various societies" and how state elites treat Islamists.[32] Other authors have argued that mainstream, mass-based Islamist parties in the Middle East actually promote principles of democracy, pluralism, accountability, and a rule of law.[33] Even in MENA countries where none of the major domestic rivals such as Islamists and secular governments has an ideology or organizational structure nurturing democracy, liberalization, and proto-democracy can still result from the fact that repeated interactions between rivals constrains them to accept limits, compromises, and constitutional protections.[34] Morocco's Islamist parties and the historical culture of Islam are not significant barriers to the diffusion of democratic norms and practices. Morocco has a wide variety of cultural norms that have changed over time, and many are compatible with European norms of democracy. In addition to traditional patrimonialism and patriarchal values, norms of tolerance, competition, and individual rights have significant resonance in society. Women's rights in particular have been given much more salience by a variety of actors. In 1999, State Secretary for Family Affairs Said Saidi unveiled an ambitious bill to guarantee basic rights for women that sparked large demonstrations and debates. King Mohammed VI has appointed women advisors, and women are now guaranteed nearly 10 percent of the seats in the lower house. Modest though these types of changes may be, they strongly suggest that the argument that Moroccan culture is essentially inhospitable to European democratic norms is incorrect.

Of greater importance in explaining the limits of EU policies in Morocco is the EU's hypocrisy on democracy promotion. This is evident in the way the EU marginalizes Islamists but also in its position toward elections in the southern Mediterranean. Absent from most EU discourse is any significant discussion, let alone promotion, of the role of elections in a democratization process. Elections tend to be the black hole in EU policies, despite the fact that it is hard to envision any serious democratization effort that does not include credible electoral processes and institutions. Promotion of even minimal procedural democracies would require Europe to discuss issues such as unfair electoral codes, gerrymandering, restrictive election campaign laws and media laws, draconian party laws, lack of administrative impartiality, and rampant vote rigging in a variety of forms. The EU has devoted few words and little money to overcoming these problems in the southern Mediterranean Arab countries, which is a dramatic contrast with its policies toward potential candidates for EU membership. While focusing on the "transparency" of elections in Morocco, European governments have shown an aversion to calling a spade a spade when it comes to the conduct of elections.

Contradictory effects of EU economic policies on Morocco's political economy

EU economic policies regarding trade, aid, structural adjustment, and other matters affect the overall capacity of Morocco to sustain elite resource distribution and ensure political loyalty of key social groups. The contradictory effects of these policies depend upon the overall nature of the Moroccan political economy and how it responds to economic constraints and opportunities created by Europe.

Like most southern Mediterranean states, Morocco faces a number of external pressures to carry out administrative and regulatory changes with potentially important implications for distributional networks because the changes affect how decision-making is made, the rules for distributing resources, and the level of transparency. Some of the pressures are ideational, designed to provide ideological legitimacy to ideas favored by technocratic reformers. Most of these pressures emanating from the World Bank, the IMF, and the EU (via the EMP) come under the rubric of promoting "good governance" and the "rule of law." These norms are not specifically political and fit into the EU's incrementalist, bottom-up approach to Arab states. By creating or enhancing specific institutions in a piecemeal manner, the EU expects to increase market efficiency, reduce rent-seeking, and engender the predictability needed by domestic and foreign investors. To the extent that implementation of these norms reduces discretion of individuals in the government and strengthens the legal system, some specific interests may be threatened in the short run but many others will benefit over the long term.

The primary mechanisms at the EU's disposal to promote these norms are the MEDA funds and supplemental credits from the European Investment Bank (EIB). MEDA, comparable to the PHARE and TACIS programs, is designed to achieve economic transition and free trade. Grants and loans have been targeted to a variety of projects in Morocco: establishment of capital market supervisory bodies; judicial reform; structural adjustment; fiscal reform; health sector reform; poverty reduction; data collection enhancement; training of customs officials; and human rights protection. The effort has been to alter the rules and institutions affecting the allocation of resources in society and between elite economic actors. Part of this effort is an attempt to enhance information gathering and dissemination by Moroccan actors who presently prefer information asymmetries. If successful, it is believed that Moroccan decision-makers will become more constrained and ultimately more accountable.

The greatest weaknesses of the MEDA I and MEDA II programs are due to the limited amount of funds distributed and the kinds of projects funded. During the 1995–1999 MEDA I program, ECU 660 million were committed to Morocco, yet by the end of 2000 only 25 percent of the funds had actually been distributed.[35] During the same period, the European Investment Bank pledged to lend ECU 574 to Morocco. For the MEDA II period (2000–2006), the EU attempted to streamline and reformulate aid distribution. In consultation with Moroccan authorities, the EU established a Country Strategy Paper and a National Indicative Program (NIP) establishing priority sectors for aid distribution such as trade liberalization, administrative reform, and immigration control. For the 2000–2001 period, the EU approved aid worth ECU 261 million, and it expects to distribute ECU 426 million more during the 2002–2006 NIP.[36] Since 2000, the EIB has also pledged loans of more than ECU 323 million. Since 1995, Morocco has been one of the biggest MEDA recipients in the southern Mediterranean.

Yet aid has proven to be a poor instrument for transforming the Moroccan political economy. It is too little to change the strategic calculation of interests by elites, and the aid that does arrive tends to sustain existing elites and enable the buying off of would-be losers. The EU has generally been unable or unwilling to extricate Moroccan public officials from control over aid allotment and distribution. Pressures in MEDA programs for long-term institutional change have met resistance from entrenched interests with considerable capacity to drag out reform or compensate for it through "re-regulation" masquerading as "liberalization."[37] Resisters have relative dominance because potential winners from real change have limited capacity for collective action or have little influence on legislation. Moreover, administrative and regulatory reforms will not necessarily strike at the heart of Morocco's patronage networks which are fueled by extra-budgetary resources and institutions that are autonomous from the formal political system.

The "fiscal crisis" literature offers an important avenue for assessing the effects of external EU policies on the relationship between state finances and political change. When states like Morocco face sustained fiscal problems, especially in the form of high budget deficits and reduced government revenues, that usually forces them to increase direct extraction or limits their capacity to reward elites and support social spending. States may face challenges resulting from their efforts to repress social demands. To the extent that fiscal crisis alienates key segments of the political economy, it may lead to fundamental splits between policy-makers over how to respond or it may produce defection of the private sector via capital flight or via siding with the opposition.[38] If disgruntled social actors then demand political representation, the process of democratization may be furthered. Many Arab governments since 1986 have faced fiscal crises, often related to declines in oil revenues or incapacity to service external debt, and in response have adopted structural adjustment policies. A concomitant initial response was often to begin a process of controlled political liberalization, as was the case in all of North Africa in the late 1980s, as a way of spreading blame for economic pain and reducing public anger.[39] Thus, a renegotiation between incumbent elites and political challengers began.

According to Giacomo Luciani, states that do not face fiscal crisis and continue to have access to external rents "will be able to postpone democratization indefinitely."[40] Even if there is fiscal crisis, states may be able to use repression that can deflect democratization pressures, although over the long term repression subjects regimes to pressures arising from international economic "intercourse" and communication. Rather than make deep institutional changes, regimes might also simply adapt to smaller revenues.

Morocco since 1986 has had a variety of fiscal problems, some of which are related to extended periods of drought. It lacks the kinds of external rents available to Egypt (debt forgiveness after the Gulf War) and Algeria (oil and gas exports). These fiscal problems have increased the importance of EU assistance and related conditionality. While government revenues and expenditures are key measures of the degree of fiscal problems, they do not necessarily account for the overall availability of patronage resources in the Moroccan economy. Sensitivity to fiscal problems is not the same thing as vulnerability. Sustainability of the system of political economy also depends on the accumulation and circulation of what could be called "extra-budgetary" resources that are not strictly dependent on formal budget considerations. These resources can influence the proclivity of elites for political defection or loyalty. To the extent that extra-budgetary resources can be maintained or increased, the *Makhzen* has been able to dampen some of the political effects of fiscal crisis. Extra-budgetary resources include: state bank credit to private actors and state enterprises; bribes; commissions and kickbacks on government spending; business profits; and proceeds of drug smuggling and other illegal activities. The EU has had a limited capacity to alter the creation and distribution of these resources by key actors. The monarchy has vast landholdings, direct stakes in the giant conglomerate *Omnium Nord Africaine* (ONA), and control over a giant slush fund called the Hassan II Fund for Economic and Social Development. ONA resources are market dependent, not budget dependent, and the Hassan II Fund has received a huge infusion of cash from the sale of a GSM (global system for mobile communication) telephone license.[41] Since patronage resources are not completely derived directly from the budget, the effects of fiscal problems on regime allies have been muted, and the King has avoided dependence on the parliament.

While the variable price for oil and gas exports contributed to fiscal crises in the mid-1980s in oil producers, declining customs revenues could produce similar fiscal problems in the future in countries like Morocco and Tunisia. One of the key threats to Moroccan government resources comes from the EU's demands for tariff reductions leading to a free trade zone between the

EU and the southern Mediterranean by 2010. Not only will this central component of the EMP decrease revenues to the central government, it will require compensatory taxes on incomes and a variety of new indirect taxes, such as value-added taxes. This requires a daunting effort to modernize tax collection and redistribute the tax burden. Moreover, if, as projected, tariff reductions increase import competition, a large number of domestic Moroccan companies will fold or face reduced profits, which also would decrease government tax revenues and increase unemployment. It is difficult to predict whether the effects of tariff reductions will change the strategic calculations of major regime allies and produce a potential democratizing effect.

Morocco also faces challenges from Europe on the export side. North Africa as a whole already enjoys liberal access to European markets for its manufactured goods, but has been losing its share of the European market to competitors from other regions. Many Moroccan exporters will have a hard time competing with new and potential members of the EU. With the exception of Algeria, North African states have relied heavily on textile exports. Moroccan companies will face stiff competition from much more efficient and low-cost producers in Asia and elsewhere as soon as the Multi-Fibre Agreement expires in 2004. In other words, their existing privileges in Europe will disappear. Also, to date Morocco has not gotten substantially better access in Europe for its agricultural exports, where the growth potential is high. Moreover, a hoped-for increase in European foreign direct investment as a result of the beginning of a Euro-Mediterranean free trade area may not occur. Absent trade liberalization between southern Mediterranean producers, a "hub-and-spoke" effect is likely, where large investments in Europe will occur instead of in the Maghrib because tariff free market access to the Middle East from Europe would be much larger than from any specific North African country. All these exports challenges may increase pressure on the monarchy and the government from exporters, but whether they increase government accountability to exporters or, instead, increase exporters' dependency on the government for subsidies and favors, remains to be seen.

In a similar vein, the effects of the EU on the Moroccan private sector have been contradictory. On the one hand, pressures for tariff reduction have scared smaller businesses into lobbying for extended protection or compensation from the government. Yet the bourgeoisie, like that in other Arab countries, fearing populism, has preferred a controlled political opening and thus has tended not to defect to the opposition.[42] Liberalization and industrial modernization programs in the Maghrib, partly funded by MEDA and encouraged by the EMP, may actually encourage new monopolies, increase the reliance of private sector manufacturers on the government, and deepen neopatrimonialism.[43] "Loyalty," to use Albert Hirschman's terms, has been a more common response than "voice" or "exit."[44] Capital inflows in the form of foreign direct investment from Europe have enhanced the mediating power of the *Makhzen* between foreign investors and the domestic private sector.

Conclusions

North African political elites and their clients face a historically unprecedented challenge from Europe and from changes in global trade and finance. It is questionable whether Morocco can reverse its continuing marginalization in the global economy without substantial changes in governance and without penalties for many domestic manufacturers. In this sense, the long-term pressures for democratization will hardly diminish. Proximity to the EU and exposure to pressures from European governments, businesses, and civil society organizations will not go away either. The EU is increasingly committed to promoting human rights norms in its common foreign policy and giving "teeth" to political conditionality in its assistance programs and association agreement with Morocco. Moroccan actors will have to deal with European-influenced changes in technology, capital flows, and trade policy.

However, it is far from clear whether the EU and individual member states actually want to promote democracy in Morocco, given their interest in stability and fear of Islamism. The exclusion of the Islamist opposition from the EMP cultural dialog, lack of MEDA funds to Islamist NGOs, and exclusion of Moroccan Islamists from European civil society initiatives are significant limitations on a bottom-up strategy to democracy promotion. Transnational networks linking EU and Moroccan actors will have limited effectiveness diffusing international norms in Moroccan civil society by ignoring Islamists or failing to recognize norms held by Islamist elites that are compatible with European interests of good governance and accountability.

Moreover, increased exposure to European political and economic forces does not guarantee a profound political change in Morocco. How the country's managers and beneficiaries of patronage process external forces will have an important role in determining whether Morocco makes the democratic transition. Since the mid-1990s, Europe has used a "softly-softly" approach in Morocco with only modest results,[45] partly because MEDA funds are limited and because the "carrot" of potential membership in the EU is not available to Morocco. Absent that carrot, the kinds of changes in incentives and risk calculations amongst party elites, private businessmen, and civil society that have occurred on the EU's eastern borders will be harder to repeat on its southern borders.

Many Moroccan elites respect the status of the EU and share with Europe the goals of accountability, transparency, human rights protection, and democracy. In this sense, cultural mismatch, Moroccan nationalism, and absence of democratic norms in Morocco are not significant factors limiting democratization. Rather, influential Moroccan elites have yet to make the instrumental calculation that EU material incentives are sufficiently large to justify elite defection from the *Makhzen* and the political networks upon which the Moroccan economy is based. Until the EU fosters material support for Moroccan actors independent of the patronage of the King and his allies, or until the EU makes the threat of sanction against the *Makhzen* credible, many elites will not risk advocacy of structural political change.

Europe has the capacity to make its threats and inducements toward Morocco more credible by focusing on the rules and institutions that currently allow the King to orchestrate resource distribution, divide political parties, and take credit for liberal ideas hijacked from true liberals in Europe and the domestic opposition. Given changes in Moroccan society and changes in the norms held by elite actors, Morocco has a realistic chance to make a democratic breakthrough that preserves a constitutional monarchy while giving predominantly secular parties a key role in representing and governing.

Notes

1 Freedom House, *Freedom in the World 2001–2002*, www.freedomhouse.org/research/freeworld/2002/essays.htm (November 1, 2002). Freedom House ranks countries on a scale of 1 to 7 that averages political rights and civil liberties, with 1 being the most free and 7 being the least free. With a score of 5, Morocco is considered to be "partly free."

2 B. Cubertafond, *Le système politique marocain*, Paris: L'Harmattan, 1997.

3 For an examination of electoral "engineering" in the 1993 and 1997 parliamentary elections, see B. Dillman, "Parliamentary Elections and the Prospects for Political Pluralism in North Africa," *Government and Opposition* 35:2 (Spring 2000), pp. 211–236.

4 For election results, see www.electionworld.org/election/morocco.htm (November 1, 2002).

5 A. R. Norton, "Political Reform in the Middle East," in L. Guazzone, ed., *The Middle East in Global Change: The Politics and Economics of Interdependence versus Fragmentation*, New York: St. Martin's Press, 1997.

6 E. Kedourie, *Democracy and Arab Political Culture*, London: Frank Cass, 1994.

7 H. Sharabi, *NeoPatriarchy: A Theory of Distorted Change in Arab Society*, Oxford: Oxford University Press, 1988.

8 D. Pipes, *The Hidden Hand: Middle East Fears of Conspiracy*, New York: St. Martin's Press, 1996.

9 S. Huntington, *The Third Wave: Democratization in the Late Twentieth Century*, Norman, OK: University of Oklahoma Press, 1991, and L. Diamond, *Developing Democracy: Toward Consolidation*, Baltimore: Johns Hopkins University Press, 1999.

10 G. Luciani, "Resources, Revenues, and Authoritarianism in the Arab World: Beyond the Rentier State," in R. Brynen, B. Korany, and P. Noble, eds, *Political Liberalization and Democratization in the Arab World: Volume 1: Theoretical Perspective*, Boulder, CO: Lynne Rienner, 1995, and T. L. Karl, *The Paradox of Plenty: Oil Booms and Petro-States*, Berkeley, CA: University of California Press, 1997.

11 For evidence of the political activism of NGOs and entrepreneurs in a recent anti-corruption movement, see G. Denoeux, "The Politics of Morocco's 'Fight Against Corruption'," *Middle East Policy* 7:2 (February 2000), pp. 165–189.

12 C. Henry and R. Springborg, *Globalization and the Politics of Development in the Middle East*, Cambridge: Cambridge University Press, 2001.

13 P. Drake, "The International Causes of Democratization," in Drake and M. McCubbins, eds, *The Origins of Liberty: Political and Economic Liberalization in the Modern World*, Princeton: Princeton University Press, 1998, p. 70.

14 P. Aliboni, "Change and Continuity in Western Policies towards the Middle East," in Guazzone, op. cit., 1997.

15 G. Joffé, "Relations between the Middle East and the West: The View from the South," in B. A. Roberson, ed., *The Middle East and Europe: The Power Deficit*, London: Routledge, 1998.

16 L. Anderson, "Democracy in the Arab World: A Critique of the Political Culture Approach," in Brynen *et al.*, op. cit.

17 Brynen *et al.*, op. cit.

18 For a discussion of how the King co-opts and fragments political parties, see M. J. Willis, "Political Parties in the Maghrib: The Illusion of Significance?" *Journal of North African Studies* 7:2 (Summer 2002), pp. 1–22.

19 A. Benhaddou, *Maroc: Les élites du Royaume*, Paris: L'Harmattan, 1997.

20 The following data is drawn from Saloua Zerhouni, "Elite Change in Morocco: More Recycling than Renewal," paper presented at the Middle East Studies Association Annual Meeting, Washington, DC, November 2002.

21 Zerhouni, op. cit.

22 A. Hammoudi, *Master and Disciple: The Cultural Foundations of Moroccan Authoritarianism*, Chicago: University of Chicago Press, 1997.

23 A. M. Maghraoui, "Depoliticization in Morocco," *Journal of Democracy* 13:4 (October 2002), pp. 24–32.

24 L. T. Hadar, "Meddling in the Middle East? Europe Challenges U.S. Hegemony in the Region," *Mediterranean Quarterly* (Fall 1996), p. 49.

25 B. Dillman, "Facing the Market in North Africa," *Middle East Journal* 55 (Spring 2001), pp. 198–215.

26 R. Youngs, "The European Union and Democracy Promotion in the Mediterranean: A New or Disingenuous Strategy?" in R. Gillespie and R. Youngs, eds, *The European Union and Democracy Promotion: The Case of North Africa*, London: Frank Cass, 2002.

27 J.-P. Tuquoi, *Le dernier roi: crépuscule d'une dynastie*, Paris: Editions Grasset, 2001.

28 Ibid.

29 The acronym "MEDA" refers to "Mesures D'Accompagnement."

30 S. Haddadi, "Two Cheers for Whom? The European Union and Democratization in Morocco," in Gillespie and Youngs, op. cit.

31 Ibid.

32 G. Kramer, "Islam and Pluralism," in Brynen *et al.*, op. cit., p. 123.

33 See A. Moussalli, ed., *Islamic Fundamentalism: Myths and Realities*, Reading: Ithaca Press, 1998, and A. S. Tamimi, *Rachid Ghannouchi: A Democrat within Islamism*, New York: Oxford University Press, 2001.

34 G. Salamé, ed., *Democracy Without Democrats? The Renewal of Politics in the Muslim World*, London: I.B. Tauris, 1994.

35 See http://europa.eu.int/comm/europeaid/reports/meda_2000_en.pdf (November 8, 2002).

36 See http://europa.eu.int/comm/external_relations/morocco/intro (November 8, 2002).

37 See B. Dillman, "International Markets and Partial Economic Reforms in North Africa: What Impact on Democratization?" *Democratization* 9:1 (Spring 2002), pp. 63–86.

38 For a detailed examination of the impact of economic crises on authoritarian regimes, see S. Haggard and R. Kaufman, "The Political Economy of Authoritarian Withdrawals," in Drake and McCubbins, op. cit.

39 Norton, op. cit.

40 G. Luciani, "The Oil Rent, the Fiscal Crisis of the State and Democratization," in Salamé, op. cit., p. 134.

41 For more on the Fund, see G. P. Denoeux, "Morocco's Economic Prospects: Daunting Challenges Ahead," *Middle East Policy* 8:2 (June 2001), pp. 66–87.

42 E. Bellin, "Contingent Democrats: Industrialist, Labor and Democratization in Late-Developing Countries," *World Politics* 52 (January 2000), pp. 175–205.

43 O. Schlumberger, "Arab Political Economy and the European Union's Mediterranean Policy: What Prospects for Development?" *New Political Economy* 5:2 (2000), pp. 247–268.

44 A. Hirschman, *Exit, Voice, and Loyalty: Responses to Decline in Firms, Organizations, and States*, Cambridge, MA: Harvard University Press, 1970.

45 R. Gillespie and L. Whitehead, "European Democracy Promotion in North Africa: Limits and Prospects," in Gillespie and Youngs, op. cit.

9 Conclusion

The European Union and democracy promotion

Paul J. Kubicek

In recent years, the European Union has emerged as an important actor in world politics, one with a very ambitious agenda. The EU has introduced a common currency, is considering a variety of institutional reforms, and is developing a military capability. However, by far its largest project is expansion to its east and south, with thirteen candidate countries approved at the December 1999 Helsinki Summit. According to the communiqué from that gathering, democracy promotion is to be an integral component of the EU's enlargement strategy. In other words, shaping other states' domestic politics is now a task of the EU, and it has, on occasion, used an array of political and economic blandishments and threats to press its democratization agenda. Moreover, as seen in the cases of Croatia, Ukraine, and Morocco, democracy is a EU concern (at least at the rhetorical level) even in those states not in the queue for membership.

Despite this turn in policy, the EU's role in democracy promotion remains, in Whitehead's words, "undertheorized" and subject of "scant attention."[1] Of course, the same could be said of the general issue of external promotion of democracy, although this topic has received treatment by some authors in the academic literature.[2] Unfortunately, however, there has been little effort to test hypotheses across a variety of countries in order to understand under what conditions democracy promotion by external actors is more likely to be successful.

This volume has aimed to fill this gap in the literature. There are, of course, a variety of issues relating to EU enlargement – e.g. financial costs, loss of national sovereignty, public opposition or support for ascension to the EU – but our focus has been on the connection between EU expansion (or, in Croatia, Ukraine, and Morocco, EU initiatives that do not include any promise of expansion) and political change in a given state's domestic political arena. Of course, this is a complex topic, and it is often difficult to disentangle and identify particular "causes" of democratization or the failure to democratize. However, these difficulties have not stopped some analysts – and EU officials – from celebrating past EU "success" in promoting democracy in Southern Europe. More recently, the EU has been lauded for its work in Eastern Europe, and indeed one sees that those states in the front of the membership queue are the ones with the strongest democracies in the region. However, as noted in Chapter 1, this apparent success does not demonstrate that the EU played a decisive role in these states, where democracy was never seriously questioned as a goal by any political elites and where democratic outcomes are arguably "over-determined." Indeed, as noted in Chapter 1, even proponents of EU activity will concede that the EU's role has been "more assumed than proven."[3]

Rather than focusing on clear-cut success stories, our objective has been to assess EU interaction with "reluctant democratizers" in the region, those states where some (or many) aspects of political liberalization met domestic political resistance. In some cases, such as Latvia, this resistance was limited in scope and eventually overcome; in other states, such as Ukraine, democracy suffers on a variety of fronts and democratic consolidation is far from assured. We believe these cases offer a better opportunity to assess cause/ effect in terms of EU efforts to advance the democratization agenda, because one can look at a variety of EU policies as well as different outcomes in the target states. Although his language and concerns are slightly different than ours, we concur with the view of Thomas Carothers, who notes

> [indeterminate cases] much better illuminate the strength and weaknesses of democracy assistance than do societies that moved rapidly to successful democratic consolidation – or those that have lapsed from an initially positive transition to some form of dictatorship. In gray-area cases, external democracy assistance is neither a dispensable supplement to a strongly propelled process nor a futile rocket off an impenetrable wall. Instead, the assistance becomes more deeply drawn into the local processes of the attempted political transition, resulting in a more thorough testing of the strengths and weaknesses of the program.[4]

The preceding chapters reveal that EU policy has varied across time and from country to country. In some cases, the EU has applied direct pressure. In others, the EU has acted in a subtler manner, or, arguably, even turned a blind eye to democratic shortcomings. The responses of target states have also varied, ranging from fulfillment of EU demands to partial reform to outright obstinacy against the EU.

This reality is, without doubt, complex, and in order to make sense of it and provide some direction for the case studies, we have posited a number of hypotheses that could explain the success or failure of EU policy. These were enumerated in Chapter 1 (see Table 1.1), and organized into two blocs: one set for the notion of convergence and another for conditionality. To review, convergence refers to a more passive process, one in which norms and practices spread through diffusion, socialization, and at times even a recognition by decision-makers that they are the "proper" path to successful development and governance. Conditionality is a more active strategy of the would-be democracy promoter, one in which carrots and/or sticks are employed to affect the instrumental calculations of targeted political elites. To distinguish between the two most explicitly, convergence refers to the spread of norms and conditionality refers to policy change based upon interests. Of course, a state may democratize due to both, and norms can affect interests and interests can affect norms. However, one can, through case studies, assess the relative effects of each in a particular environment. Moreover, one can imagine a variety of factors that might produce democratic convergence or democracy through use of conditionality. These factors shape our hypotheses, which are listed, together with the conditions that would confirm and disconfirm them, in Table 9.1

Table 9.1 Summary of hypotheses on the European Union and democratization

Convergence	Hypothesis confirmed if	Hypothesis disconfirmed if
Cultural match	Target state shares norms with EU and democratizes or Norms differ and democratization stalls	Norms are similar but democratization stalls or Norms differ but democratic norms are accepted
Novelty of environment (competes with nationalism)	New elites/states more open to new norms and outside influence Not relevant in older, established states	New states/elites resist outside norms and influence
Nationalism of new states	Elites of new states will resist outside pressure Not relevant in older, established states	New states resist nationalist temptations and accede to EU norms
Status of persuader	If EU held in high regard, EU more likely to influence or If EU held in low regard, EU influence will be low	If EU held in high regard, democratization stalls or If EU held in low regard, democratization proceeds
Spillover	Rhetoric of reform spills over into policy Not relevant if there is no rhetoric	Rhetoric of reform does not lead to policy transformation
Transnational networks	If there are transnational networks, the spread of norms is easier or If networks are lacking, norms will not spread	Norms spread despite lack of transnational networks or Networks exist, but norms do not spread and democratization stalls
Soft tactics preferred	Softer tactics facilitate movement toward democratization	Soft tactics produce little or no policy shift

Table 9.1 (Continued)

Conditionality	Hypothesis confirmed if	Hypothesis disconfirmed if
Sizable carrots	Sizable carrots help overcome reluctance to democratize or Lacking carrots, states will not democratize	States democratize despite lack of sizeable incentives or Sizeable incentives fail to spur democratization
Real sticks	Punishment or threat of same compels democratization or Lack of sticks coincides with reluctance to democratize	Sticks fail to produce democratization or Democratization occurs without threat/use of sticks
Lack of alternatives	States with alternatives to EU will be more reluctant to accede to EU pressure or States lacking alternatives will give in to EU pressure	States with alternatives to EU give in to EU pressure or States with no alternatives to EU hold out on democratization despite EU pressure
Transnational networks	If there are transnational networks, democratization is more likely or If networks are lacking, it will be easier to maintain the status quo	If there are transnational networks, but reform is not forthcoming or Reform emerges despite the lack of transnational networks
Gray zone democracies	Pseudo-democracies can confuse policy by pointing to "progress" and thus escape sanction and win benefits Not relevant if state is clearly viewed as non-democratic or there is no liberalization	Pseudo-democracies are pushed by EU to complete or deepen democratization, presenting no special problems

Evaluating the evidence

The time has now come to assess which hypotheses best explain the record of EU democracy promotion in the countries we have considered. Drawing upon the evidence and arguments made in the previous chapters, one can present a "scorecard" for each hypothesis. This is presented in Table 9.2.

A more detailed assessment of each country is given below, but before moving ahead some general comments about Table 9.2 are in order. Note that the table indicates several things for each hypothesis in each country. First, it asks whether or not a condition is present or absent (e.g. Is there a cultural "match"? Were carrots employed? Did the state lack alternatives?).

It then assesses whether or not the condition (or lack thereof) produces the hypothesized effect. In cases where the signs match (condition and positive effect present or condition absent and no positive effect), the hypothesis is considered confirmed, and both boxes are then filled in. For example, in Latvia one sees that carrots were employed (+), and there was a change in policy attributable to these carrots (+). In contrast, in Ukraine there are no really sizable carrots (e.g. membership) on the table (−), and little movement toward democratic consolidation (−). Both cases thus confirm the hypothesis, albeit by different means. Looking across the rows then, one can ascertain which hypotheses are most commonly confirmed by our cases.

Some caveats are in order. First, rarely does a given "score" rely solely upon quantitative, irrefutable evidence. As a consequence, the evaluations rest upon a subjective assessment of the evidence, primarily "process-tracing" in the case studies to divine cause and effect as well as statements, judgments, and actions taken by leaders of the EU and the target country. Critics may disagree with the evaluation in a particular case, and I can only ask them to turn to the more detailed arguments and evidence presented in the chapters. Second, in some cases one sees evidence of a certain condition present at one time and absent at another (most frequent in Slovakia due to its democratic "arc"), or working at one level in society and absent at another (e.g. cultural match with the masses but cultural mismatch with elites). In these cases, I have indicated a ±, indicative of the fact that the condition is present in some form, but at some times or among some important actors may be lacking. If the hypotheses are confirmed in both cases (e.g. in the presence and absence of the condition), the result is a positive; if it is disconfirmed, it is negative; if it is confirmed in one case and disconfirmed in another or there is uncertainty about its effect, again one sees a ± in the "Effect" box. Third, in some cases the condition is simply not relevant or data on it were not presented in the chapter. This accounts for the N/A scores for some hypotheses. Finally, since there are more hypotheses than cases, one cannot do any sort of rigorous statistical test to determine which ones work best. However, I think the assessment as presented allows one to make several general conclusions about EU efforts to promote democracy, and these are presented below.

Now let us summarize the findings in each country as a way of explaining the "scores" presented in Table 9.2.

Latvia

Latvia constitutes the most successful case of democratic consolidation among those we have considered, and, given EU involvement in Latvia, especially on the citizenship and language issues, one can expect a correlation between EU engagement and democratization. However, was the EU truly instrumental, and, if so, how?

Chapter 2 by Nils Muiznieks and Ilze Brands Kehris provides great detail about the diplomatic efforts of EU, OSCE, and other Western organizations

Table 9.2 Evaluation of hypotheses in seven countries

Hypothesis	Latvia		Slovakia		Romania		Turkey		Croatia		Ukraine		Morocco	
Convergence	Condition present	Effect present	Condition present	Effect present	Condition present	Effect present	Condition present	Effect present	Condition present	Effect present	Condition present	Effect present	Condition present	Effect present
Cultural match	+	+	±	+	±	+	±	−	+	−	±	+	−	−
Novelty	±	−	+	−	N/A		N/A		+	−	+	−	N/A	
Nationalism	+	+	+	+	N/A		N/A		+	+	+	−	N/A	
Status	+	+	±	+	+	−	−	−	+	−	+	−	+	−
Spillover	N/A		N/A		+	+	+	−	+	−	+	−	N/A	
Networks	+	+	+	+	±	+	±	±	−	−	−	−	−	−
Soft tactics	±	±	+	−	+	−	+	−	+	−	+	−	+	−
Conditionality														
Carrots	+	+	±	+	+	+	±	±	−	−	−	−	−	−
Sticks	+	+	±	+	+	+	±	±	−	−	−	−	−	−
Lack alternatives	+	+	±	+	±	+	−	−	+	+	−	−	−	−
Networks II	+	+	+	+	+	+	±	±	−	−	−	−	−	−
Grey zone	+	−	+	−	+	+	+	+	+	+	+	+	+	+

Notes:

+   Factor present/hypothesis confirmed
−   Factor absent/hypothesis disconfirmed
±   Factor both present and absent at different times or among different forces/hypotheses confirmed and disconfirmed at different times
N/A   Not relevant – variable either missing or not considered

and states to influence citizenship and language legislation in Latvia. In general, one can trace a rather direct line between European intervention in the Latvian political arena and adoption of legislation more accommodating to non-Latvian minorities. The logic of carrot and stick was clearly at work, as the Latvians' desire to join the Council of Europe and the EU overcame (although just barely) the resistance of more nationalist-minded politicians. However, Latvians did not simply roll over when faced with external pressure. Muizineks and Kehris illustrate quite clearly how the EU had to be adamant in its position and win over important Latvian allies. Ultimately, "the liberalization of the legislation was dependent on the precarious domestic balance of power, which succeeded in keeping the nationalist impulses in check."[5]

The case study illustrates the importance of both private and public diplomacy, the former arguably "softer" as it is hidden from public view. The larger question, however, is whether Latvia's acquiescence to EU pressure was simply due to instrumental calculations in line with conditionality or if there was some transference of norms as well. This is a difficult issue to resolve, as one can "see" the logic of conditionality at work more easily than the internalization of norms. While the authors do point to some groups in Latvia that "come to internalize the standards through international exposure and socialization," they note in conclusion that "cold calculation of potential lost international prestige, not the internalization of Western norms stayed the hand of those wanting to regulate language use in a manner inappropriate for a democracy in the EU."[6] Indeed, it seems safe to assert that had it not been for explicit use of conditionality by the OSCE and EU, the citizenship and language laws in Latvia would be very different – and less in line with accepted Western practice for protection of minorities – than they are today.

Slovakia

Slovakia is one of the more interesting cases in this volume. As Kevin Deegan Krause notes in Chapter 3, it is the only country to experience such pronounced movement away from democracy after 1989 and then dramatically improve its democratic standing; hence, a democratic "arc." Many would be quick to credit the EU for improvements in Slovakia's democratic record, as the EU and other outside organizations took a keen interest both in the 1998 elections that ousted Mečiar and in the 2002 elections that kept him from returning to power.

Kevin Krause, however, argues that the EU had a "surprisingly small role" in this process. He notes that the transfer of norms was problematic. While many Slovaks were predisposed to the EU and the "return to Europe," this view was not shared among the elite, who embraced nationalist arguments and "came by the mid-1990s to regard Western support for specific efforts at democratization as sufficient reason to reject such ideas."[7] Rather than persuading Mečiar and company of the merits of their arguments, EU overtures only seemed to harden attitudes of Mečiar and his supporters, eventually prompting them to launch a clearly anti-EU campaign.

However, one might argue that the hardball tactics of conditionality were the ones that were ultimately successful, and indeed there is a correlation between EU involvement (specifically employment of sticks by noting Slovakia's failure to meet the EU's political criteria for membership) and change of government in Bratislava. Krause, however, makes two important arguments on this score. The first is that the EU efforts were not decisive in switching voters' minds or getting out the vote; Mečiar was likely on his way out for other reasons. Secondly, he notes that the incentives on offer had no appeal to the government under Mečiar, thus precluding any sort of favorable response by him to EU overtures. He maintains

> EU conditions ultimately failed to bring about political reform under the Mečiar government, because its main incentive – membership – depended on the very condition – accountability – that Mečiar sought most to avoid. The EU had nothing to offer Mečiar to compensate for what it demanded from him.[8]

In this way, one sees a clear limit to the use of conditionality, and how one cannot make facile judgments about costs and benefits. Mečiar was not going to cave in. The carrots on offer were not attractive to him, and the sticks – refusal to grant Slovakia membership in the EU – were not especially painful to him. These same carrots and sticks, however, did matter to other political actors, and they are helping guide Slovakia at present through the ascension process. Thus, one sees a number of ± scores in the Slovak case, reflecting a polarization in Slovak politics along the axis of the EU. True, in the end Mečiar lost power and Slovakia's democratic record and prospects for joining the EU have improved. However, one should be cautious in drawing a clear connection between EU democracy promotion and political outcomes in Slovakia, as the ability of the EU to influence politics in Slovakia has been very dependent upon who is currently in power in Bratislava.

Romania

Romania stands out among our cases because it is the only one where elites previously ambivalent, if not hostile, to many democratic norms, have, it appears, adapted their behavior. As a consequence, Romania is inching toward democratic consolidation and membership in the European Union while under the leadership of Iliescu and the former communists. William Crowther in Chapter 4 recounts the ups and downs on the country's path to "Europe."

It is quite clear that in the years after Ceauçescu's ouster, Romania was one of the most "reluctant democratizers" among East European states. True, there was rhetoric of reform and "joining Europe," but actual policy fell short of these objectives, and arguably there was a cultural disjuncture that prevented the immediate adoption of European norms, as the Romanian government was dominated by officials from the *ancien régime*. On a related note, Crowther suggests that Romania attempted to play a pro-Russia strategy for a while, which allowed it to fend off pressure from the West. The twin goals of Europe and democracy, however, remained popular with the population, and when the first post-Ceauçescu government's policies led the country nowhere, regime change became possible. At the same time, opposition groups, which were weak and fractured in the early years, had begun to coalesce, offering some form of a "transnational network" through which outside influence could play a more important role. Indeed, Crowther notes that "[little] could be done by the EU and other external actors to influence its [the first Iliescu government] activities . . . because of the lack of a viable domestic alternative to the regime."[9]

The victory of Emil Constantinescu obviously bolstered the country's relationship with the West, even if all the promises of political and economic progress could not be met. However, it became clear in the mid-1990s even before the 1996 elections that the carrot of membership in EU figured more and more prominently in Romanian debates over reform. "Business as usual" would entail high costs for the government, particularly given the incongruence between its rhetoric and policy. To remedy this problem, policy began to shift, and the EU played a "vital" role in this process. Carrots and sticks thus worked, although Crowther suggests that norms may also have played a role, as those who had possessed dubious democratic credentials now, again in power, seem committed to keeping the country on the reform path.

At present, the EU is closely monitoring the situation, especially in light of the surprisingly high vote tally for the far right in 2000 elections. The EU has stated firmly that it expects progress to the made, and the government, not beholden to the far right, has been able to push through reforms. Romania is an electoral democracy, but further progress may be hampered because of ambiguities in the "gray zone" which make it difficult to measure democratic progress. Nonetheless, the domestic political environment, combined with the attraction of EU membership, augur well for further progress in Romania.

Turkey

It is a bit difficult to write something definitive on EU–Turkish relations, given that they remain very much a work in progress. While Turkey has remained a "reluctant democratizer" in past decades, events in 2002 give some hope that Turkey will indeed liberalize its political system and, given the salience of the EU in contemporary Turkish politics, one might be tempted to draw a direct line between EU policy and reform efforts in Turkey. Indeed, one could argue that the movement toward liberalization in Turkey was spurred by the EU decision in 1999 to consider the Turkish candidacy for membership. That decision has given pro-reform elements in Turkish civil society added leverage with which to challenge the Kemalist status quo.[10]

That said, some lessons can be gathered from Thomas W. Smith's review of Turkish–EU relations on the central question of human rights in Chapter 5. As far as "cultural match" is concerned, one encounters two discourses in Turkey: one that attempts to place Turkey with the West, and another that emphasizes Turkey's own traditions or special circumstances that preclude immediate adoption of Western practices. This also hampers any sort of rhetorical "spillover," as the rhetoric itself is often ambiguous, and complicates the perception of the EU, as some in Turkey remain suspicious of EU motives and refuse to recognize the legitimacy of EU interest in Turkey's domestic politics. For both conditions, however, the key point is that norms are not changing. Movement toward reform, to the extent that it does exist, has been associated with aspects of EU conditionality. On the positive side, there is a growing network of NGOs in Turkey pushing for reform, not only human rights groups but also more powerful business lobbies such as TUSIAD, and through this one sees some signs – not yet decisive – of a "boomerang effect" that could assume more and more importance. However, it seems clear that soft tactics and reliance upon processes of "convergence" or democratic "diffusion" have produced little fruit in Turkey to date.

What the Turkish case does appear to demonstrate (with the caveat that the final outcome of democratic consolidation in Turkey is pending) is that conditionality, under the proper circumstances, can be used effectively. The key, as Smith notes, is offering a big enough carrot. Before the prospect of EU membership was extended, "the pace of liberalization had been glacial."[11] However, ultimate success for the EU may depend on its ability to employ sticks as well, as past admonishments and half-hearted sanctions have done little to further Turkish reform. Moreover, Turkey has been able to employ the US card to get around European criticism of its human rights record. At present, it has constructed a "Potemkin" human rights regime, and a series of partial measures have been adopted while actual practice on the ground is changing much more slowly, if at all. Indeed, for every step forward, there is often a step back: another ban on a political party or politician from the Turkish side, and, on the European front, a refusal in October 2002 to set a date on accession talks due to continued shortcomings on human rights. Notably, Turkish leaders have proven to be skilled in exploiting the "gray zone" as well, accentuating the positive and pointing to special circumstances or legal justifications to excuse actions designed to limit political competition or target anti-Kemalist groups. The sweeping victory of the Islamic-oriented Justice and Development Party (AK) in the November 2002 election may also mark a democratic opening, provided that AK members do in fact abandon their Islamist past in favor of a liberal future. Thus, there is some reason for optimism in the Turkish case, most particularly as the new prospect of EU membership may create a "virtuous circle," so that the EU can anchor the ongoing reform process.

Croatia

Because of the wars of Yugoslav secession, Croatia possesses a number of features not seen in other cases. Nonetheless, this is not sufficient reason to exclude the country from comparative consideration, and, indeed, lessons can be learned of the relative failure of the EU to push successfully a democratization agenda in the country. Clearly, as Stephen M. Tull notes in Chapter 6, "the Croatian case underscores an important point: how difficult it can be to find a foothold for democratization programs in societies undergoing major upheaval."[12] Most specifically, what stands out in the Croatian case is the strength of the nationalist agenda within the Croatian leadership, so that it "could not (or did not want to) connect the dots between domestic democratization and EU assistance and/or membership. That is, convergence would not occur given the conflicts Europe had with a nationalizing agenda – an agenda which would always have priority in the HDZ leadership."[13] Thus, while the idea of Europe and its norms had some attraction for Croats, this was not sufficient to give the EU's political agenda a foothold in the country. Nationalist ideals presented a "firm limit to the EU's tapping into alternative fountains of liberal democracy."[14] Despite some lip-service in Zagreb to EU ideals, transnational networks were not empowered to assist the EU. Given the conflicts between the external and internal agendas, it would have taken a Herculean effort for the EU to prevail.

In Chapter 6 Tull demonstrates clearly that the EU was not up to this task. It did not have the carrots or sticks to offer, and lacked a coherent approach to the region. True, over time policies evolved and arguably became more effective in the realm of conflict management, but the democratization agenda barely got off the ground. Tull suggests that a stronger-handed approach would have had more success, and currently, with Tudjman out of the picture, the EU may be able to offer more incentives for reform to Croatia. Interestingly, the relative political isolation of Croatia during the war (the Croats did receive more international sympathy than the Serbs, but the Croats hardly had an American or Russian card to play against Europe) did not compel Tudjman and company to accede to all EU demands. Again, nationalism trumped any other concerns, and, arguably, the exigencies of war allowed Zagreb to capitalize on the "gray zone" hypothesis – in the sense that there were elections, Croatia was seen to be more democratic than Serbia, and that some democratic shortcomings could be justified by the war.

In short, then, there were substantial domestic hurdles to democratization, and EU efforts were inadequate to overcome this resistance. At present, of course, the environment is much more precipitous for EU efforts to advance democratization in Croatia. With the war concluded, Tudjman gone, and Croats eager to join the EU, Brussels will have greater influence in Zagreb. Hopefully, it has learned some of the lessons outlined by Stephen M. Tull and will be more successful in the immediate future.

Ukraine

If one can point to signs of progress in other cases, stagnation reigns in Ukraine. Despite hopes for democracy in the immediate post-Soviet period, Ukraine has languished both politically and economically, and, under the Kuchma regime, appears to have taken significant steps backwards. Ironically, however, the EU and other Western actors have stepped up their involvement in Ukraine, even as the country's democratic credentials have become increasingly discredited.

How does one explain this? On one level, one can point to a cultural "mismatch," as Ukraine continues to be ruled by elements from the old Soviet *nomenklatura*. In contrast to hypotheses about the novelty of the environment, Ukrainian leaders did not constitute a *tabula rasa* on which the West could impose its values. At the same time, however, a nationalist discourse has been employed only periodically – far less prominently than in the Croatian case – to justify the state's democratic shortcomings. The EU is lauded by actors across the political spectrum and the discourse of the "European choice" is marked, but neither seems to have helped the course of genuine political liberalization. Civil society also remains weak, and, arguably, those with a vested interest in the current system (including much of the economic elite) are at best equivocal about implementing reforms suggested by the EU. While there are, of course, a number of barriers to democracy in Ukraine (e.g. political disengagement and cynicism, wide gaps between rich and poor), suffice to say that one sees little notion of democratic "convergence" beyond the rhetorical level.

Unfortunately, the EU has been unable or unwilling to adopt a more active strategy with regard to Ukraine. Membership is not on the table, and to date the EU has refrained from offering substantial carrots or employing significant sticks. At the same time, Kyiv has tried to play the game of geopolitics to garner Western (particularly American) support against Russia. This may change in the post-September 11 environment, (and revelations about the selling of radar equipment to Iraq do not help the Ukrainian cause), but Kuchma has also indicated he is willing to play the Russia card against the West. Moreover, because the state does have competitive elections and democratic shortcomings are more connected to the Byzantine nature of the statist system and political corruption rather than to overt repression (although some individuals do complain of actions by state secret services), Ukrainian leaders and their would-be supporters in the West can point to some democratic "progress" to prevent democracy promoters from cutting off aid or pushing their criticisms too far (e.g. witness how quickly the Gongadze case dropped off the agenda of foreign states).

While the above analysis might suggest that the EU play tougher with Ukraine, at present at appears that Western states are looking toward the post-Kuchma era, hoping for the emergence of a new leader who will do more than offer lip-service to democracy and the notion of a "European choice."

Morocco

Morocco is unique among our cases on two counts: it has been excluded, on geographic grounds, from joining the EU, and it has failed to launch a democratic transition. The EU has engaged Morocco through the Euro-Mediterranean Partnership, but this initiative significantly differs with EU agreements with candidate countries. As Bradford Dillman argues in Chapter 8, the EU has stressed economic liberalization and "good governance" over democratization. Given the various internal obstacles to democratization, the "tepidness" of the EU on basic questions such as free and fair elections has helped stymie the democratization process in Morocco.

If one turns to our hypotheses, a few things stand out. "Carrots" have clearly been insufficient, at least on questions of democratization. Dillman also points out in that "aid has proven to be a poor instrument for transforming distributional networks because it sustains those networks and enables the buying off of would-be losers."[15] Sticks have also been lacking. Dillman suggests, provocatively, that the rationale, in part, is that the EU is not really interested in democracy – particularly democratization from below – for fear of an Islamist victory. Thus, little has been done to change the cost/benefit calculation of political elites in Morocco, and little effort has been made to promote change in the broader political economy that at present limits prospects for liberalization. The result – glacial movement (at best) toward democracy – is predictable.

It is a bit harder to assess norm diffusion, given the apparent dearth of democratic norms held by the existing political elite in Morocco, as well as the middle classes who would be nervous about democratization. Clearly, norm promotion – meaning norms of democracy, as opposed to transparency or human rights – has not been a priority of the EU. Dillman does not focus on cultural mismatch between the EU and Morocco, and although the EU is recognized as important, this has not led to any democratic norm diffusion. Overall, it is clear that the "softly-softly" policy of the EU – whose primary objective is economic liberalization, which might lead (someday) to a democratic transition – has not advanced the democratization program. Interestingly, Dillman notes that the Moroccan elite has responded to EU pressure on questions of human rights and "good governance," which suggests that a more active EU policy – and one that can navigate the various channels of Moroccan domestic politics – might be able to accelerate political liberalization, if not help launch democratization.

General conclusions

Now that we have looked in brief at these cases, what can be said more generally about the hypotheses advanced in this volume? Returning to Table 9.2, one can discern a few patterns. Some hypotheses are strongly confirmed by our cases; others fare rather poorly. In general, what one sees is that the hypotheses on conditionality (admittedly ones that have clearer lines of cause and effect than those on convergence) appear to hold up far better. Unfortunately, they often are confirmed in cases where conditionality was *not* employed. In other words, one can associate reluctance to democratize with insufficient outside pressure or inducement to democratize. Notably, seen clearest in the cases of Latvia, Romania, and Slovakia, when the EU did extend sizable carrots and/or threaten with significant sticks – and here we are talking primarily about the offer of membership in the EU itself – there has been a clear shift in tone, if not policy, of the "reluctant democratizer." The one exception to this rule has been Turkey, but arguably with more time Turkey will meet EU demands on human rights and other issues, although, as Thomas W. Smith notes, there is still significant resistance in Turkey to adopting the entire package of reforms demanded by the European Union.

Of course, matters are not simple so that one can argue that conditionality always works or is easy to apply. Among our writers, Krause most clearly notes the ambivalent influence of the EU in Slovakia, and his arguments have resonance in other countries as well. The problem is twofold. First, it may be very difficult for the EU to offer real incentives to truly "reluctant democratizers." Sure, membership may be great for the country, but would the required political reforms be good for the existing leadership? This was clearly a concern for Mečiar, but also had relevance for Tudjman in Croatia, and remains a great concern for Turkish generals, Kuchma in Ukraine, and the King, the *Makhzen*, and other elites in Morocco. Thus, rather than pinning its hopes on the existing authorities, the EU and democracy promoters must hope for (if not work for) regime change. This is, of course, a delicate matter. Here issues such as building grassroots political parties and networks, assisting a free media, and developing links with actors in civil society are relevant in order to build transnational networks for change. Our cases reveal that in some cases this may be possible – one might point to some success in Romania, Latvia, potentially Turkey – but this is easier said than done. Indeed, what is clear from our studies is that the external democracy promoter – no matter how well intentioned or funded – will need to develop domestic allies in order to get some sort of "beachhead" from which democracy can be advanced. In cases where elites remained entrenched and links with civil society are lacking (as remains the case in Morocco and Ukraine) it is difficult to be sanguine about prospects for democratization, at least in the near to medium term.

Some other hypotheses fare fairly well in our cases. If a state has alternatives to the EU – as has been the case with Turkey and Ukraine – it is harder for the EU to use conditionality. In cases where there was no real alternative to the EU – Latvia, Romania after 1992 – the notion that we "must" accede to Europe's demands can be more powerful. Pridham's notion of difficulties of pushing open "gray zone" or partial democracies is also frequently relevant, as it gives both sides an ability to point to "progress" while democratic consolidation remains elusive. This can be seen in Romania, Turkey, Morocco, and Ukraine, although, on a more hopeful note, the EU has not let Latvia or Slovakia get away with such claims as the prospect of membership became more real. In other words, the EU shows more willingness to push democratization as talks of ascension advance and views democratization in black/white terms, whereas it pursues a more laissez-faire attitude toward democratization and tolerates "grayness" when there is no serious discussion of membership, as in Morocco and Ukraine.

While one can generally point to support in most cases for the hypotheses relating to conditionality, those on convergence do not fare so well. Again, part of the problem may be that evidence for these hypotheses is often harder to marshal, but one can note that the conceptually simplest hypothesis – Checkel's claim that novelty of environment may facilitate outside influences – fails to be supported, in some cases because elites are not really "new" and in others because they choose to play the nationalism card. There is some support for the idea of cultural match or proximity, which notes that external norms must have some resonance with preexisting internal ones, and this hypothesis has been tentatively confirmed in a study looking at foreign NGO efforts to promote democracy in post-communist states.[16] Insofar as one can judge preexisting norms in the states we consider, those with more of a desire to be "European" or "return to Europe" (the latter of which implicitly suggests cultural affinity to Europe) have been, over time, more willing to accede to EU demands, even if some elites in countries like Romania, Latvia, and Slovakia initially dragged their feet on some reform issues. The status of the EU – again, judged primarily by public announcements – does not matter that much, as elites are willing to give lip-service to the EU but not give in to EU suggestions for reforms or try to justify their special circumstances requiring democratic shortcomings. Rhetoric – insofar as one can identify it – also rarely "spills over" into substantive change, although it may help prevent some democratic backsliding. In general, however, the key point is that movement toward democracy or democratic consolidation does not occur with solely soft tactics, and, with the possible exception of Romania, one does not see convincing evidence of a change in norms among those leaders who have been "reluctant democratizers." Mendelson notes in her study that "the diffusion of norms does not occur . . . [in the manner] that the literature suggests."[17] Those that have prevented democratization in these states do not become inoculated with democratic values associated with the EU or a broader diffusion of values. They must either be ousted from power or be persuaded by judicious use of carrots and sticks.

Again, tracing the spread of a norm can be difficult and it may take a longer time span to identify its role, but our case studies confirm that EU efforts, when they work, are usually because of pressure that changes the instrumental calculations of domestic decision-makers, not their norms. In a sense, this should hardly be surprising. Democracies frequently can take root without total adherence to democratic norms among elites or the population at large.[18] At present, as one Turkish writer noted, governments are more apt to respond to EU directives like students doing homework: they do it because the "teacher" tells them to do so, not because they themselves see any merit in it.[19] However, just as one hopes that academic experiences foster intellectual curiosity, one could argue that internalization of democratic norms arises only with lived experience under democracy. Once a state has embarked upon a democratic course, the EU, of course, can and has acted by moral example as a type of "guardrail" to keep a nascent democratic system moving ahead. Convergence, then, may yet be a long-term factor, something we will eventually see, and indeed, one can speak of a convergence of democratic norms today among existing EU members. However, for democracy promotion *today*, conditionality is more likely to be effective, and the lessons of this study help identify better when and how it might work. We close with a consideration of these issues.

Policy implications

Although this is a work primarily about the EU, we note that several states and international organizations are interested in democracy promotion. Moreover, our hypotheses are not unique to the EU as an organization. Thus, we would suggest that our work has policy implications both for the EU and for the broader community of would-be democracy promoters.

What sort of policy implications and recommendations stand out? Clearly, one can point to the efficacy of conditionality, if it is applied rigorously and in fortuitous circumstances. As Tull suggests with the case of Croatia, if the EU defines conditions and pursues the democratization agenda with some degree of consistency, it is likely to be more successful. As we have seen, however, conditionality has not always been applied rigorously. Apologists of the EU might argue for the efficacy of softer tactics, hoping not to push the targeted states' elites into a corner and alienating them (this argument has been frequently invoked with respect to Turkey and Ukraine in particular). However, one sees little evidence for democratic movement with soft tactics alone. Conditionality has worked in virtually every case in which it has been applied, and in the Turkish case one can see that it has to date energized the reform process in Turkey.

However, one must be careful before encouraging all would-be democracy promoters to wholeheartedly pursue policies based on conditionality. One clear point is that there must be substantial carrots or sticks at stake. The EU may be uniquely positioned on this score, as membership is a major attraction to many, and the EU has clear incentives not to admit non-democratic countries. The costs of continuing to aid reluctant democratizers and forgoing conditionality are not so clear (e.g. is the United States really harmed by supplying a non-democratic Ukraine with aid?) for individual countries or other organizations (not to mention NGOs), and many will not have sizable carrots to offer anyway. True, if all parties could agree to conditionality and enforce sanctions on states that drag their feet on reforms, political change would be more likely. But again, as an expanding literature on the spread of international norms demonstrates in numerous contexts,[20] transnational networks play a crucial role in producing a "boomerang effect" and increasing the costs to reluctant democratizers. In cases where such pro-democracy networks are not present (e.g. Morocco), conditionality, even if pursued, will not easily yield results. The larger point may be that conditionality is less likely to work with the most intransigent authoritarian states and leaders (e.g. think of Iraq or North Korea) or where there is a clear case of cultural mismatch (e.g. perhaps Saudi Arabia), but it can work in cases where external promoters can work together with pro-democratic elements to produce change.

These caveats in mind, however, it is clear from our case studies that the EU (and, by implication, other actors) have not always done as much as they could to promote democracy among reluctant democratizers in Europe or along its periphery. EU rhetoric and norms need to be bolstered by stronger policies to encourage political change. Specifically, the EU should re-emphasize that all European states could join the EU and accept in principle applications from all countries, while at the same time emphasizing the criteria necessary to join. This would help change the discourse in a number of states, such as Ukraine, Croatia, and, beyond our case studies, Albania, Serbia, Belarus, and Russia. At present, EU membership seems so far away for these states that there is little impetus to undertake radical reforms or stay committed to the democratic path. A better path for the EU would be to do what it has done with Turkey, which is to accept the application despite the country's democratic shortcomings and then put the ball back in the applicant state's court by saying, in essence, "We are more than ready to accept you, but you will have to fulfill this criteria." Then, of course, it is imperative that the EU offers assistance to pro-democratic forces in that state and not hesitate to speak out when practice falls short of democratic principles.

The EU, of course, cannot do everything by itself, and other organizations and states, particularly the United States, have to support the democratization agenda. Outside Europe, the carrots may not be quite as attractive, but aid and trade benefits could be linked to political liberalization or democratic progress, particularly in states with groups already pushing the authorities for change. While critics might charge that conditionality is a risky strategy, I would argue that it would end the practice of Western states hypocritically supporting corrupt, authoritarian regimes that have never demonstrated any propensity for liberalization (Egypt comes to mind) and create positive incentives for change. Although derided at the time, few now doubt that the emphasis on human rights put forward by the Carter presidency helped foster political liberalization in a number of countries.[21] Moreover, one should recognize that "constructive engagement" has borne little fruit on the democratization question, whether it has been pursued in Ukraine, Russia, China, Latin America, or South Africa.

The larger point, demonstrated in several of our case studies, is that reluctant democratizers are often *not* tough nuts to crack. With an active and rigorous democratization program, rooted in conditionality, the EU has had clear success. The task now is to learn from these positive experiences and extend the agenda and policies to the democratic holdouts in Europe and beyond.

Notes

1 L. Whitehead, "The Enlargement of the European Union: A 'Risky' Form of Democracy Promotion," in Whitehead, ed., *The International Dimensions of Democratization: Europe and the Americas*, Oxford: Oxford University Press, 2001 (expanded edition), p. 416.
2 The preeminent writer remains Geoffrey Pridham. For a concise explication of the main issues on this topic, see his "The International Dimensions of Democratization," in Pridham, ed., *The Dynamics of Democratization: A Comparative Approach*, London: Continuum, 2000.
3 G. Pridham, "The International Dimension of Democratization: Theory, Practice, and Inter-regional Comparisons," in G. Pridham, G. Sandford, and E. Herring, eds, *Building Democracy? The International Dimension of Democratization in Eastern Europe*, London: Leicester University Press, 1994, p. 7.
4 T. Carothers, *Assessing Democracy Assistance: The Case of Romania*, Washington, DC: Carnegie Endowment for International Peace, 1996, pp. 7–8.
5 N. Muiznieks and I. B. Kehris, "The European Union, Democratization and Minorities in Latvia," Chapter 2 of this volume, p. 30.
6 Ibid, p. 30.
7 K. D. Krause, "The Ambivalent Influence of the European Union on Democratization in Slovakia", Chapter 3 of this volume, p. 56.
8 Ibid, p. 56.
9 W. Crowther, "The European Union and Romania", Chapter 4 of this volume, p. 87.
10 P. Kubicek, "The Earthquake, Civil Society, and Democratization in Turkey: An Assessment with a View Toward Eastern Europe," *Political Studies* 50 (June 2002), pp. 759–776.
11 T. W. Smith, "The Politics of Conditionality," Chapter 5 of this volume, p. 111.
12 S. M. Tull, "The European Union and Croatia," Chapter 6 of this volume, p. 132.
13 Ibid, p. 132.
14 Ibid, p. 132.
15 B. Dillman, "The European Union and Democratization in Morocco," Chapter 8 of this volume, p. 174.

16 S. Mendelson and J. Glenn, eds, *The Power and Limits of NGOs*, New York: Columbia University Press, 2002.

17 S. Mendelson, "Conclusion: The Power and Limits of Transnational Democracy Networks in Postcommunist Societies," ibid., p. 243.

18 Examples might include West Germany and Japan. One important volume that takes up this theme is G. Salamé, ed., *Democracy Without Democrats? The Renewal of Politics in the Muslim World*, London: I.B. Tauris, 1994.

19 C. Ülsever, "What Kind of Country do We Want?" *Turkish Daily News*, July 18, 2000.

20 The best source remains T. Risse, S. Ropp, and K. Sikkink, eds, *The Power of Human Rights: International Norms and Domestic Change*, Cambridge: Cambridge University Press, 1999.

21 This point is raised in several chapters of Whitehead, op. cit.

Index

Abikis, Dzintars 44, 49–50
Albania 3, 137, 138
Albright, Madeline 42
Algeria 174, 179, 183, 184, 191
Ataturk, Mustafa Kemal 111, 118, 126

Badinter Commission 141
Bahceli, Devlet 124–5
Berzino, Indulis 48
Birkavs, Valdis 37, 41, 45–6
Birkelbach Report 8, 116
Blair, Anthony 41
Bosch, Herbert 67–8, 70–2
Bosnia and Herzegovina 136, 137,
    140–1, 145

Ceaucescu, Nicolae 89–91
Charter of Fundamental Rights of the
    European Union 117
Checkel, Jeffrey 6, 14, 16, 48, 163, 165,
    211
Chrisopher, Warren 35
Ciorbea, Victor 99–101
Clinton, William 42, 100
Common Security and Foreign Policy
    116
Commonwealth of Independent States
    (CIS) 150
conditionality 4, 7, 17–19, 198–200,
    202, 210–14; see also under individual
    countries
Constantinescu, Emil 95, 99–103,
    106–7, 205
contagion effect 1, 4–6
control, as means for democratization
    4–5
convergence 4, 6–7, 12–13, 198–9,
    210–12; see also under individual
    countries

Copenhagen Criteria 1, 4, 7, 18, 21,
    111, 117, 127, 160, 167
Council for Security and Cooperation in
    Europe (CSCE): see Organization for
    Security and Cooperation in Europe
    (OSCE)
Council of Europe: in Croatia 132; in
    Latvia 30–8; in Ukraine 153, 155,
    163–4, 167
Croatia 24, 132–49, 207–8; attraction
    of Europe 135, 144; conditionality in
    145, 207–8; convergence in 144–5;
    declaration of independence
    139, 141; democratic shortcomings
    137; EU aid to 136–8; EU
    democratization efforts 144–6; EU
    diplomacy during war 139–43;
    "gray zone" democracy, as 207;
    membership in EU 138; nationalism
    in 144–6, 207; public opinion 144;
    Stabilization and Association
    Agreement 137–8; post-Tudjman
    government 132, 138
cultural match 13–14, 199, 202; see also
    under individual countries
Czech Republic 2, 10, 12, 22

Dayton Accord 145
democratic consolidation 21–2
Dzurinda, Mikulas 63, 69

Egypt 174, 184, 191
Erbakan, Necmettin 114, 126
Erdogan, Recep 126
Estonia 10, 22
Euro-Mediterranean Partnership (EMP)
    16, 175, 180, 184–7, 192
European Bank for Reconstruction and
    Development (EBRD) 9, 105, 144

European Community Humanitarian Office (ECHO) 137
European Convention on Human Rights 116–17
European Court of Human Rights 47, 118
European Investment Bank 123, 189–90
European Union: Central Europe 2–3, 9–11; relations with Southern Europe 2–3, 8–9; *see also individual countries*

Fischer, Joschka 45, 116
France, relations with Morocco 186
Freedom House 22, 57–8, 113, 174

Gheorghiu-Dej, Gheorghe 89–90
Gongadze, Georgii 153, 158, 162, 208
"gray zone" democracies 19, 200, 202; *see also individual countries*
Greece 2, 8; Turkey, relations with 121, 127

Hassan II, King 174, 176–7, 179, 183, 185–6, 191
High Commissioner on National Minorities (HCNM): *see* Organization for Security and Cooperation in Europe (OSCE)
Hungary 2, 3, 10, 22
hypotheses on democratization 12–20, 198–201, 210–14; *see also* conditionality; contagion effect; control; convergence; cultural match; nationalism; novelty of environment; spillover effects; status of persuader; transnational networks

Iliescu, Ion 23, 90–6, 99, 102–4, 106–7, 204–5
International Monetary Fund (IMF): in Morocco 180, 189; in Romania 90, 100–1; in Ukraine 162
international norms 6–7, 13–16, 211–12

Jetbu, Briss 178

Kinakh, Anatolii 154
Kohl, Helmut 41, 67
Kosovo 144–5
Kovac, Michal 61–2, 68
Krasts, Guntars 39–42
Kravchuk, Leonid 152
Kristopans, Vilis 45

Kuchma, Leonid 17, 24, 152–9, 162, 164–5, 168, 208
Kurds, in Turkey 19, 24,

Latvia 22, 30–55, 201–3; Accession Partnership 42; citizenship policies 32–43; conditionality in 35–42, 46–8, 50–1, 201, 203; contagion effect 50–1; cultural match 50–1; demographics 30, 43; independence 32; language issues 43–50; membership in EU 30, 37, 42; nationalists in 36, 39–41, 47, 51; NATO membership 30, 37; referendum 42; Russia, relations with 33; spillover in 50; status of persuader 51
Lazarenko, Pavlo 152
Lome Convention 1, 116

Maastricht Treaty 1, 116, 136
Macedonia, Former Yugoslav Republic of 137–8, 144
Mečiar, Vladimir 3, 17, 23, 56–61, 63–4, 66–82, 203–4
MEDA (Mesures D'Accompagnement) 123, 187, 189–90, 192–3
Melnychenko, Mykola 153, 158
Milosevic, Slobodan 24, 94, 142–3, 146, 154
Mohammed VI, King 14, 25, 174, 177–8, 183, 185, 188
Moldova 151
Morocco 24–5, 174–96, 209; civil society in 179, 187, 193; conditionality 186, 188–9, 193–4, 209; democratic shortcomings 174–8, 186; denied membership in EU 24, 174–5; economy 179, 190–2; elections in 174, 176–8, 188; EMP in 175, 180, 184–7, 192; EU aid to 185–90, 193, 209; EU trade with 180, 184–6, 192; "exceptionalism" 181–2; external factors for democracy 178–81; France, relations with 186; human rights in 176, 186–7; Islamic groups in 176–9, 187–8, 193; *Makhzen* 177, 179, 181, 183–4, 191, 194; military 179; political culture 178–9, 188, 193; political economy 182–4, 189–93; political parties in 176–8, 187–8; political reform in 175–7; Spain, relations with 186; Western Sahara issue 179, 185–6; womens' rights 188

Nastase, Adrian 104–5
nationalism, as factor for
    democratization 14, 199, 202; in
    former Yugoslavia 133–4; *see also
    under individual countries*
North Atlantic Treaty Organization
    (NATO) 18; *see also under individual
    countries*
novelty of environment 14, 199, 202;
    see also under individual countries

Ocalan, Abdullah 122
Organization for Security and
    Cooperation in Europe (OSCE) 112,
    132; High Commissioner on
    National Minorities (HCNM) 31–42,
    44–7, 49–51; in Latvia 30–51

Partnership for Peace 155, 159
Patten, Christopher 162, 164
PHARE (Poland and Hungary
    Assistance for the Restructuring of
    the Economy) 1, 9–10, 16, 66, 93,
    100, 175, 189
Piskinsut, Sema 125
PKK (Kurdistan Workers' Party) 115,
    122
Poland 2–3, 10–12, 22
Poos, Jacques 135
Portugal 2–3, 8
Prodi, Romano 37, 42
Putin, Vladimir 158

"reluctant democratizers" 2, 11–12,
    22–5, 198
Roman, Petre 93, 99, 101, 103
Romania 23, 87–110, 204–5;
    Association Agreement with EU 97;
    communist regime 89–90;
    conditionality in 90–1, 98, 107,
    204–5; corruption 105; democratic
    shortcomings 90–3, 105, 107–8;
    economic reform 92–3, 96, 100–1,
    105; elections 92, 95, 99, 102–3; EU
    aid 93, 104; "gray zone" democracy
    105–6; historical development 88–9;
    membership bids for EU 97, 108;
    nationalists in 92–3, 95–6, 98, 102–3;
    National Salvation Front (FSN)
    91–3, 95–9; NATO membership 97,
    100; novelty of environment in 98;
    political parties 91–6, 99–104, 107;
    public opinion 91, 102, 108; Russia,

relations with 93–4, 96–7; spillover in
    81
Russia 3; Latvia, relations with 33;
    Romania, relations with 93–4, 96–7;
    Ukraine, relations with 150, 155, 158,
    168, 208; West, relations with 162

Santer, Jacques 45, 67
Serbia and Montenegro, Republic of
    145
Slovakia 10, 22–3, 56–86, 203–4;
    conditionality in 56–7, 68–72, 81–2,
    203–4; convergence in 64–6, 81–2;
    democratic shortcomings 57–62,
    69–70; elections 56, 63, 69, 73, 81;
    EU aid 66, 80–1; EU criticism of
    66–8; government criticism of EU
    73–7; membership bid for EU 10,
    67–9, 73–7; minorities in 67, 69;
    nationalism in 65–6, 76–7; NATO
    referendum 70–1; political culture
    64–5; political parties 57, 59, 63,
    77–9; public opinion 64–5, 77–80;
    separation of powers 61–3
Slovenia 2, 10, 135, 138–40
Solana, Javier 161
Spain 2–3, 8, 12; relations with
    Morocco 186
spillover effects 15, 199, 202; *see also
    under individual countries*
status of persuader 14, 199, 202; *see
    also under individual countries*

TACIS (Technical Assistance for CIS)
    9, 16, 66, 156, 159–60, 175, 189
tactics for democratization 16, 199, 202
transnational networks 15–16, 18–19,
    199–200, 202, 213; *see also under
    individual countries*
Treaty of Amsterdam 117
Treaty of the European Union (TEU):
    see Maastricht Treaty
Tudjman, Franjo 3, 17, 24, 132, 137–9,
    142–4, 146, 207
Tudor, Corneliu Vadim 102–3
Tunisia 3, 174, 191
Turkey 23–4, 111–31, 205–7; Accession
    and Partership Accord 111, 120–1;
    Association Agreement with EU 8,
    111, 118; conditionality in 9, 111,
    116–21, 127–8, 205–7; constitution
    113, 118, 121–2; Customs Union
    Treaty 111, 118–19; democratic

shortcomings in 113–15, 121–2; EU
aid 123; EU trade 125; "gray zone"
democracy, as 206; Greece, relations
with 121, 127; human rights
problems 113–15, 121–2; Islamists
113–15, 126–7; Kurds 113–15, 118,
122, 126; membership bids in EU
9–10, 18, 23, 118–19; military 113,
115, 124; nationalists 124–5; NATO
membership 112; political culture
112; public opinion 123–4, 127;
transnational networks 124–6;
TUSIAD 125–6, 206; 2002 elections
126–7, 206
Tymoshenko, Yulia 154–5

Ukraine 24, 150–73, 208–9; Chernobyl
159, 162–3; Common Strategy with
EU 24, 153, 155, 161–2, 167;
conditionality in 160, 167–9, 208–9;
convergence in 166–7, 169; Crimea
150–1; cultural match in 164–5;
democratic shortcomings 12–5, 168;
economy 151–2; elections 152–5;
"European Choice" 10–1, 155–7; EU
aid 159–60; EU membership for 167,
169; EU trade 161; "gray zone"
democracy, as 168, 207; nationalism
in 165, 208; Non-Proliferation Treaty
(NPT) 151, 155, 159; novelty of
environment 165, 208; Partnership
and Cooperation Agreement (PCA)
151, 155–6, 159–61, 163, 167;
political parties 152, 154–5; public
opinion in 153, 157–8; Russia,
relations with 150, 155, 158, 168,
208; scandals in 153–4, 162; spillover
in 166; status of persuader 165–6
Ulmanis, Guntis 36–9, 41

van deer Stoel, Max 31, 33–4, 36, 41–2,
44–6, 48–9
van den Broek, Hans 38, 41, 46, 67–8,
70–2
Verheugen, Günter 48, 104, 120
Vike-Freiberga, Vaira 46–7

Whitehead, Laurence 2, 6, 8–9, 197
World Bank 105, 180, 189
World Trade Organization (WTO) 156

Yilmaz, Mesut 119, 124–5
Yugoslavia 133–6; dissolution of 139,
141; European diplomacy toward
135–6
Yushchenko, Viktor 154, 158, 162